The front book-cover title is purposefully understated to avoid any association with all the get-rich-quick books. Actually the complete promise contained in this book is . . . not only:

How to Live Rent Free

BUT ALSO

Mortgage Free
Tax Free (legally)
Job Free (soon)
and
Energy Free also

BY: JIM ANDERSON
SUCCESSFUL REAL ESTATE INVESTOR

I

. . . I DID THIS 3 TIMES IN 3 YEARS . . . WITHOUT ANY PRIOR EXPERIENCE . . . AND YOU CAN TOO!

II

HERE IS AN ATTAINABLE DREAM . . .

A Note From The Author . . .

One of the most important decisions in your life will be how to invest your savings . . . will your decision give you 30 years of peace, security and happiness . . . or will your investment decisions give you grief for the next 30 years. Most people are just too casual and too trusting as to how they invest their hard earned bucks.

You probably do not know that for as little as $15,000 (or the current equity in your own home), you can purchase a 4 unit apartment building and get on your way to financial independence.

Immediately you will begin to live rent-free . . . in several more years you will also clear a regular income from these units by following the rules set forth in this book. As the rents on your Property continue to increase with inflation, while your Mortgage stays the same (until it ends in a pay off), you will eventually probably want to quit your regular salaried job . . . and just enjoy life.

James W. Anderson

OUR QUAD

Here is what our gushing oil-well (without the risk) does for us:

- We live rent free.

- My Real Estate Brokers office is rent free.

- Our rent from the 3 tenants pays the mortgage, taxes, interest, insurance; plus maintenance and improvement costs to increase the rents.

- Then with continued inflation our tenants rents continue to rise, even without improvements.

- The property value also continues to increase, like your home which was tripled in the past five years.

- If you double the rents in 3 to 5 years . . . you have simultaneously doubled the property value (merely by using the 8x's annual rental principal to arrive at the value).

- Your mortgage payments actually decrease, since your effective salary income increases while your mortgage stays at cheap 1980 money. (That's called "leverage")

- With all the above advantages we pay little or no Income Tax on our salaries because we now have an apartment building as a tax shelter (like our rich Senators).

GIVE THE FINGER TO INFLATION . . . BUY A QUAD OR A DUPLEX AND ENJOY 30 YEARS OF PEACE AND PROSPERITY.

I did it 3 times in 3 years without any previous experience . . . **and you can to.**

This book dedicated to

Andrée

who gave support and
assistance to this project.

"SOME OF MY BEST FRIENDS ARE TENANTS"

THE HOW TO LIVE RENT FREE BOOK

Library of Congress. Catalogue Card No. 78-113752

HARD COVER   ISBN 0-932574-00-9

QUALITY PAPERBACK   ISBN 0-932574-03-3

Printed in the United States of America.

TO YOU BIG CITY PEOPLE "HOOKED" ON RENTING

A word about the "rental-syndrome" that I was caught-up-in in New York City for some years myself. As I heard one man, about to retire say, after working all his life in New York City. . . (and renting all his life). . . "IN RETIREMENT ALL I CAN AFFORD IS THE YMCA IN MIAMI BEACH."

A Publisher, in his late 50's recently conscious-raised to his wife: "You know, I have a high paying job. . . but I don't own anything." Believe it or not, it is not even too late for this Publisher to change his errant ways and to "own something" which will be a help in his old age (just around the corner). Tomorrow this Publisher could get sick or lose his "high paying job". . . maybe his Pension would help his wife. . . but they would definitely have to move out of their fancy and high priced apartment on Fifth Avenue.

Anybody that "works for a living" should have "something working for them" also. . . that "something" can be a safe investment like a QUAD.

The "rental syndrome" is the strongest in New York City, where it is just "the way of life in the big-apple". Actually Europeans readily say that "NYC is not the USA". But as the New Yorkers like apartment living. . . some of them can change their errant-ways and buy a QUAD (a brownstone in one of the 50 redeveloping-areas in the NYC area).

And even for the New Yorkers. . . if they can stick out their hand to pick up the rent checks. . . this book will do the rest.

THE HOW TO LIVE RENT FREE BOOK

(24 Chapters)

written by

JAMES W. ANDERSON

Registered Real Estate Broker in Florida
Author of books on Real Estate
Owner of Apartment Buildings
Manager of Apartment Buildings

"Peace of mind and prosperity through wise investments"

BRUN PRESS   NEW YORK-PARIS

WINTER HEADQUARTERS AND PRIMARY
CORRESPONDENCE & ORDER CENTER:

701 N.E. 67 STREET
MIAMI, FLORIDA 33138
305/756-6249
(if no answer, call again, we probably went sailing)

THIS IS NOT A PHONY BOOK, WRITTEN FROM THE IVORY TOWER . . .

Throughout this book there are more than one dozen "actual forms used by the Author, and not made up, just for this book." Each actual form is so-noted. Most Publishers will not allow "actualities" like this in their books . . . saying that they do not "look neat" . . . to this the Author said, "baloney . . . I am dealing with the Public's life savings, and I want to give them all of my actual knowledge from the firing line after having actually done all of this." The Author wisely then, kept artistic control of this book and therefore broke through, eliminated and changed many old fashioned methods in the Publishing Industry . . . all for the benefit of you, the reader.

As an example; Anderson herein exhibits the Lease Form (one of many) that HE USES, and recommends . . . AND THEN, this Lease Form in this book is one that ANDERSON ACTUALLY WROTE UP, FOR AN ACTUAL TENANT (names blanked out, of course). Now . . . this Lease shows the reader Anderson's special insight into the proper way to fill out a Lease (which 99% of the current small apartment owners do not do properly). Anderson's Lease is a tough one . . . properly tough to increase his Property value by having only STAR-TENANTS.

Anderson's dozen or so Actual Forms in this book then, may not be totally esthetic to the Publisher's Book Designer in New York City (but what do they really know about this subject any way, since most of them are Renters), but the Reader will appreciate such PROVEN INFORMATION DIRECT FROM THE FIRING LINE . . . information that has made Author Anderson a very comfortable and happy and secure life . . . and hopefully it will do the same for readers all over the World. This book is also available in French, German and Spanish, for the Author realizes, that when you deal in "money," the reader wants to learn it in his Mother-tongue.

WHY RENT-FREE WORKS IN THE 1980'S

The remarkable thing about the Rent-Free-Movement is that HOMES ARE OVERPRICED because there is a big demand for them . . . while QUADPLEXES ARE UNDERPRICED because they have not been discovered (yet) by the Masses.

Your home is your solution to your skyrocketing inflation dilemma . . . you are sitting on an oil well and don't even realize it, while you remember your Granny's "wise Depression words" . . . MY HOME IS FREE AND CLEAR. That was good in the '30's . . . but in the '80's your home and its big increase in value can be your inflationary solution and salvation.

Let us say that you bought your home 5 to 10 years ago for about $20,000/$30,000 ... today that home is worth $75,000 or more . . . and you owe less than $10,000 on this home . . . so you have over $50,000 in equity. $20,000 of this $50,000 equity can allow you to live rent-free; mortgage-free, tax-free (legally) and soon job-free and with no energy worries. So read this book 2 or 3 times (don't scan it for you will have scant success). Remember, you have not done this project yet, as I have and it involves your life's fortune; and it can allow you to live like a millionaire for the rest of your life without any financial worries. Your only worry will be to get to the Cruise ship on time, or to get the dog to the kennel before you take off for a Summer along the Riviera. I did it without any previous experience in my spare time . . . and you can too. But you must get motivated and active . . . and get away from the TV set and the can of beer . . . later you'll be drinking wine and champagne. Welcome to a lifetime (with me) of peace and prosperity.

SOME DEEP THOUGHT

The Author unconsciously planned the gold and red cover color combination to look "Bible-like" or "dictionary/encyclopedia-like" (without being disrespectful at all) . . . that is: A BOOK OF GREAT IMPORTANCE TO THE WORKING MASS PUBLIC OF THE WORLD . . . for the Author reasoned, "Am I not dealing with the most important thing in a person's life? . . . that is . . . SHELTER . . . A ROOF OVER YOUR HEAD?" Some thinking people countered that food is more important . . . "I agree with them to an extent," and Anderson continues, "BUT PEOPLE EAT THEIR FOOD, UNDER THE ROOF THAT I RENT THEM." This book then, is on a most profound subject, dating back to the prehistoric cavemen . . . that is MAN'S NEED AND SEARCH FOR A ROOF OVER HIS HEAD.

Incidentally, after the book's second printing, the Author heard a coincidental Biblical quote which confirms these thoughts . . . "the foxes have holes, and the birds have nests . . . but the Lord never provided for a place for Man's head to rest." (Amen).

With, then, this book, Author James W. Anderson is telling his readers how to provide for "a place for Man's head to rest", ie, HOW TO LIVE RENT FREE.

HOW TO LIVE RENT FREE ENTERPRISES INC.
Book; Volume I; Volume II; Tapes; Newsletter; Seminars; Lectures; Advocate-Broker Offices Coast to Coast.
Jim Anderson Approved Quad-Plexes; Regular Television Program, Radio Program, Newspaper Column; Syndicated.

COUPON-ORDER FORM ON PAGE 52

"How To Live Rent Free" featured in Associated Press; UPI; NBC News; CBS News; ABC News; Voice of America; and 100's of "talk" Radio/TV Programs locally, Coast to Coast. This book is "Required-Stock" (5 copies per store) in the 750 Walden Book stores Nationally. Also progressive independent bookstores order through their Distributors, such as, Ingram Book Co., Nashville, Tenn.
ISBN, $10 pb. 0-932574-01-7. $25 lux. HC. 0-932574-00-9. Library of Congress No. 78-113752. Copyright, 1978.

A SPECIAL THANK YOU

TO

MY MOTHER

CECELIA ANDERSON

AMERICA'S FIRST SALESWOMAN

1888-1980

CASH WILL NOT BE YOUR BIGGEST PROBLEM IN ACQUIRING YOUR FIRST APARTMENT BUILDING . . . BUT . . . PROCRASTINATION WILL

It is my estimate that procrastination stops most people from going into business for themselves. Most people are "mañana" people. Lets face it, most people are just plain lazy and should not be in business for themselves. They should just continue on their salaried jobs, or face up to it, and say to themselves: I am going to quit all this wasted effort in dreaming about something that I know I will never do. Its like an alcoholic who is finally on the road to recovery when he finally admits he IS an alcoholic . . . he will cure himself. Similarily, when you finally admit that you are a procrastinator . . . then you will be on the road to curing yourself. I did, and I stopped being a procrastinator.

I know I lost several fortunes just through procrastination. It was a good idea . . . and a lot of talk (mainly at cocktail parties) . . . but NO ACTION. I guess I had ten subjects for books . . . before I wrote the first book in a ten year period. After I wrote the first it was a lot easier to write this. It's the same in buying apartment buildings.

XIII

TABLE OF CONTENTS

JIM ANDERSON'S
"HOW TO LIVE RENT FREE" BOOK

SPECIAL SECTIONS

IF YOU CAN AFFORD A HOME . . . YOU CAN
AFFORD YOUR OWN APARTMENT BUILDING
. . . AND LIVE THERE RENT FREE . . . OR . . .   1

— How to own your own Duplex, even if you
  don't have the down payment, and soon live
  there rent free.   10

YOU HAVE A SECRET WEAPON AT YOUR
DISPOSAL . . . SO DON'T TREAT BUYING AN
APARTMENT BUILDING CASUALLY LIKE
BUYING A LOAF OF BREAD   15

— How to find your own, free, Advisor-Broker   27

WILL YOU CHOOSE TO LIVE IN ONE OF
YOUR APARTMENT UNITS?   45

YOU REALLY DON'T KNOW NOW WHAT TYPE
APARTMENT BUILDING YOU WILL BUY.
WATCH OUT FOR THE "SEXY-LEMON"   53

— Quick analysis forms to compare inspected
  buildings   59

HOW TO DETERMINE WHAT IS A FAIR PRICE
TO PAY   65

— Three ways to insure that you pay less than
  Market-Price for your first building   68

Page No.

Chapter 1

IF YOU CAN AFFORD A HOME . . . YOU CAN AFFORD YOUR OWN APARTMENT BUILDING . . . AND LIVE THERE RENT FREE . . . OR . . .

TABLE OF CONTENTS

Library of Congress

NOW IF YOU READ THIS BOOK VERY, VERY
CAREFULLY, AND THEN APPLY YOUR NEW
LEARNING WITH THE ENTHUSIASM AND
KNOWLEDGE THAT YOU WILL NEVER,
NEVER AGAIN HAVE TO WORRY ABOUT
MONEY. AND THAT YOU CAN TRAVEL AND
ENJOY LIFE THE WAY YOU WANT TO FOR
THE REST OF YOUR LIFE . . . YOU WILL
HAVE ESCAPED THE RENT-RUT; THE
MORTGAGE-RUT; THE JOB-RUT; AND THE
TAX-RUT THAT KEEPS THE MAJORITY OF US
SHACKLED IN THE SYSTEM-RUT. COME JOIN
ME ON THE RIVIERA IN THE 1980'S . . . I
DARE YOU.

"IF YOU CAN AFFORD A HOME . . . YOU CAN AFFORD TO OWN YOUR OWN APARTMENT BUILDING . . . AND LIVE THERE RENT FREE."

I WAS AMAZED THREE YEARS AGO WHEN I DE-CIDED TO RELEASE MYSELF FROM THAT BIG OLD MILLSTONE AROUND MY NECK (MY HOME) BY BUY-ING AN APARTMENT BUILDING, THAT I COULD AF-FORD THE APARTMENT BUILDING FOR ACTUALLY LESS MONEY THAN THE EQUITY I HAD FROM THE SALE OF MY HOUSE.

IT WAS GOODBYE TO THAT WARM AND COM-FORTABLE, THAT CHARMING OLD MILLSTONE AROUND MY NECK . . . THE OLD HOMESTEAD. FINALLY I REALIZED THAT MY HOME WAS A REAL LUXURY FOR WHICH I PAID THE TAXES, THE UP-KEEP, THE INSURANCE; AND EVERYTHING ELSE, JUST FOR ME AND MY WIFE TO LIVE THERE AND TO TRY TO KEEP UP WITH THE MORTGAGE PAY-MENTS.

FINALLY, I DECIDED THAT LIFE WAS TOO SHORT

AND SWEET TO CONTINUE WITH THAT KIND OF LIVING FOREVER, AND THAT IF I COULD ACQUIRE A THREE TO FIVE UNIT APARTMENT BUILDING, WHICH WOULD INCLUDE A NICE AND SPECIAL APARTMENT FOR ME AND MY WIFE... THEN MAYBE I COULD LIVE RENT-FREE... WORK LESS AND BEGIN TO LEARN ABOUT SOME OF THE NICER ASPECTS OF LIFE IN BEAUTIFUL TROPICAL FLORIDA. THINGS LIKE GOLF, TENNIS, FISHING, MY FAVORITE HOBBY, OR JUST LAZING IN A HAMMOCK. ALL THESE THINGS THAT I HAD DENIED MYSELF FOR MUCH TOO LONG A PERIOD IN MY LIFE.

IN OTHER WORDS, I DECIDED TO STOP BEING THE "WORK-UNIT" AND TRANSFERRED INTO A MORE FREE AND INDEPENDENT-SPIRIT. ALL OF THIS TRANSFORMATION DEVELOPED BECAUSE I FINALLY REALIZED THAT I, AS A HOME OWNER COULD BECOME AN APARTMENT OWNER AND THAT I COULD COLLECT THOSE RENT CHECKS JUST AS WELL AS THE NEXT GUY ... YOU ARE LIVING "ON TOP OF AN OIL-WELL" (YOUR MILLSTONE)... AND PROBABLY DON'T EVEN KNOW IT!

"IF YOU CAN AFFORD A HOME . . . YOU CAN AFFORD
TO OWN YOUR OWN APARTMENT BUILDING . . .
AND LIVE THERE RENT FREE."

I REALIZED THAT I COULD GAIN MORE FREEDOM
AND INDEPENDENCE FROM MY DAILY WORK
GRIND . . . AND THAT IF I GOT FIRED OR IF AN-
OTHER RECESSION HIT, THAT IT WOULD NOT MEAN
A REAL STRUGGLE FOR SURVIVAL . . . FOR NOW I
WOULD BE LIVING RENT FREE.

YOU WILL BE SURPRISED TO LEARN THAT THERE
ARE PLENTY OF 3 AND 5 AND 7 UNIT APARTMENT
BUILDINGS AVAILABLE FOR SALE WITH A RE-
QUIRED DOWN PAYMENT OF BETWEEN $10,000 AND
$20,000. MANY COMMERCIAL PROPERTIES IN FACT,
REQUIRE LESS OF A DOWN PAYMENT THAN A
HOUSE. YOU WILL PROBABLY HAVE $3,000 TO
$5,000 OR MORE REMAINING IN EQUITY FROM
YOUR HOUSE SALE, AFTER YOU PURCHASE YOUR
APARTMENT BUILDING. AND THAT IS ALWAYS RE-
COMMENDED REGARDLESS OF WHAT KIND OF BUSI-
NESS YOU GO INTO. THE SMALL BUSINESS ASSOCIA-
TION SAYS THAT "NO CASH RESERVES ARE THE

REASON FOR MOST BUSINESS FAILURES", AND THIS INCLUDES OF COURSE THE RISKY TYPES OF BUSINESSES, LIKE BARS, RESTAURANTS, MOTELS, SMALL STORES AND SHOPS ETC. EVERYONE GOING INTO A NEW ENDEAVOR SHOULD HAVE A CASH RESERVE FOR THE UNEXPECTED.

THEN ALSO, THIS CASH RESERVE WILL COME IN HANDY, SHOULD YOU WISH TO DO SOME SIMPLE, BASIC AND INEXPENSIVE IMPROVEMENTS WHICH WILL ALLOW YOU TO INCREASE THE RENTS, AND TO BECOME MORE INDEPENDENT SINCE YOUR INCOME WILL AGAIN INCREASE FROM THE INCREASED RENTS. ALSO, ALL SMART PROPERTY OWNERS ARE CONTINUALLY CONCERNED WITH IMPROVING THEIR PROPERTY, BECAUSE DETERIORATION WILL DEFINITELY LOWER THE VALUE OF YOUR PROPERTY DESPITE THE CONTINUAL UPWARD SPIRAL OF PROPERTY VALUES OVER THE PAST FIFTY YEARS.

REGARDING THE RISK: TO MY MIND, THE APARTMENT BUILDING BUSINESS IS NOT NEAR THE RISK OF THE OTHER TYPE BUSINESS VENTURES LISTED

"Real estate is the best investment. More money is made from the rise in real estate values than from all other sources combined.

William Jennings Bryan

"The big fortunes of the future will be made in real estate."

John D. Rockefeller

"I advise women to invest in real estate. It is the collateral to be preferred above all others and is the safest means of investing money."

Hetty Green

"Land can't run away, can't burn up; it can't be stolen and hidden away out of sight. It represents the most solid, substantial and permanent investment possible."

Col. H. Oswald

"Buying real estate is not only the best way, the quickest way, and the safest way, but the only way to become wealthy."

Marshall Field

"Ninety per cent of all millionaires became so through owning real estate. More money has been made in real estate than in all industrial investments combined."

Andrew Carnegie

"No investment on earth is so safe, so sure, so certain to enrich its owner as real estate."

Grover Cleveland

"Land monopoly is not the only monopoly, but it is by far the greatest of monopolies—it is a perpetual monopoly, and it is the mother of all other forms of monopoly."

Winston Churchill

"IF YOU CAN AFFORD A HOME . . . YOU CAN AFFORD TO OWN YOUR OWN APARTMENT BUILDING . . . AND LIVE THERE RENT FREE."

ABOVE. OWNING AN APARTMENT BUILDING MEANS THAT YOU OWN A SOLID PIECE OF PROPERTY WITH A BUILDING ON IT. REFER TO ANY LONG TERM STUDY YOU WISH AND YOU WILL LEARN THAT REAL ESTATE PROPERTY HAS IRREGULARLY BUT STEADILY AND GREATLY INCREASED IN VALUE OVER THE PAST FIFTY YEARS.

SECONDLY, EVERYONE NEEDS A ROOF OVER HIS HEAD. PEOPLE CAN EAT AT HOME AND THEY DO NOT HAVE TO GO OUT TO YOUR RESTAURANT, BAR OR TAVERN, AND THE PUBLIC DOES NOT HAVE TO BUY "THAT DOOHICKEY" THAT YOU PLAN TO MAKE A FORTUNE WITH IN YOUR NEW SHOP . . . BUT A ROOF OVER THEIR HEADS? SHELTER IS PRIMARY.

SO IF YOU PURCHASE A POTENTIALLY ATTRACTIVE BUILDING, IN A CONVENIENT LOCATION, COMFORTABLE UNITS, PRICED RIGHT . . . HOW CAN YOU GO TOO FAR WRONG? YOU CAN GO WRONG, ONLY

IF YOU PAID TOO MUCH FOR YOUR BUILDING INI-
TIALLY, OR IF IT WAS A BAD BUY IN ONE OF MANY
OTHER RESPECTS. AN INDEPENDENT-EXPERT CAN
BE OF GREAT HELP HERE, IN PREVENTING YOU
FROM MAKING A BAD BUY THAT COULD BURDEN
YOU FOR THE REST OF YOUR LIFE. CONVERSELY,
IF THE INDEPENDENT-EXPERT HELPS YOU MAKE A
GOOD SELECTION, YOUR HAPPINESS IN LIFE WILL
BE GREATLY INCREASED FOR THE REST OF YOUR
LIFE. SO, THE STAKES ARE BIG AND IMPORTANT . . .
THIS IS NOT LIKE GOING OUT TO BUY A LOAF OF
BREAD, AS TOO MANY CASUAL PEOPLE WILL DO.

THE HAPPY END TO MY PARTICULAR STORY
THAT BEGAN THIS CHAPTER, IS THAT TWO YEARS
AFTER THE PURCHASE OF MY FIRST APARTMENT
BUILDING (5 UNITS) I HAVE IMPROVED THE PRO-
PERTY (SPENT ABOUT $5,000), SIMULTANEOUSLY
INCREASED THE RENTS TO ALMOST DOUBLE . . . SO
THAT TODAY, TWO YEARS LATER, I NOT ONLY
LIVE RENT FREE, BUT I CLEAR A PROFIT ON THIS

"IF YOU CAN AFFORD A HOME . . . YOU CAN AFFORD
TO OWN YOUR OWN APARTMENT BUILDING . . .
AND LIVE THERE RENT FREE."

APARTMENT BUILDING OF $300 MONTHLY, AND I

WORK LESS NOW AT MY REGULAR JOB. NOT BAD

FROM A $15,000 DOWN PAYMENT TWO YEARS AGO,

HUH? ALL BECAUSE I FINALLY GOT RID OF THAT

OLD MILLSTONE AROUND MY NECK, MY HOME. AND

INCIDENTALLY I LIVE BETTER NOW THAN IN MY

FORMER HOME THAT WASN'T TOO CHARMING. MY

APARTMENT IS A SHOWCASE VILLA-MANSION TYPE

THAT WOULD RENT FOR $450 MONTHLY, SHOULD I

MOVE OUT. AND, MY $72,000 APARTMENT BUILDING

(WITH RENTS DOUBLED) IS NOW WORTH $144,000. NOT

A BAD TWO YEARS WORK?

THERE ARE 47,000,000 HOME OWNERS IN THE USA,

ALONE. AS WE GO INTO THE SPIRALING INFLATION

OF THE 1980'S, MANY OF THESE HOMEOWNERS WILL

SELL THEIR "MILLSTONE" (THEIR HOME) AND

PURCHASE A QUAD-PLEX (4 UNITS). THESE WISE

PEOPLE WILL LIVE RENT FREE IMMEDIATELY WHILE

THE RENTAL INCOME FROM THE OTHER 2 OR 3

UNITS WILL PAY OFF THE MORTGAGE, ITS INTEREST,

AND THE TAXES AND THE INSURANCE. AS INFLA-

TION RISES, SO WILL YOUR TENANTS RENTS: BUT

YOUR MORTGAGE STAYS THE SAME (THAT'S CALLED

9

LEVERAGE). IN JUST 2 OR 3 YEARS THESE RENTAL INCREASES WILL GIVE YOU AN ADDITIONAL INCOME BESIDES LIVING RENT FREE. THIS QUAD-PLEX WILL GIVE YOU FINANCIAL SALVATION AS WE GO INTO THE INFLATIONARY SPIRAL OF THE 1980'S.

AND YOU CAN LIVE RENT FREE, ANYWHERE IN THE WORLD. SHELTER IS NOT A NECESSITY, JUST IN FLORIDA (WHERE I CHOOSE TO LIVE) . . . OR EVEN IN THE USA . . . SHELTER IS NECESSARY WORLDWIDE (UNLESS YOU ARE A SQUATTER, OR A CAVEMAN . . . AND SOME MOTHERS IN LAW LIVE RENT FREE) . . . IN FACT . . . WANT TO LIVE RENT FREE IN TAHITI? BUY A QUAD PLEX THERE, AND DO IT!

HOW TO OWN YOUR OWN DUPLEX APARTMENT BUILDING . . . EVEN IF YOU DON'T HAVE THE DOWN PAYMENT . . . AND SOON LIVE THERE RENT FREE . . . AS WE ENTER THE INFLATIONARY SPIRAL OF THE 1980's.

YOU CAN PURCHASE A NICE DUPLEX IN MOST AREAS FOR $25,000, AND A $2,500 DOWN PAYMENT . . . BUT YOU DON'T HAVE THE DOWN PAYMENT. FOR THIS, I SUGGEST THAT YOU GET A "FRIENDLY LOAN" FROM

"IF YOU CAN AFFORD A HOME . . . YOU CAN AFFORD TO OWN YOUR OWN APARTMENT BUILDING . . . AND LIVE THERE RENT FREE."

A RELATIVE; "SECURED" IN A BUSINESS-LIKE FASHION IN WRITING ON THE DEED; FOR ABOUT A 3 YEAR PAYOFF AT A GENEROUS INTEREST RATE. DON'T BE CHEAP (ESPECIALLY WITH RELATIVES) OFFER A POINT OR TWO OVER EXISTING INTEREST RATES TO INSURE GETTING A "YES". IF YOU CAN'T GET A FRIENDLY LOAN, GET AN 'UNFRIENDLY LOAN' FROM A LOAN COMPANY. THIS IS EASY ENOUGH, SINCE YOU ARE A WORKING ADULT . . . (YOU GET A 3 YEAR LOAN SOMETIMES FOR MORE THAN $2,500 TO PURCHASE A CAR!)

1. YOU WILL BE ABLE TO FIND DUPLEXES, WHERE THE RENT FROM THE OTHER UNIT WILL MORE THAN COVER YOUR MONTHLY PAYMENTS ON THIS SHORT-TERM, DOWN PAYMENT LOAN. DON'T GIVE UP . . . KEEP LOOKING UNTIL YOU FIND JUST THE RIGHT DUPLEX FOR YOU.

ADDITIONALLY, YOU FIND A DUPLEX WHERE THE OWNER WILL DO YOUR FINANCING INSTEAD OF A

BANK. (SEE CHAPTER ON "NO-FRILLS FINANCING"). WITH OWNER FINANCING YOU IMMEDIATELY SAVE THE HUNDREDS OF DOLLARS THE BANK CHARGES YOU FOR "CLOSING COSTS." (WHICH YOU MAY NOT HAVE). AN OWNER LOAN IS CALLED A P.M.M., ie, PURCHASE MONEY MORTGAGE. AGAIN, DO NOT DESPAIR . . . SHOP FOR DUPLEXES UNTIL YOU FIND OWNERS WHO WILL FINANCE YOU . . . THEN TAKE THE BEST ONE. OWNER FINANCING IS NOT THAT DIFFICULT, I BOUGHT 3 IN 3 YEARS ON THIS BASIS.

2. SO NOW, INSTEAD OF PAYING RENT . . . YOUR MONTHLY PAYMENTS ARE GOING TO THE FORMER OWNER OF THIS DUPLEX AS MONTHLY PAYMENTS ON THE LONG TERM MORTGAGE. THESE PAYMENTS WILL NORMALLY BE HIGHER THAN YOUR SHORT TERM MONTHLY PAYMENTS . . . BUT SO WHAT . . . YOU ARE PAYING OFF YOUR OWN BUILDING INSTEAD OF COLLECTING A FILE DRAWER OF RENT RE-CEIPTS . . . AND YOU HAVE EFFECTIVELY STOPPED YOUR OWN INFLATIONARY CLOCK, THE DAY YOU

"IF YOU CAN AFFORD A HOME . . . YOU CAN AFFORD
TO OWN YOUR OWN APARTMENT BUILDING . . .
AND LIVE THERE RENT FREE."

MADE THE PURCHASE . . . BY LOCKING IN YOUR
LONG TERM LOAN . . . TO BE PAID OFF WITH "CHEAP"
DOLLARS IN THE 1980'S. THE ENTREPENEURS CALL
THIS "LEVERAGE"; BUT YOU ARE USING LEVERAGE
IN A VERY CONSERVATIVE WAY AND FOR A VERY
GOOD CAUSE . . . PERSONAL INVESTMENT . . . FREE
RENT . . . TAX SHELTER, BECAUSE YOU NOW PAY
LESS OR NO INCOME TAX ON YOUR SALARIED
INCOME.

3. IN 3 YEARS, YOUR TENANTS' RENTAL PAYMENTS
HAVE PAID OFF YOUR SHORT-TERM LOAN (HIS RENT
TO YOU HAS PROBABLY INCREASED ALREADY WITH
THE INFLATIONARY SPIRAL) . . . AND NOW YOUR
TENANTS' RENT CHECKS PAYS OFF ALL OR THE
MAJOR PORTION OF YOUR LONG TERM MORT-
GAGE . . . AND IF NOT IMMEDIATELY . . . VERY SOON,
YOU WILL BE LIVING RENT FREE IN YOUR OWN
DUPLEX.

BUYING TIP: SHOP AND SAVE... ITS YOUR MONEY. NORMALLY YOU PURCHASE A DUPLEX AT ABOUT 6 TIMES ANNUAL RENTAL... HOWEVER, YOU WILL KNOW THE "MARKET" IN YOUR AREA AFTER SHOPPING AT LEAST 5 DUPLEXES. YOU CAN ALSO GET FREE PROFESSIONAL ADVICE BEFORE AND, EVEN AFTER THE SALE. (SEE CHAP. "YOUR SECRET WEAPON."

4. AS A DUPLEX OWNER (SOUND GOOD?) YOU NOW HAVE YOUR OWN TAX-SHELTER TO AVOID, QUITE LEGALLY, PAYING ALL OR MOST OF THE INCOME TAX ON YOUR SALARY. (SEE CHAPTER, "YOUR PERSONAL OIL-WELL (DUPLEX) WITHOUT THE RISK.")

"WILL EVERYONE DO THIS?" AUTHOR ANDERSON IS ASKED AFTER LECTURES... HIS REPLY... "NO, BECAUSE WE ARE MADE UP OF 90% "DREAMERS" AND 10% "DOERS". THE DOERS WILL BUY THE DUPLEXES; THE DREAMERS WILL BE THE RENTERS.

CHAPTER TWO

"YOU HAVE A SECRET WEAPON. DON'T TREAT
BUYING AN APARTMENT CASUALLY, LIKE BUYING
A LOAF OF BREAD

BUYING YOUR APARTMENT BUILDING WILL BE ONE
OF THE MAJOR MONETARY DECISIONS OF YOUR
LIFE. IF YOU ARE SUCCESSFUL IN MAKING A GOOD
PURCHASE, YOU WILL BE REWARDED WITH A HAP-
PIER LIFE IN MANY FINANCIAL AND SELF SATISFY-
ING WAYS OVER THE LIFETIME OF THAT OWNER-
SHIP. CONVERSELY, IF YOU MAKE A POOR PUR-
CHASE, YOUR LIFE WILL BE SORRIER FOR IT MANY
TIMES OVER THE OWNERSHIP TERM, AND THAT
COULD BE TEN YEARS OR FOR THE REST OF YOUR.
LIFE.

SO DON'T BE CASUAL ABOUT THE PROJECT TO PUR-
CHASE AN APARTMENT BUILDING. AS AN EXAMPLE,
HAVE YOU OR A FRIEND EVER TAKEN A "STOCK
TIP" FROM "SOMEONE IN THE KNOW", ONLY TO
LOSE YOUR MONEY. AND MAYBE IT WAS A BIG
CHUNK OF YOUR LIFE'S SAVINGS WHICH YOU WILL
NEVER RECOVER. DO YOU MAYBE KNOW A FRIEND

WHO INVESTS HIS LARGE SUM OF MONEY THROUGH A STOCK BROKER WHO HAS ONLY A SMALL SUM OF MONEY IN THE MARKET. THIS IS HOW CASUAL PEOPLE CAN BE WITH THEIR SAVINGS THAT THEY HAVE WORKED SO HARD TO ACQUIRE. I HAVE HEARD MACHO-TYPE MEN WHO TELL ME "YEA, I'M GOING TO BUY AN APARTMENT BUILDING." WHEN I INQUIRE IF THEY OWN OR EVER HAVE OWNED ONE THEY USUALLY CASUALLY SAY, "NO", AS IF TO SAY ("WHAT'S THE BIG DEAL ABOUT BUYING AN APARTMENT BUILDING?") TO THIS I WOULD AN-SWER . . . "MAYBE THIRTY YEARS OF ANGUISH."

SO BE CAREFUL. IF YOU DO NOT HAVE EXPE-RIENCE IN THIS FIELD . . . DON'T EXPECT YOUR FRIENDLY REAL ESTATE SALESPERSON TO GUIDE YOU DOWN THE PATH TO WEALTH, FORTUNE AND CONTENTMENT AS A NEW APARTMENT OWNER. MAYBE YOU DO NOT KNOW THAT THE REAL ES-TATE AGENT HAS A FIDUCIARY TRUST WITH THE SELLER . . . NOT YOU THE BUYER. THIS IS EVEN

"YOU HAVE A SECRET WEAPON. DON'T TREAT
BUYING AN APARTMENT CASUALLY, LIKE BUYING
A LOAF OF BREAD"

TAUGHT IN REAL ESTATE SALES CLASSES. IT IS
ALSO TAUGHT IN THESE CLASSES "CAVEAT EMP-
TOR", WHICH MEANS "BUYER BEWARE". THE
AGENT AND THE SELLER ARE NOT OBLIGATED IN
ANY WAY TO TELL YOU OF ANY DEFICIENCIES IN
THE APARTMENT BUILDING. THE ONLY THING THE
AGENT AND SELLER ARE BOUND BY LAW TO TELL
YOU IS "HIDDEN CONSTRUCTION ELEMENTS"... IF
YOU ASK. LIKE WHAT IS INSIDE THE WALLS, UNDER
THE ROOF, ETC. THEN, LATER, IF YOU HAVE FALSE
STATEMENTS IN WRITING OR WITNESSED BY A PRO-
PER PERSON, THEN YOU CAN COLLECT DAMAGES.
ALL OF THIS IS TAUGHT TO THE AGENTS IN CLASS,
WHEN THEY ARE APPLYING FOR A REAL ESTATE
LICENSE ... SO CAVEAT EMPTOR.

NOW THINK BACK TO WHEN YOU BOUGHT YOUR
HOME. DO YOU EVER RECALL AN AGENT TELLING
YOU "NOT" TO BUY THIS OR THAT HOME? OF
COURSE NOT. THE AGENT'S JOB IS TO SELL ... AND
"BUYER BEWARE."

SECONDLY, THE AGENT PROBABLY DOES NOT OWN ANY APARTMENT BUILDINGS. SO HOW CAN THE AGENT GUIDE YOU DOWN THE PATH TO WEALTH AND FORTUNE IF THE AGENT HAS NOT DONE IT FOR HIMSELF IN HIS CHOSEN PROFESSION? THAT'S LIKE A STOCK BROKER I ONCE HAD FOR A SHORT TIME IN MY YOUTH, WHO ALWAYS PLAYED THE HORSES. IT ALWAYS MADE ME UNEASY AND I FINALLY DUMPED HIM.

THERE ARE TWO ANSWERS TO ALL OF THESE CONSCIENCE-RAISING THOUGHTS AS TO HOW YOU CAN FOLLOW THE SUCCESSFUL PATH TO WEALTH AND FORTUNE IN THE APARTMENT OWNERSHIP BUSINESS.

1. DO A LOT OF WORK AND INVESTIGATING YOURSELF AND LEARN WHAT IS A GOOD BUY FROM A BAD BUY.
2. EMPLOY AN INDEPENDENT-EXPERT. I SAID A REAL EXPERT, AND THAT IS A PERSON WHO

"YOU HAVE A SECRET WEAPON. DON'T TREAT BUYING AN APARTMENT CASUALLY, LIKE BUYING A LOAF OF BREAD"

NOW OWNS APARTMENT BUILDINGS AND MANAGES THEM HIMSELF, AND NOT ONE WHO PUSHES THE BUTTONS FROM HIS "IVORY TOWER."

"Buying Income Property? Ask the Man Who Owns One!'

FOR HOW CAN AN INDEPENDENT-EXPERT PROPERLY GUIDE YOU DOWN THE PATH TO WEALTH AND FORTUNE . . . IF HE HAS NOT DONE IT FOR HIMSELF? ? ? IF YOU ARE SUSPICIOUS, LOOK AT HIS BUILDINGS. AT LEAST REQUIRE IT IN WRITING THAT CURRENTLY HE OWNS X BUILDINGS, WITH X UNITS, AND HE MANAGES THEM HIMSELF. A REAL ESTATE BROKER WHO BECOMES YOUR INDEPENDENT-EXPERT WILL NOT PUT THAT IN WRITING IF IT IS NOT TRUE, BECAUSE THIS TYPE OF DECEIT IN SUCH A FIDUCIARY RELATIONSHIP BETWEEN YOU AND THE EXPERT, COULD CAUSE THE BROKER-EXPERT TO LOSE HIS LICENSE. AND THESE LICENSES ARE TOO HARD TO GET THESE DAYS.

19

INCIDENTALLY, I ONCE FIGURED IT UP, THAT IT TOOK ME THREE YEARS, 2000 HOURS OF STUDY AND CLASS, AND ABOUT $1,000 TO BECOME A REAL ESTATE BROKER IN FLORIDA. THAT IS ABOUT WHAT IT TAKES TO BECOME A LAWYER. SO NO BROKER WILL JEOPARDIZE HIS LICENSE WITH UN-TRUTHS IN A FIDUCIARY ARRANGEMENT. NOW NOTICE I SAID FIDUCIARY ARRANGEMENT . . . FOR WHEN YOU EMPLOY THE BROKER-EXPERT TO AD-VISE YOU (NOT TO SELL YOU), BUT TO ADVISE YOU ON WHAT TO BUY . . . YOU HAVE SET UP A FIDUCI-ARY RELATIONSHIP (A TRUTHFUL AND TRUST-WORTHY RELATIONSHIP) IN YOUR PURCHASE OF AN APARTMENT BUILDING. THIS IS NOT THAT OFTEN DONE BY THE "CASUAL BUYER", BUT IS THE ONLY SMART WAY TO BUY REAL ESTATE . . . AND IT COSTS YOU NOTHING. BECAUSE IF YOU EMPLOY A BROKER-EXPERT (NOT A NON-BROKER-EXPERT), THEN THIS BROKER-EXPERT CAN SHARE IN THE SIZEABLE SALES COMMISSION THAT THE SELLER PAYS TO HIS REAL ESTATE AGENT. EXAMPLE: SAY

"YOU HAVE A SECRET WEAPON, DON'T TREAT BUYING AN APARTMENT BUILDING CASUALLY, LIKE BUYING A LOAF OF BREAD

YOU PURCHASE A $100,000 APARTMENT BUILDING THROUGH A LISTING BROKER. IN THAT SALES PRICE YOU PAY IS A 5% TO 7% SALES COMMISSION PAID TO THE LISTING BROKER. IF YOU HAVE PLAN-NED AHEAD AND EMPLOYED YOUR OWN INDEPEND-ENT-EXPERT-BROKER, BY A LITTLE USED STATE-MENT, YOUR BROKER-EXPERT CAN SHARE IN 30% TO 40% OF THAT $5,000 TO $7,000 COMMISSION, WHICH AMOUNTS TO ABOUT $2,000 TO $3,000. THAT IS NOT A BAD DAY'S WORK FOR THE EXPERT, AND YOU HAVE GOTTEN THE SERVICE FREE. NOW, IN YOUR AGREEMENT WITH THE BROKER-EXPERT, IF YOU CAN GET A FURTHER AGREEMENT FOR SOME FREE ADVICE, AFTER THE SALE, IN THE OPERA-TION AND MANAGEMENT OF YOUR NEW APART-MENT BUILDING, IMAGINE WHAT A GENIUS YOU HAVE BEEN? FOR HAVE YOUR EVER RUN INTO AN AGENT WHO AFTER HE SOLD YOU A PROPERTY, WAS AVAILABLE TO HELP YOU, AFTER THE SALE? ? ? RARELY, IF AT ALL. INCIDENTALLY THE

SELLER PAYS THE COMMISSION . . . YOU DO NOT.

FURTHER, REGARDING POINT No. 1 ABOVE . . . "CONFUCIUS SAY; BEST HELPING HAND IS AT END OF RIGHT SLEEVE." THIS MEANS FOR SECURITY, HELP YOURSELF. INSPECT MANY BUILDINGS ON YOUR OWN BUT WITH THE GUIDANCE OF YOUR BROKER-EXPERT. SINCE I WAS TOTALLY NEW TO THIS AREA, AND NEW IN APARTMENT INVESTING THREE YEARS AGO, AND I DID NOT KNOW ABOUT THE POSSIBILITY OF HIRING A BROKER-EXPERT COST FREE, I LOOKED AT OVER 100 APARTMENT BUILD-INGS BEFORE I BOUGHT THE FIRST ONE. FOR I NOT ONLY HAD TO LEARN ALL THE VARIOUS PROFIT POTENTIAL GUIDELINES, BUT I ALSO HAD TO LEARN ABOUT THE VARIOUS AREAS AND WHICH LOCATION WAS THE BEST FOR ME. EVEN WITH YOUR ABILITY TO HIRE YOUR OWN FIDUCIARY-BROKER-EXPERT, I WOULD STILL RECOMMEND THAT YOU LOOK AT ABOUT TEN BUILDINGS, AND REQUEST YOUR EXPERT TO THEN LOOK AT

"YOU HAVE A SECRET WEAPON. DON'T TREAT
BUYING AN APARTMENT CASUALLY, LIKE BUYING
A LOAF OF BREAD"

THE FINAL TOP THREE THAT YOU LIKE PERSONAL-
LY. THEN HAVE YOUR EXPERT "GRADE" THE FINAL
TOP THREE AS TO PROFIT POTENTIAL, CONSTRUC-
TION, LOCATION, ETC.

FURTHER, REGARDING POINT No. 2 ABOVE.
LUCKILY, I HAD A LITTLE ADVICE FROM A NEW
REAL ESTATE BROKER FRIEND, WHO WAS NOT IN-
VOLVED IN THE PURCHASE OF THE BUILDING. I DID
NOT ASK TOO MUCH OF HIM BECAUSE I FELT
GUILTY ABOUT TAKING HIS TIME. IF HE WOULD
HAVE EXPLAINED TO ME WHAT I HAVE JUST EX-
PLAIN TO YOU IN THIS CHAPTER ABOUT THE COST
FREE FIDUCIARY EXPERT RELATIONSHIP I AM
CERTAIN THAT I WOULD HAVE GRABBED THE OP-
PORTUNITY TO GAIN HIS COMPLETE ADVICE ABOUT
MY PURCHASE. I WAS THEN LIKE YOU PROBABLY
ARE RIGHT NOW. I DID NOT KNOW THAT SUCH A
SERVICE WAS AVAILABLE. AND MAYBE IT SOUNDED
SO GOOD THAT YOU COULD EVEN BE SUSPICIOUS

UNLESS YOU GOT THE COMPLETE EXPLANATION, AS YOU ARE GETTING IN THIS BOOK.

MY REAL ESTATE BROKER NEW FRIEND WAS A RARE FRIEND INDEED. HE TAUGHT ME MANY OF THE THINGS I AM WRITING ABOUT IN THIS BOOK. HE ALSO WAS MY FIRST TEACHER AT THE UNIVERSITY OF MIAMI WHERE I ENROLLED IN THE REAL ESTATE COURSE TO GAIN MY LICENSE. HE ADVISED ME WITHOUT ANY REWARD... THAT IS RARE INDEED. OBVIOUSLY YOU OR I WOULD TRUST STATEMENTS MADE BY SUCH AN EXPERT, FOR HE HAD NOTHING TO GAIN, REGARDLESS IF I BOUGHT OR DID NOT BUY. YOU CAN DO PRACTICALLY THE SAME THING SINCE YOU NOW HAVE THE SECRET OF GAINING A FIDUCIARY RELATIONSHIP WITH AN INDEPENDENT EXPERT BROKER AT NO CHARGE TO YOURSELF.

FURTHER, YOU GO TO A LAWYER WHEN YOU NEED LEGAL ADVICE, YOU GO TO AN ACCOUNTANT

"YOU HAVE A SECRET WEAPON. DON'T TREAT BUYING AN APARTMENT BUILDING CASUALLY, LIKE BUYING A LOAF OF BREAF"

WHEN YOU NEED BOOKKEEPING ADVICE, WHY NOT GO TO AN INDEPENDENT EXPERT WHEN YOU ARE ABOUT TO PURCHASE AND APARTMENT BUILDING WHICH IS PROBABLY ONE OF THE BIGGEST INVEST- MENT DECISIONS IN YOUR LIFE? BELIEVE ME, IT IS DIFFERENT WHEN YOU BUY AN APARTMENT BUILD- ING VERSUS WHEN YOU BUY A HOME AND YOUR INDEPENDENT-EXPERT-BROKER WILL PROBABLY EVEN SAVE YOU MONEY ON THE PURCHASE PRICE, FOR IF THE ASKING PRICE OF THE BUILDING THAT YOU SELECT IS $100,000, YOUR EXPERT MAY REC- OMMEND THAT YOU OFFER $85,000 OR $90,000 AND HE WILL TELL YOU AND THE SELLER WHY THEY SHOULD ACCEPT THE LESSER PRICE, IE, BECAUSE OF THIS AND THIS AND THIS, ETC.

SO, YOUR SECRET WEAPON IN BUYING AN APART- MENT BUILDING IS TO MAKE AN AGREEMENT, IN WRITING, WITH A REAL ESTATE BROKER, WHEREBY THE BROKER IS REPRESENTING YOU IN A FIDUCI-

ARY RELATIONSHIP, AND THAT WITH HIS EX-
PERTISE IN OWNING AND MANAGING APARTMENT
BUILDINGS, THIS BROKER WILL TO THE BEST OF
HIS ABILITY, ADVISE YOU AS TO WHAT TO BUY,
AND HE WILL BE AVAILABLE TO ADVISE YOU IN
THE OPERATION AND MANAGEMENT OF YOUR
APARTMENT BUILDING AFTER YOU BUY IT. ALL
THIS SERVICE AND ADVICE FROM YOUR INDEPEND-
ENT BROKER EXPERT IS AT NO COST TO YOU IN
MOST CASES. IF, AS EXAMPLE, YOU DECIDE TO PUR-
CHASE A BUILDING THAT IS NOT LISTED THROUGH
A REAL ESTATE AGENT, BUT IS FOR SALE PRIVATE-
LY, BY THE OWNER, THEN YOU WILL OWE THE EX-
PERT BROKER WITH WHOM YOU MADE THE AGREE-
MENT AN ADVISORY FEE OF ABOUT 4% OF THE
GROSS COST. BUT REMEMBER, YOU WILL ALSO
GAIN THIS EXPERT'S KNOWLEDGE... AFTER THE
SALE, PER YOUR SAME AGREEMENT. FURTHER, I
HAVE FOUND NOT TOO MANY GOOD BUYS FROM A
PRIVATE INDIVIDUAL WHO IS NOT REPRESENTED
BY A BROKER. THIS PRIVATE OWNER USUALLY HAS

"YOU HAVE A SECRET WEAPON. DON'T TREAT BUYING AN APARTMENT CASUALLY, LIKE BUYING A LOAF OF BREAD"

AN INFLATED PRICE ON HIS PROPERTY, AND IS JUST WAITING FOR THE "SUCKER" WHO THINKS HE IS GETTING A BARGAIN. THE OWNER WHO REALLY IS SERIOUS ABOUT SELLING HAS LISTED HIS PROPERTY WITH A BROKER, AT A FAIR AND MARKETABLE PRICE, WHICH CAN STILL BE NEGOTIATED DOWN BY A KNOWLEDGEABLE BUYER.

HOW TO FIND YOUR OWN FREE ADVISOR BROKER (YOUR SECRET WEAPON) AND THEN HOW TO DRIVE THE RIGHT AND COMPLETE BARGAIN WITH HIM.

BELIEVE IT OR NOT RARELY WILL YOU BE ABLE TO FIND SUCH AN ADVISOR BROKER IN THE "YELLOW PAGES" ... FOR I SAY OFTEN IN INTERVIEWS AND LECTURES THAT REAL ESTATE IS AN UNCREATIVE BUSINESS AND MANY PEOPLE GOT INTO IT BECAUSE THERE WAS NOTHING ELSE TO DO. THIS IS YOUR CHALLENGE FOLKS TO DRIVE THE RIGHT BARGAIN (FREE) WITH THE RIGHT BROKER. YOU MAY WANT TO LET HIM READ THIS BOOK IF HE IS UNCONVINCED TO "DO IT YOUR WAY". I FIND BROKERS QUITE OFTEN ARE BOOK BUYERS WHEN I

27

MAKE A BOOK STORE APPEARANCE . . . AND THEY PROUDLY TELL ME SO, ADDING THAT THEY ARE ALWAYS INTERESTED IN "A NEW APPROACH." BELIEVE IT OR NOT, HOWEVER, WHEN I WAS FIRST DEVELOPING THESE IDEAS SEVERAL YEARS AGO, I ASKED A REAL ESTATE SCHOLAR FRIEND OF MINE ABOUT BECOMING "AN ADVISOR BROKER" . . . HE NAIVELY RECOUNTED THAT ON OCCASION HE WOULD ADVISE A CUSTOMER IN A PURCHASE . . . "FOR A $5,000 FEE" BELIEVE IT OR NOT. WHEN I TOLD THIS "SCHOLAR" THAT I PLANNED TO DO IT "FOR FREE" . . . "BY MERELY TAKING ONE HALF OF THE SELLER'S COMMISSION WHICH IS DUE ME, SINCE I QUALIFY AS THE-COOPERATING-BROKER IN THE ANTIQUE-STYLE REAL ESTATE BUSINESS BY BRINGING THE BUYER HALF OF THE TRANSACTION INTO THE DEAL" . . . TO THIS DAY I DO NOT THINK HE AGREES WITH MY PREMISE . . . OR EVEN UNDERSTANDS . . . AND HE HAS BEEN IN THE REAL ESTATE BUSINESS, AS A BROKER, FOR ABOUT 40 YEARS. I EVEN TOLD THIS BROKER, THAT "FOR EVERY ONE

"YOU HAVE A SECRET WEAPON. DON'T TREAT
BUYING AN APARTMENT CASUALLY, LIKE
BUYING A LOAF OF BREAD."

$5,000 CUSTOMER FEE YOU GET . . . I WILL GET 25
CUSTOMERS, SINCE MY CHARGES ARE FREE." TO
THIS DAY, I JUST DON'T THINK HE UNDERSTOOD
WHAT I WAS SAYING . . . ALTHOUGH I SAID IT TO HIM
IN A NUMBER OF CLEAR AND DIFFERENT WAYS . . .
BUT DO NOT BE DISCOURAGED . . . YOU NOW HAVE A
$25 BOOK IN YOUR HAND THAT YOU CAN SHOW TO A
DOUBTFUL BROKER . . . AND YOU MAY JUST OPEN UP
A NEW CAREER TO HIM, THAT IS, ADVISING THE
BUYER (IF HE QUALIFIES) AT NO FEE . . . SINCE HE
SHARES ("COOPERATES") IN THE COMMISSION THE
SELLER PAYS.

1. FIRST, YOU MUST FIND A REAL ESTATE BROKER
   IN AS CLOSE AN AREA TO YOU AS POSSIBLE WHO
   OWNS AT LEAST ONE APARTMENT BUILDING. IT
   MAY SOUND STRANGE TO YOU, BUT MY RE-
   SEARCH SHOWS THAT ONLY ABOUT 1% TO 5% OF
   THE BROKERS OWN APARTMENT BUILDINGS . . .
   SO HOW CAN THEY SHOW YOU THE WAY TO FAME,
   WEALTH AND FORTUNE IN THE APARTMENT
   BUILDING BUSINESS . . . IF THEY DON'T OWN ONE

THEMSELVES... YET EVERY DAY, BUYERS ARE BUYING APARTMENT BUILDINGS FROM BROKERS WHO DON'T OWN ONE... THEY POSSIBLY RENT AN APARTMENT THEMSELVES. DO YOU KNOW WHY SUCH A SMALL PER CENT OF BROKERS OWN AN APARTMENT BUILDING? I GET TWO FREQUENT ANSWERS FROM THE BROKERS... A) "WE DON'T HAVE THE CAPITAL"... (SHAME ON YOU SLICK BUYERS AND SELLERS FOR SNOOKERING SALES COMMISSIONS AWAY FROM THE POOR DEFENSE-LESS BROKERS... BUT WE ALL HEAR IT CON-STANTLY... ("LET'S CUT-OUT-THE-BROKER"). B) BROKER'S ALSO TELL ME AS REASONS WHY THEY DON'T OWN APARTMENTS... "I DON'T WANT TO CLEAN THE JOHNS... AND I DON'T WANT THOSE SATURDAY NIGHT CALLS"... TO THIS, I REPLY (AS I LAUGH MYSELF ALL THE WAY TO THE BANK, ON A LEISURELY MONDAY MORNING)... "I DON'T CLEAN THE JOHNS ... AND I DON'T GET THOSE SATURDAY NIGHT CALLS" (SEE CHAPTER ON TURNING GOOD-TENANTS INTO STAR-

"YOU HAVE A SECRET WEAPON. DON'T TREAT
BUYING AN APARTMENT CASUALLY, LIKE
BUYING A LOAF OF BREAD."

TENANTS) . . . I AM A PROBLEM SOLVER, AND THIS
BUSINESS SURE WAS WAITING FOR ME TO COME
ALONG, FOR SOMETIME, EVEN IN COLOMBUS,
OHIO, YOU WILL WANT TO TELL A DOUBTING
BROKER ABOUT HOW I OPERATE, FREE TO THE
BUYER, FOR IN MY TRAVELS ON LECTURES AND
BROADCAST APPEARANCES, I HAVE YET TO MEET
A REAL ESTATE BROKER WHO COMES UP TO ME
AND SAYS: "I DO THE SAME THING, HERE." . . . SO,
YOU MAY HAVE TO USE ME AND MY CREATED
BUYER-SERVICE ON SOME LESS ENTERPRISING,
BUT QUALIFIED BROKER. AS I SAY ON MY BUSI-
NESS CARD, AND THIS IS STEP NO. 1 FOR YOU TO
LIVE RENT FREE . . . "BUYING INCOME PROPER-
TY . . . ASK THE MAN WHO OWNS ONE." REMEMBER
THAT "BEAUTLINE" TO ADVERTISE PACKARD
AUTOMOBILES BACK IN THE 1930'S? . . . TO ME IT
IS MORE APROPOS TO BUYING A QUAD PLEX . . . IT
IS YOUR LIFE'S SAVINGS . . . AND IT CAN MEAN 30
YEARS OF HAPPINESS. . . RIGHT?   THEN DON'T
TREAT THIS VENTURE LIKE BUYING A LOAF OF

BREAD ... SO IF YOU ARE LOOKING TO BUY AN APARTMENT BUILDING ... FIND A BROKER WHO OWNS APARTMENT BUILDINGS ... HE BELIEVES IN THE BUSINESS LIKE YOU AND I DO, AND HE WILL BE ABLE TO EARN HIS NO-COMMISSION FROM YOU ... BUT DEFINITELY DON'T GO TO YOUR UNCLE HARRY, WHO JUST GOT HIS REAL ESTATE LICENSE, AND RENTS AN APARTMENT HIMSELF ... THIS IS BUSINESS ... YOUR LIFE'S SAVINGS ... 30 YEARS OF HAPPINESS ... UNCLE HARRY JUST IS NOT QUALIFIED ... FIND YOUR ADVISOR BROKER EXPERT WHO WILL CHARGE YOU NOTHING ... THAT IS YOUR FIRST JOB ... AND IT REALLY WON'T BE THAT DIFFICULT, WHEN YOU REALIZE THE SITUATION AS WE HAVE JUST DISCUSSED IT.

2. NOW YOU MUST DRIVE THE RIGHT BARGAIN WITH THIS NO-COST-BROKER. AT THIS POINT, YOU MAY BE UNKNOWINGLY SAYING ... ("THAT GUY SURE HAS GUTS") ... TO THAT I SAY, "BALONEY" ... I

"YOU HAVE A SECRET WEAPON. DON'T TREAT
BUYING AN APARTMENT CASUALLY, LIKE
BUYING A LOAF OF BREAD."

DO IT FOR BUYERS. WHY CAN'T SOME QUALIFIED
BROKER DO IT FOR YOU IN YOUR OWN HOME
TOWN? SOON, PERHAPS, I WILL BE PROVIDING
EVEN MORE EXPERT AND LOCALIZED HELP FOR
YOU TO FIND THAT "RIGHT MR. ADVISOR-
BROKER" . . . SO IF YOU HAVE DIFFICULTY . . .
THIS WILL BE YOUR FIRST SUBJECT OF INQUIRY
TO ME PER YOUR" 90 DAY BOOK SERVICE
GUARANTEE".

BARGAINING POINTS: BASICALLY WHAT MY
AGREEMENT STATES IS AS FOLLOWS AND YOU
WILL POSSIBLY HAVE TO SHOW THIS TO YOUR
LOCAL AND QUALIFIED BROKER TO SELL HIM ON
THE IDEA THAT IT IS PROFITABLE . . . I DO IT . . .
WHY CAN'T HE?

A) I LOOK AT THE TOP THREE CHOICES OF A MINI-
MUM TOTAL OF AT LEAST TEN APARTMENT
BUILDINGS THAT MY CLIENT-BUYER HAS
LOOKED AT ALONE, BUT POSSIBLY WITH MY

BEHIND THE SCENES DIRECTION AS TO WHERE
TO GO, AND WHO TO CONTACT . . . FOR IF THE
BUYER WANTS HIS ADVISOR BROKER TO
QUALIFY IN SPLITTING THE COMMISSION OF
THE SELLING BROKER . . . THEN ON EACH
APARTMENT VISIT (WITHOUT THE AD-
VISOR) . . . YOU, THE BUYER MUST TELL THE
SELLING-BROKER: "I HAVE BEEN SENT BY
MR. ...., MY (ADVISOR) BROKER . . . DO YOU
COOPERATE?" THIS IS THE KEY TO SELL YOUR
ADVISOR BROKER THAT YOU IN FACT WILL
NOT CUT HIM OUT OF HIS HALF SHARE COM-
MISSION FROM THE SELLER . . . AND FURTHER
THAT YOU COMPLETELY UNDERSTAND "CO-
OPERATION" IN REAL ESTATE TERMINOLOGY.
(I even had produced a 4 page legal document which
protects the Advisor Broker and the Buyer (you) . . . I
am not selling, only trying to help . . . but if either
you or your Broker would find it helpful to your
agreement . . . (this form clearly outlines responsib-
ilities to each other) . . . . you or your
Advisor Broker (who may want to specialize in this

"YOU HAVE A SECRET WEAPON. DON'T TREAT BUYING AN APARTMENT CASUALLY, LIKE BUYING A LOAF OF BREAD."

area of real estate) can order a copy of my 4 page Buyer-Advisor agreement for $20.00. (I paid $400 to have my law firm check it for legality . . . after I wrote it . . . so if I get 20 orders for this four-page legal form . . . at least my legal fee is paid back.) FURTHER, NOW . . . IF YOU DO NOT IMMEDIATELY MENTION "COOPERATE" TO THE SELLING BROKER . . . THEY SOMETIMES GET "CANTANKEROUS," AND TELL YOU THAT 'NOW" THEY WILL NOT COOPERATE BECAUSE IT WAS NOT MENTIONED AT THE VERY BEGINNING OF THE INTRODUCTION. THIS IS HOW "HAIR-LINE" THIS STODGY OLD BUSINESS IS OPERATED . . . BUT AS SOMEONE ONCE SAID (I AM QUITE SURE) . . ." YOU MUST PLAY BY THE CURRENT RULES CORRECT?"

B) I ALSO ASSIST IN THE NEGOTIATION . . . THE INSPECTION . . . AND GIVE ADVICE ON THE PROFITABILITY OF THE BUYERS TOP THREE CHOICES. IF I DO NOT RECOMMEND ANY OF

THE TOP THREE CHOICES . . . I WILL EITHER
RECOMMEND A LOWER BID-OFFER . . . IF THAT
FAILS WITH THE SELLERS . . . I AGAIN SEND MY
BUYER-CLIENT "PACKING" OFF AGAIN, LOOK-
ING FOR MORE BUILDINGS FOR ME TO GRADE
AND SUGGEST OFFERING PRICES. AS AN
ADVISOR BROKER, I SHOULD BE WILLING TO
DO THIS MUCH . . . FOR I AM LOCKED IN ON
THE DEAL, IF MY BUYER BUYS, THAT IS ALSO
IN MY AGREEMENT.

C) I ALSO INSIST ON A "TOKEN-REFUNDABLE-
FEE"; IN FRONT, FROM MY BUYER-CLIENT . . .
THIS WEEDS OUT THE "DOERS" FROM THE
"DREAMERS" . . . FOR IF MY BUYER CLIENT IS
WILLING TO PAY ME A REFUNDABLE FEE
(WHEN I GET MY HALF OF THE COMMISSION
FROM THE SELLER AND THE SELLING BRO-
KER) . . . THEN I PRETTY WELL KNOW THAT I
AM DOING BUSINESS WITH A "DOER" . . . AND
THAT LITTLE "REFUNDABLE FEE" IS PEANUTS
TO THE HALF COMMISSION FROM THE SELLER
THAT I WILL EVENTUALLY GET.

"YOU HAVE A SECRET WEAPON. DON'T TREAT BUYING AN APARTMENT CASUALLY, LIKE BUYING A LOAF OF BREAD."

D) THEN I ALSO GIVE MY "BUYER CLIENT" 3 MONTHS FREE ADVISORY SERVICE... SPECIFICALLY, ONE TEN MINUTE TELEPHONE CALL WEEKLY FOR THE FIRST 3 MONTHS PLUS THREE, ONE-HOUR VISITS TO THE NEW BUYERS PROPERTY (ONE PER MONTH) TO SUGGEST WAYS OF IMPROVING THE PROPERTY AND APARTMENTS CHEAPLY FOR ANTICIPATED RENT INCREASES. AGAIN, YOUR BROKER SHOULD GLADLY DO THIS FOR YOU... AS I DO THE SAME FOR MY CLIENTS... ITS A NICE DEAL FOR BOTH BUYER AND BROKER AND IT SURELY BEATS GETTING "SNOOKERED OUT OF COMMISSIONS ALL THE TIME," AS MOST BROKERS EXPERIENCE ALL TOO OFTEN. AGAIN... USE ALL THE "SELL" I HAVE LISTED, OR BETTER YET, LET YOUR QUALIFIED BROKER READ THIS BOOK, FOR I FIND ALL TOO OFTEN, THAT "PROFESSIONALS" ARE JUST TOO SET IN THEIR WAYS, AND WILL NOT LISTEN TO A NEW WAY OF MAKING MONEY... UNLESS IT IS

PRESENTED TO THEM. . . BY ANOTHER PROFES-
SIONAL. . . THIS TIME THAT PROFESSIONAL IS
ME. . . I CREATED THIS TYPE OF A BUYER
SERVICE. . . I FIND IT PROFITABLE. . . AND I AM
CERTAIN YOUR QUALIFIED BROKER WILL
ALSO FIND IT PROFITABLE, IF HE WILL JUST
LISTEN. . . AND WITH AN OPEN MIND.

INCIDENTALLY, I EVEN PROVIDE THIS SERVICE FOR
A BUYER FOR A FIVE YEAR PERIOD JUST IN CASE
SOMETHING COMES UP THAT DELAYS THIS "DOER"
FROM "DOING" IT. . . HOWEVER, I WILL NOT GO PAST
GRADING FOR OFFERS; ABOUT TEN BUILDINGS. . .
FOR THAT MEANS MY BUYER HAS LOOKED AT 35
BUILDINGS. . . AFTER THAT MUCH EXERCISE, I WILL
KEEP MY REMAINING AND PROMISED NO COST
SERVICES AVAILABLE TO MY BUYER WHEN HE DOES
FIND WHAT HE WANTS. . . FOR BY NOW, I HAVE
TAUGHT HIM ALL THE TRICKS OF LOOKING. . . AND
IF HE KEEPS ME "IN THE DEAL" (COOPERATION) THEN
HE STILL HAS MY PROFESSIONALISM FOR "CONTRACT

"YOU HAVE A SECRET WEAPON. DON'T TREAT
BUYING AN APARTMENT CASUALLY, LIKE
BUYING A LOAF OF BREAD."

FOR SALE" "CLOSING" AND THE THREE MONTHS OF
FREE TELEPHONE AND IN-PERSON APARTMENT
ADVISORY SERVICE, AFTER THE SALE IS MADE.

PARDON THE LENGTH I HEREIN WENT THROUGH TO
GIVE YOU JUST THE "JIST" OF WHAT I DO FOR MY
BUYER CLIENTS. I FEEL THAT THERE WILL SOON BE
ADVISOR BROKERS ALL ACROSS THE U.S.A. . . . . AS
THEY CONTINUALLY BUY MY BOOK AND LEARN
WHAT A NICE AREA OF THE REAL ESTATE BUSINESS
BEING AN "ADVISOR BROKER" CAN REALLY BE. AND
LASTLY. . . AND AGAIN. . . I AM NOT SELLING MY
SERVICE AS A BROKER, PER SE. . . BUT SINCE I HAVE
CREATED THIS ENTIRE PROCEDURE, AND SINCE AT
FIRST YOU MAY FIND A QUALIFIED BROKER NOT
WILLING TO "GO ALONG WITH SUCH A DEAL" (LIKE
MY "SCHOLAR" BROKER). . . THEN YOU MUST USE ME
AS A SUCCESSFUL EXAMPLE FOR YOUR BROKER TO
CONSIDER LIKEWISE. (INCIDENTALLY, THAT $400
LEGAL FORM THAT I WILL SELL FOR $20 (four pages)
IS TITLED "EXCLUSIVE RETAINER AGREEMENT TO

LOCATE REAL PROPERTY", (SHOULD YOU OR YOUR ADVISOR BROKER WISH TO ORDER A COPY, WITH MY WRITTEN APPROVAL FOR (NAME) BROKER TO USE SAID FORM)... REMEMBER, YOU MUST SPECIFY A REGISTERED REAL ESTATE BROKER NAME WHEN ORDERING THIS FORM.

E) AND LASTLY NOW, IF YOU HAVEN'T GIVEN UP (AND "DOERS" DO NOT GIVE UP)... YOU CAN SEE WHY 99% OF THE BUYERS OF HOMES, CONDOS OR APARTMENT BUILDINGS BUY THEM IN THE WRONG WAY... FOR THEY LOOK AT THE REAL ESTATE ADS, OR THE "FOR SALE" SIGNS... AND THEN CONTACT THE SELLING BROKER. THIS SELLING BROKER'S PRIME FIDUCIARY (TRUST) IS TO THE SELLER WHO HIRED HIM... AND IF HE GETS YOU TO BUY SOMETHING THAT ISN'T WORTH IT... WELL HE'S JUST DOING HIS JOB. WHEN YOU EMPLOY YOUR OWN ADVISOR BROKER... YOU ARE APPOINTING HIM AS YOUR PURCHASING AGENT AND HIS No. 1 LOYALTY IS TO YOU...

"YOU HAVE A SECRET WEAPON. DON'T TREAT BUYING AN APARTMENT CASUALLY, LIKE BUYING A LOAF OF BREAD."

YET ITS ONLY YOUR LIFE'S SAVINGS. . . ONLY POSSIBLY 30 YEARS OF HAPPINESS OR GRIEF. . . SO 99% OF PROPERTY BUYERS HAVE BEEN DOING IT IN THE WRONG WAY, BY GETTING LITTLE FREE AND PROFESSIONAL HELP ON THIS MOST IMPORTANT UNDER-TAKING. . . SO, IF YOU DON'T COMPLETELY UNDERSTAND THE PAST FEW PAGES, DON'T DESPAIR. . . PROBABLY YOUR BROKER DOESN'T EITHER (AS I HAVE TALKED TO A FEW THAT DIDN'T). . . SO READ THIS SECTION AGAIN AND AGAIN UNTIL YOU COMPLETELY UNDERSTAND IT. . . FOR IT IS YOUR LIFE'S SAVINGS. . . IT CAN MEAN 30 YEARS OF HAP-PINESS. . . AND IT IS YOUR FREE AND SECRET WEAPON THAT 99% OF REAL ESTATE BUYERS DO NOT TAKE ADVANTAGE OF. . . NOW WITH THIS BOOK IN NATIONAL AND WORLD DIS-TRIBUTION. . . I HAVE A FEELING ALL OF THESE PAST BUYER ERRORS WILL BE COR-RECTED. . . FOR HEAVEN KNOWS. . . THE REWARDS ARE THERE FOR "DOERS."

AS AN EXAMPLE OF WHAT I AM TALKING ABOUT...
HERE IS WHAT THE DUSTY OLD FLORIDA REAL
ESTATE LAW BOOK SAYS ABOUT THE 99% IN THE
FIRST PARAGRAPH No. 7.08 ENTITLED "MISREPR-
ESENTATION"... AND THEN THE NEXT CHAPTER,
WHICH DEALS WITH THE SMART 1% WHO BUY PRO-
PERLY (AND NOT LIKE A LOAF OF BREAD)... WHICH
BEGINS: "A BROKER MAY DEVELOP A CONFIDEN-
TIAL RELATION..." READ THIS CAREFULLY... IT
COULD SAVE YOU YOUR LIFE'S FORTUNE... OR
GIVE YOU 30 YEARS OF HAPPINESS. EVERY STATE'S
LAW BOOKS ON REAL ESTATE ARE BASICALLY THE
SAME, BECAUSE WE ALL GET OUR BASIC LAW FROM
ENGLAND WHICH SAID, LONG AGO: "YOU CANNOT
SERVE TWO MASTERS... NEITHER CAN A BROKER...
ALTHOUGH SOMETIMES HE TRIES. (See Exhibit.)

7.08 Misrepresentation. Almost any misrepresentation made by a broker to his employer is fraudulent unless the employer knows the statement to be false. A person who employs a broker has a contractual right to rely on his truthfulness and fidelity. When the broker is employed by the owner to sell a piece of property, the purchaser has only a limited right to rely upon the statements of the broker. The broker may puff or exaggerate the value and prospects of the property, especially when the purchaser is present in the locality and may easily see or investigate for himself. The purchaser ordinarily should not rely on representations as to boundaries and title. If the broker knows the truth as to these matters and deliberately misrepresents or conceals them he is guilty of fraud.

A broker may develop a confidential relation with a purchaser which binds him to exercise good faith. If he invites the trust of the purchaser, or if he knows, or ought to know, that the purchaser is uninformed of the matters about which he makes representation, and he knows that the purchaser is relying on his statements he must be truthful. In dealing with those who are uninformed the broker should be extremely careful that his statements and opinions are truthful and sound, or he should advise such people not to rely upon him, but to check his statements with some disinterested party.

Jim Anderson's "No Frills Seminars" Available Soon in Your Home Town Sponsored by Your Local "Advisor-Broker"™

Have your local prestige-broker call Jim Anderson for details
on his "One Day No Frills Seminar"
backed up by expert-free-advice to help the seminar students
to make their first quadplex or home investment.

Contact:

JIM ANDERSON
701 N.E. 67 St., Miami, Fl. 33138
305/756-6249

WILL YOU CHOOSE TO LIVE IN ONE
OF YOUR APARTMENT UNITS?

I am certain that you have already a definite "yes" . . . or a
definite "no" to this very personal question.

But don't "shoot from the hip" with a quick answer to
this question that maybe you have not clearly and carefully
studied. When you are in business for yourself, be flexible . . .
don't be rigid on anything . . . even be it your own
domicile . . . especially when you are considering going into
the domicile business.

I asked this question of a "Buyer". . . "Do you plan to
live in one of the units in your apartment building?" "Definitely not" was the quick answer from this gentleman. He
mumbled a few more hackneyed phrases like "not wanting to
be bothered by the tenants" . . . and "the apartment would
not be suitable for his desired lifestyle."

First, I explained "the other side" to that age old wives-
tale that the tenants would be a bother to him.

If you are an apartment building owner, you had better
be concerned about your apartment building, as you would
be concerned with any other business venture you entered.
You cannot expect an apartment building to run itself any
more than you would expect your grocery store or restaurant
to run itself. That is to say, "absentee management" is not
the most satisfactory way to manage a building or any other
kind of business. Did you ever hear the old bartender
joke? . . . "two dollars for me; one dollar for the boss." You
should be involved in your apartment buildings unless you
are a big operator with dependable management people.

Further I explained that this "bother" should be welcome to an owner, because who should be more concerned
about a faucet leaking than the owner? I tell my tenants
"thank you" when they tell me something is not working
properly in the apartment. (Obviously not damage, tenant-

caused, which will also be fixed promptly; but paid for by the tenant. See another Chapter). I try to fix the malfunction myself, or have it fixed, by one of my low cost, professional Craftsmen. And pronto.

Tenants are grateful for prompt service, because most owners are not prompt. The old-time-landlord is famous for never fixing anything promptly. I like to fix things pronto, so the building will not deteriorate, and instead, will appreciate at an even greater pace.

For what happens when that leaky faucet was left unattended? In some areas, your water bill can go up dramatically. What happens when a leaky roof is left unattended? You can have a much bigger bill for new plaster inside and then a new room paint job. All this extra expense, caused by a tenant who had not "bothered you?"

I strongly urge my tenants to let me or my managers know when anything is not working properly. I tell them that we want these apartments to be in first class working order. What tenant wouldn't like to hear this? Don't you also believe that the tenant will be more careful of your property also? It's also a good pitch (when sincere) for a future rent increase, for what tenant has not been looking for an owner attitude like this?

I urge the tenants' cooperation, by alerting the tenant that sometimes a small problem can become much bigger and more costly to me later on, and I therefore want to know immediately, when damage has occurred. Then, of course if the damage is tenant-caused, you merely sit down with the tenant and refer to your complete tenant Lease Agreement (wherein tenant responsibility is clearly spelled out) and you work it out for Mr. Tenant to foot the bill or lastly to take the repair out of Mr. Tenant's Security Deposit, with a letter sent to Mr. Tenant explaining the repair, with a bill enclosed for the expense. You can probably be assured of a more careful Mr. Tenant in the future.

Once, a very nice tenant had not "bothered me" about dampness in the wall from a roof leak. When I finally discovered it on one of my regular inspections, the wall was an unsightly black mildew. Left much longer, I would have had a big plasterer's expense; instead, all it took was some "sealer" and some touch-up paint for a like-new appearance. And I called my dependable roofer-Craftsman, who had guaranteed the job, and he fixed the leaky roof, no charge.

Another nice tenant, who did not want to "bother me," casually told me almost six months afterward that "the air conditioner did not work, but not to bother because we don't like air conditioning anyway." I really had to gulp hard on this one, from such nice and well-meaning tenants, because my one year service guarantee had now expired. Luckily, I develop a good, but firm relationship with my suppliers; and as a building owner you must   "Go to the top" when such a problem occurs (for no regular line-manager could now extend this guarantee). So, I got the air conditioner repaired on the expired guarantee; because of this innocent mistake.

So now, I tell . . . urge . . . remind . . . thank . . . do anything to let my tenants know that it is no "bother", when they have to tell me that something is not working correctly in their apartment.

To this Buyer's second comment about "desiring a better lifestyle than could be provided in one of his apartment units," I gave the answers.

The U.S.A. is like nowhere else in the World. Wealthy and creative people of the world over the past fifty years, have decided to spend their lifestyle this way. Some of these people, being business oriented, decided to build their dream apartment building, with an apartment suite "just for them." This type building could not be duplicated today without spending a fortune. But when you coldly look at its income, etc., versus its selling price, you are getting a building value that could not be duplicated for what you paid for it. There are many of such buildings available everywhere, and instead of a condominium or another house, why not get out of your rut and try a new lifestyle? At worst, if you aren't happy after a year, move out; rent the apartment, and you can go back to your more comfortable lifestyle.

Here I want to state that I am definitely against building your own FIRST Quad or duplex UNLESS: 1) the right one for you is just not available in your area. 2) You have building experience on a home. Since building costs can really get out of hand, unless you know what you are doing, and you have a dependable, and honest Contractor.

As an example, recently we were driving in a fashionable area, and we saw an unfinished grand mansion, obviously deserted for perhaps one year. My friend said, "Why?". . . My answer, "Obviously this wealthy person just ran out of money. . . the expense of this grand mansion, was just too much, even with his wealth."

There are all kinds of owner-live-in apartment buildings available. From the ridiculous to the sublime. Don't think that you are all so dear and precious, that there has not been another like you in the past with your same financial abilities who decided in past years to buy an apartment building, and to live on-premises, in a special owner apartment. Has there been another just like you? There has probably been hundreds just like you.

Then I described my own humble beginning in Florida as a live-on-premises owner. Three years ago my first apartment building had five units which included our own elegant "villa style front unit" that today has a market rental value of $450 monthly. My initial investment on this first building was $20,000. We must entertain the "hoi paloi" since my wife is a World famous concert pianist. I delight in surprising our guests during the evening by showing them the other four units on the grounds that they did not know even existed. I show them proudly and am proud of my ingenuity to provide us with such a luxurious "home" (much nicer than our former "mill-stone"). I am content that after thirty years of adult life in a home I have found a better lifestyle for todays living than a non-productive home of just the one living quarters for wife and I; on the same size piece of land as my five units (100 foot front incidentally) where we paid the taxes, the mortgage, the yard costs, the paint, the insurance, etc., etc., just for wife and I. Obviously you can tell that I am prejudiced to this new life style, but I can say that after living in some nice homes in the midwest, in Connecticut, and in Washington D.C., today, I love this lifestyle . . . and I am taking care of my property, since no one has more incentive to do so than I. So, take your pick . . . live on premises or live away from your investment. I am simply trying to get you to get deeply involved with a serious decision on the matter, instead of a casual decision made up of old wives-tales rumors.

Incidentally, for even less than the two above examples . . . for maybe less than $15,000, there are 4 or 5 units available, where 4 units are not as big, maybe one bedroom and where the last unit is a spacious two bedroom for the owner.

So, you can own an apartment building and have it either way. You can live on premises or you can live off premises. But if you live off premises, I would advise that you arrange to live conveniently nearby, at least the first year or so, so you can visit the property often. Incidentally, a manager charges, among other things, how far he is from the building, for driving there takes time, and as they say, "time is money."

Someone should visit the property at least once a week, even more often is preferred. At least at the beginning when you are getting to know your tenants. Maybe you will find one especially dependable tenant that you may consider giving a ten to twenty dollars rent discount to "look after you interests at the property," to report any problem (for you to solve), and to possibly "accept" (not collect) the rent from the other tenants. You now have taken reasonable steps to properly manage your property as off-premise owners. Get to know your tenants and your helper tenant. Very soon you will know who is dependable and who is not, and if a closer eye is necessary to manage this property when you do not live there, you will be first to know.

Lastly, if you choose to do so, and you can afford the reduction in return on your investment; you can employ a professional to entirely manage your apartment building. A professional manager's fee ranges at around ten per cent of the gross rents collected by him. Sometimes there are other charges (depending on the size of the building, with larger buildings getting more service for less charges) such as: a percent for renting vacant units. A percent of all maintenance bills, etc. These charges also average about ten percent. Also a consideration will be made by the Manager as to how convenient it is to his office base. How old is the building? Are the units priced right and in demand in a good location?

When I purchased my second and then my third building (about a year apart), I planned some "cosmetic" work around the property at the very beginning to get to know the tenants, the neighbors, and the neighborhood. This can be very enlightening to you, the new owner, and will let you know if your visits should be more than once a week later on. I discovered a noisy tenant who was actually depreciating my property by making the other tenants miserable. Usually the tenants will not complain. If they are not happy, they will just move. Finally I had to ask this noisy tenant to vacate his property, now all is serene, my tenants are happy and my property's value has been improved. At another building, I found a messy tenant who threw papers on the property and not in the garbage (as agreed to in my special tenant agreement. Another chapter) This less serious but important problem was solved easily. The tenant agreed to be neater, and again I improved the value of my new property. You will encounter numerous simple little problems like the two above which you will handle with equal ease of just good old common horse-sense. But you, the owner, must make visits to the property to discover what is going on. That is also just good old common horse-sense to realize it. . . and to act accordingly. That is why you always hear bad reports on people who have invested but are absentee-owners.

Secondly, I like the current tenants to see some "action" and fix-up at this newly sold property, which usually goes down a little in maintenance repair and cosmetic-look when it is for sale.

In conclusion from what probably was a rigid "no" to the question as to whether you will live on-premises, I hope that at least now you can see another valid side to the question. Personally, I also feel that people too often get into a rut in lifestyle (such as living in an old millstone) and a person can actually look and think younger and happier . . . in a new type environment. And you may actually discover a nice new lifestyle to replace that nice but really impractical and demanding old "millstone" currently dangling around your neck . . . and maybe strangling you. You may enjoy living on premises, and an owner on premises can't help but improve the value of the property. After a test, if you don't agree, rent that unit and live elsewhere and just collect the rent checks and have a more happy and stable life and income, that we can reasonably be certain will gradually increase over the years, as most property in good neighborhoods has done over the past thirty years.

Re-building. . . On the brighter side, I saw a Builder recently advertise a new QUAD; all 2 bedrooms for $107,000. Now figure it out. . . if they each rent for $250/MO. that's $12,000 annual rental, which comes out at about 8 times annual rental, on a new building. Not bad, and that is how you figure, when you build a Quad. Its never emotionally as how you buy a millstone. . . such as; how many baths to luxuriate yourself (maybe you will get a heart attack keeping up with the payments in the inflationary spiral of the 1980's). . . or does it have a swimming pool. . . or a three car garage. . . no my friends, even the best QUAD. . . you buy on a business like and slide rule basis. . . not emotionally. . . and you will not get financially hurt in the Quad-plex business.

WRITE THE AUTHOR REGARDING ANY QUESTIONS YOU MAY HAVE, AFTER READING THIS BOOK

To: James W. Anderson
P.O. Box 370034, Miami, Fl., 33137

I have finished reading your 24 chapter book **HOW TO LIVE RENT FREE**, and I have the following questions to ask you.

1. _____

2. _____

3. _____

Comments: _____

NAME _____

ADDRESS _____

CITY_____STATE _____ ZIP_____

- -

SEND THIS BOOK AS A GIFT TO A FRIEND

To: James W. Anderson, P.O. Box 370034, Miami, Fl. 33137

Enclosed find check or money order for $_____
(check one or more boxes, then add up your total money)

☐ Volume I   ☐ $11 paperback   ☐ $25 luxury hardcover

☐ Volume II   ☐ $15 paperback   ☐ $25 luxury hardcover

☐ TALKING BOOK (audio-cassettes, 2 reels, 3 hours) ☐ $25

☐ JIM ANDERSON'S MONTHLY RENT-FREE NEWSLETTER ☐ $50

Please send to:

NAME_____

ADDRESS _____

CITY _____ STATE ____ _____ ZIP_____

CHAPTER FOUR

WATCH OUT FOR THE SEXY-LEMON

The above Chapter title may sound silly and foolish to you, but I recall that I did not end up with anything like I originally set out to buy as my first apartment building purchase.

I thought that all that I could afford was a nice home for me and my wife, with maybe one or two units tucked in the back as rental units. Here is where I discovered, but only after getting active and looking at some buildings, that apartment buildings do not require as big a down payment as homes. Therefore you can purchase a more expensive building normally, than a home, for the same down payment.

So as it developed, we got our nice home, but it included five units . . . not three units as originally I thought was all I could afford.

Also you will find that as you look and inspect and look and inspect somemore, that your ideas will change as you see the various apartment buildings that are for sale. And here is a strong recommendation . . . don't be "old and set in your ways" and refuse to see some buildings that you think are just not right for you. This beginning is very important. Treat it with care and with the importance it deserves. You are talking about a lifetime of joy or a lifetime of frustration as you go around inspecting buildings. Don't be lazy either. Don't expect your Broker to do all your leg work. He can guide, help, advise . . . but you are the one whose personal tastes are in command. So get out of the easy chair and make this one of the most active times of searching for something very worthwhile. Confucius say: "Best helping hand is at end of right sleeve." If you never realized that, get smart quick and adapt.

You will enjoy this building inspection period for the rest of your life. Years later you will look back on it as one of the most satisfying experiences in your lifetime. And you will be rewarded by learning the full scope on what is available for sale . . . what is the Market like, high? low? Additionally you will be surprised and I guarantee you will not be wasting your time if you go to inspect three to five buildings that your Advisor-Broker suggests . . . after he gets to know your personal situation better through conversations with you in discussing your desires. So open your vistas . . . take off the blinders . . . explore . . . for this is a very important decision and you should know all of the many possibilities available to you in consideration of your personal and financial requirements.

Make up your own check-list as you go around inspecting buildings. For you will forget later when you are reviewing various buildings that interest you. Note such things as number of floors, clusters of buildings versus one building, large or small grounds, landscaping? (lush, or not much?), modern kitchens and baths? Sizes of the apartment rooms? Closet sizes? Storage space? Patios or recreation area? Off -street parking? Attractive street and area as you approach the building? Attractive building entrance? Building on noisy or congested street? Washer and Dryer on premises? (In Florida I also like to provide a clothes line for the many people who prefer to dry clothes by the Florida Sun instead of the Utility Co., Florida Power and Light. I say why not use the J.C.P. & L. instead of the F.P. & L.?) Location is important of course, and I will do an entire Chapter on this subject. Nearby shopping? Nearby Public transportation? (This will become increasingly important in the 1980's with the ever growing energy shortage.)

Are there added attractions near by like water or a park? All these considerations and others and some of your own personal likes and dislikes will become imprinted in your mind as you continue to inspect building after building. And I recommend that you inspect at least ten apartment buildings the first time around, to become your own expert.

Together with your notes and the checklist you have made of all your inspections, you will soon discover what you actually would like to buy and what financially you can buy.

Your choices should now be narrowed down to your top three favorite apartment buildings that you like and can afford. Now this is where your Advisor Broker becomes valuable to you. With his professional experience he will inspect these top three buildings with you, and he will rank them and sit down with you and tell you why.

Your advisor Broker may rank your No. 1, his No. 3 . . . or maybe say that your No. 1 is a very poor buy at the current price. Here he may advise you to make a reduced offer, at a price where the building will become profitable for you to operate it . . . and he will back up his reduced offer with cold hard facts to the Selling-Broker and the Owner as to why your reduced price offer is valid.

However from all the initial work you did in inspecting all those buildings, I do believe that consideration should be given to the Buyers favorite types of buildings. Everyone has a different feeling about architecture, layout, area, etc. . . . this we call the sex-appeal of a building. But you certainly do not want to end up buying a sexy-lemon, and then spending the rest of your life sweating to make that building a paying proposition, only to find that this is an impossible task; and likewise an impossibility to resell the building even for what you paid, much less a profit, because you paid too much for it in the first place. So beware of the sexy-lemon . . . your Advisor-Broker has seen many of them and he can help you greatly here at this important and decisive time.

There are many good and even sensational bargains out there to be had . . . so why buy the sexy-lemon without an Advisor-Broker whose services can cost you nothing for all his professional know how and years of experience. Maybe your Advisor Broker will not recommend any of your first–round choices for a number of reasons he will give you. Maybe he will recommend that you offer considerably less for one or two of your choices. Otherwise he may recommend that the process begin anew on more apartment buildings, but this second-effort can be very quick and rewarding because now you and your Advisor-Broker know pretty clearly what you require, and your Advisor Broker can probably find that building quickly for you, if it exists and is for sale.

On a radio interview, the program host got quite intrigued with the investment-in-apartment-building-business and he asked me, "If many people follow your suggestions, and purchase apartment buildings . . . how big is the supply?" My answer was clear and correct, "Because of the great depreciation tax deductions alone, there will always be good buildings for sale. Because when the current owner takes his depreciation out of a building over a fixed period of years, then he will probably want to sell, so the new owner can start the depreciation all over again." This answer, plus normal commerce with a number of Sellers and a number of Buyers that will always be there assures us that there will always be good and profitable apartment buildings for sale.

Another thought on this Chapter's topic is this: if you feel you may live on-premises in one of the apartments, you will even be more personally selective in choosing a building. And only you will be able to decide in this personal area of a selection. Then your Advisor-Broker will tell you if you should purchase that building, and at what price it becomes a decent purchase for you.

Some personal considerations are: Do you require a special, larger and nicer apartment as the tenant-owner? There have been many such buildings built over the years for their original tenant-owner.

Do you want to live near water, near golf, near tennis, or near your Club?

You may be a handy man who wants to purchase some older building at a low cost and then fix it up into a real money maker as I did with my second building purchase.

All of these and other personal requirements will be unleashed from inside you as you inspect all the various apartment buildings that are for sale. You will have pleasure, gain enlightenment, and find it very rewarding as you inspect more buildings for the perfect selection . . . for you . . . with the advice of your Advisor-Broker.

Some Buyers say: "When is the right time to buy?" I heard the best answer at the Diplomat Hotel, where I lectured recently, on an "Own Your Own Business Expo," produced by the Publisher of the "Business Opportunities" magazine. When some one asked him that question . . . he snapped back in a quick and startling fashion, and said . . . "NOW" . . . to which the questioner from the audience asked "why not yesterday?" . . . to which Mr. Foley beautifully replied . . . "YOU WASTED A DAY." And that about sums up the "when to get into business." Oh sure, there are peaks we may sometimes see and wait for a down-slide . . . but the Quad plex business is so attractive, and offers you free rent, pay less or no taxes, you have an inflationary edge, you have the big time leverage of the mortgage on not just a millstone . . . but four income producing units . . . I can hardly imagine the time that I would hesitate in buying my first Quad-Plex . . . I may wait for the best time (if it ever comes) to purchase my second Quad-plex . . . but my first one . . . "one day late . . . is one day wasted."

Renegotiated-offers: Here is where your Broker can really earn his no-fee. Countless stories are told of the Buyer telling the Seller "the building is not worth the price" . . . to which the Seller orders the Buyer off his Property. This type "emotional-negotiation" never happens when you let your Advisor Broker handle this delicate part. He can coldly tell the Seller or through the Seller's Broker "why" the Property is overpriced. He may say something like, "look, you're asking ten times annual rental . . . the "market" is 6 or 7 times . . . I may get my client (you, the Buyer, all pre-arranged) to go 7 or 8 times annual rental . . . how about it." The Seller hopefully will see the light and casually say, "well, make an offer." That is your signal to make a fast-but-casual offer, and you probably got the building at your price.

There are bargains out there for another reason that you should know. Many small apartment owners for some reasons operate them "like a candy store", that is, they allow the tenants to run the building instead of vice-versa. If my tenant EVER gets out of line, I am the first one to remind the tenant: "Hey Mr. Tenant . . . I own the Property . . . remember?" I am sorry to say that most small building owners do not run their Property this way, so they have themselves to blame . . . but to your advantage, you will find a building, quite frequently, where "Owner must sell quickly." Probably, that Owner, has run his building like a candy store, with the Tenants in charge . . . and he wants to sell, even at a loss (or no gain; which is still a loss) . . . sit tight and make a lean offer . . . and perhaps you have just "stolen" your first apartment building which can be rightfully managed, with the Owner in charge, and not the Tenants, if you just follow the principals listed herein to insure "star-tenants"

Also, there will never be a total lack of Properties, because as good as this Quad-Plex business sounds to you (and it is, as stated) . . . there 90% procrastinators (the dreamers) . . . and 10% "doers". The "doers" will sell their millstones . . . buy the Quad's . . . however, some of those "Dreamers" will make you excellent tenants.

Several off-beat ways to make a good deal: For you prospective Quad owners who don't like apartment building areas . . . there are situations, where you can find a Quad, nextled in a beautiful neighborhood of private homes. This Quad is quite legal in most cases (but check zoning) since it probably exists under what is called a "Grand Father Clause," meaning that this building was here a long time, and although this is a private home neighborhood, it is very nice, and perfectly legal. I have one of these . . . and I love it.

Also, sometimes, you can find a duplex on a large and expensive lot in the highest priced part of town; which will allow you to build another duplex in the rear. Don't turn up your nose until you see many chic two-duplexes on one deep lot . . . separated tastefully by much foliage (Palm Beach, a chic, city beautiful has many). While you laughed, someone else just made a fortune. Take off your "blinders," remember?

PART ONE. QUICK ANALYSIS FORM TO COMPARE BUILDINGS (Primary)

Copy this form for use over and over. Just so you give proper credit to the James W. Anderson book "How to Live Rent Free", Box 370034, Miami, Florida.

Interestingly, when you lay out visually, comparable facts about a group of buildings that you have inspected . . . revealed in front of you will be great inconsistencies among the various buildings you are looking at. This visual comparison will help you toward a correct decision.

ASKING PRICE

BROKER/OWNER?

No. UNITS

EXISTING MORT.?

MORT. ASSUMABLE?

ITS INT. RATE?

MO. PYMT/No. MO'S.

OWNER TAKEBACK MORT.

_____ % INT. _____ No. YRS.

PART ONE CON'T. QUICK ANALYSIS FORM TO COMPARE BUILDINGS (Primary)

ANNUAL RENTAL INCOME

PRICE _____ X'S RENTAL

TENANTS PAY UTIL.?

TOTAL EXPENSES

AREA "LOOK"

APT. "LOOK"

NEAR WATER/PARK

LANDSCAPING?

MODERN KITCH'S?

MODERN BATHS?

APT. ROOM SIZE

CLOSET SIZE?

APT. STORAGE AREA

PART ONE CON'T. QUICK ANALYSIS FORM TO COMPARE BUILDINGS (Primary)

GENERAL STORAGE

PATIO/REC AREA

OFF-STREET PARK?

WASHER-DRYER

BLDG. CONSTRUCTION

YEAR BUILT

LOT SIZE

TYPE ZONING

ROOF CONDITION

APPLIANCES COND.

AIR CON. No. & COND.

OTHER

OTHER

PART TWO. QUICK ANALYSIS FORM TO COMPARE BUILDINGS (Secondary)
These are secondary buy-considerations but also important to consider after inspections.
It is important to compare these after making primary considerations. "How to Live Rent Free" Jim Anderson.

UNIT SIZES, SQ. FT'

No./SIZE (5-1 BR)

POTENTIAL ANNUAL RENT

COST PER UNIT

TAXES, City

TAXES, County

TAXES, Other

INSURANCE

"HOUSE" UTILITIES?

WATER/SEWER

EST. MAINTENANCE COST

PART TWO CON'T.   QUICK ANALYSIS FORM TO COMPARE BUILDINGS   (Secondary)

COST OF LICENSES

$ WASTE COLLECTION

MGR. COST

STREET "LOOK"

NOISY/QUIET STREET

CONGESTED STREET?

ENTRANCE "LOOK"

NEAR AIRPORT/HOSP.

NEAR RAPID TRANSIT

NEAR SHOPS/BUSES

No. FLOORS/ELEVATOR?

BLDG. CLUSTER VS ONE?

LARGE/SMALL LOT

PART TWO CON'T. QUICK ANALYSIS FORM TO COMPARE BUILDINGS (Secondary)

NEAR 24 HOUR STORE

NEAR ATTRACTIONS

NEAR RESTAURANTS

SWIMMING POOL

CLOTHES LINE

APTS. ZONED LEGAL?

OTHER

OTHER

OTHER

OTHER

OTHER

CHAPTER FIVE

HOW TO DETERMINE WHAT IS
A FAIR PRICE TO PAY?

Prices of apartment buildings are guided by the RENTAL INCOME TO GROSS PRICE RATIO. This is also call the RENT MULTIPLE. These terms simply mean that you should under normal circumstances pay no more than five to seven times the annual rental income as a fair price for the apartment building.*

Therefore, if you are looking at an apartment building that delivers $10,000 in annual rentals (if you plan to live in one unit, the fair rent for that unit must be included) . . . then that building is fairly priced somewhere between $50,000 and $70,000.

A five times rent-multiple is usually a combination to some degree of an older building, in a poor neighborhood, needing some repairs.

A seven times rent-multiple is for a well kept building, probably newer, and in a better location and neighborhood.

Occasionally, an excellent apartment building will come available that will merit an eight to ten times rent-multiple price, especially if there are great personal considerations and advantages as to why you personally would want to live in this building. Say its in the best area, maybe waterfront, with an owner perfect penthouse. Then in this type situation, I would overlook some of the strict business-like formulas and say to you, "this apartment is overpriced according to the normal standards of buying apartments, but looking at it from your personal viewpoint, isn't it nice to have a lovely personal home where you will enjoy living just as much as your personal home . . . its in a great location . . . and you have the water . . . maybe even your own dock, and yet, for perhaps the equity you have in your home, you have a group of apartment units to pay the taxes, the insurance, etc. and you can live rent free. From my viewpoint this is a nice situation for the ultra particular person who would have initially thought they "would never be caught dead living in their own apartment building." And there are some of these special situations of special apartment buildings around town that can change your mind about living on premises.

Continuing on pricing... "negotiation" and "timing" and your not being overly anxious in front of the seller or selling Broker, all will play important roles in what you can end up purchasing your desired apartment building. Just like your past experience in buying a home, or anything of value ... these three factors will come into play in varying degrees that can get you a price reduction.

Does the owner have to sell because he is leaving town, or of ill health, etc.? But these reasons are overworked and often untrue. If you know the reason is true; then it can help you.

Does the owner need cash badly. Again is this need verified and proven to be true?

Is business generally bad with properties moving slowly? Maybe yours is the first legitimate offer the Seller has had in several months. If so, negotiating downward has great possibilities.

This is one time when the normal negotiating considerations are used as in any major purchase, be it a home, and auto, or an apartment building. But, in apartment building buying, these negotiation ploys should be used, along with the rent-multiple rule as a good guideline to a fair price to pay, and a price that will enable you to make a profit.

You will find that an owner who offers his property for sale without a Real Estate Agent, really isn't totally serious about selling, unless he can find that rare "fish" who is not informed as to how apartments are valued and priced every day. These owner-sellers have their property overpriced, and are just waiting for some "fish", probably from up North, to catch the bait. Otherwise they just don't sell and really don't care if they sell or not. I know some Owners that put out the "For Sale by Owner" sign every Fall as the tourist traffic from up North begins. And I have known these Owners to snag a few "fish."

HOW TO DETERMINE WHAT IS
A FAIR PRICE TO PAY

I have personally checked out this Owner-Sale about twenty five times. When I discuss the owners' asking price in relation to the annual rent income (and they normally try to avoid this subject completely), but I say to the owner, "but you are asking ten times annual rental and the average is five to seven times annual rental . . . aren't you overpriced . . . or is your property so exquisite and perfect as to merit a price that is ten times annual rental?"

My reply from the owner-seller is usually silence or a blank stare . . . if it is on the telephone . . . the owner just hangs up . . . because I am not the "fish" that Mr. Owner-Seller is trying to snag.

When the owner of an apartment building really, really wants to sell . . . he puts his property in a Listing with a Real Estate Broker, who will represent him in a fiduciary-relationship to sell his property as quickly as possible for the highest price possible to the Buyer.

Similarily, if you employ a no cost Advisor-Broker to advise you and help you negotiate a purchase, you have your own fiduciary-relationship . . . but most Buyers do not think of this or know such a service is available, so most Buyers let themselves be represented by the Sellers Broker to whom the Buyer has no fiduciary-relationship.

Incidentally, your Advisor-Broker should not have apartment building listings of his own that he shows you. Your Advisor-Broker should be completely impartial as to what Broker has the Listing . . . just as long as your Advisor Broker does not have the Listing. By law your Advisor Broker must advise you if the Listing is his, in which case your Advisor Broker will earn 100% of the sales commission instead of the preferred way of his advising you on a Listing from another Broker, in which case your Advisor Broker splits the commission with the "cooperating" Broker. That is why in most cases your Advisor Broker's services are free to you, but still a little known fact by the buying Public.

Obviously your Advisor-Broker's impartiality by not offering you any of his own Listings allows you to look over the entire large market of available buildings, instead of just several from your Advisor-Broker, who incidentally is no longer impartial to what you buy or what he recommends you, if indeed he tries to sell you one of his own Listings.

Unless it is a rare value, and a one-of-a-kind which just suits you . . . tell your Advisor-Broker to sell his Listings through another Advisor-Broker and not to you . . . better yet . . . you should consider employing another Advisor-Broker.

* Of course this rent multiple supposes no extra-ordinary operating expenses against this rental base income, such as Utilities which should be paid for by the tenant, or an additional charge added to the rent for Utilities.

There are three things you can do to insure that you pay less than market-price for your first building . . . and to prepare you to KNOW a bargain when it is up for sale (probably just for a short time) only to be snapped up by you or some other knowledgeable Buyer . . .

1) This book is giving you your initial conscious-raising philosophy on this subject.

2) As this book has clearly informed you . . . employ your own no-fee Advisor-Broker (your "Secret-Weapon"). Add his knowledge of the local Market.

3) But don't take my word, or the word of your Advisor-Broker as the "complete Gospel" . . . this is your life's savings, right . . . 30 years of happiness can hinge on your right decision? So, get off your haunches. Get out of that easy chair; and carefully inspect at least ten buildings yourself. Your Broker can direct you from behind the scenes as to where to go, who to see, etc., and look at some on your own. Don't be manipulated. Also protect your Brokers so he can "cooperate" on the commission, because finding a good buy is only the beginning. There is the negotiation, inspection, Contract For Sale, after-the-sale advice from your experienced Broker; and insist that he confidentially give you his list of low cost Craftsmen.

If you do these three things, you are going to purchase a sensational bargain Quad or Duplex which will give you 30 years of happiness.

CHAPTER SIX

GIVE IT THE 5 POINT INSPECTION

The age old story of the prospective auto buyer kicking the tire of the used car as his "inspection criteria" before purchasing it, is also prevalent in property building. I am totally amazed at the stories I hear after the sale as to how the Buyer was "bilked" by believing everything he was told by the Seller and the Seller's Broker. Most Buyer's have never heard of the term "caveat emptor" which means "buyer beware". Remember, if you want to bank on a sales point of the Seller or his Broker . . . get it in writing . . . or forget it. Verbal sales pitches will give you no protection later on. Please . . . please don't be naive . . . this could be the biggest decision in your life. Why believe all verbal sales points from the sellers who legally can tell you, or not tell you just about anything.

Specifically, too many Buyers take the verbal "word" of the Owner or his Selling-Broker as to the condition of the apartment building or the home.

Before you purchase an apartment building you should employ a duly authorized inspection Company to professionally inspect your considered building in five categories: The electrical wiring system . . . the plumbing system . . . the roof . . . the basic condition of the structure and foundation . . . and a termite inspection, which will be handled and paid for by the Seller if you ask (normally) and put it in the Contract For Sale agreement. There are total Service Companies that will do all of this inspection for about $200 total; and I would recommend that you tag-along with the Inspector, and ask a lot of questions, even to the point of annoying the Inspector, This is important business to you, you can tell the Inspector, and you want to know everything about this building. The Inspector will probably gain respect for you and patiently give you all of the information you ask, as they have done for me.

A different approach to the inspection, and usually more authoritative, is to call an expert in each category. Your electrician will check the electric . . . your plumber will check the plumbing, etc., etc. If this Craftsman will become your regular maintenance man, you can be certain he will do a better job, because he would be embarrased to be called by you right after the completed sale, to fix something serious that he should have discovered on the Inspection. And this second method can be actually cheaper if you have a good craftsman available in each category. They will give you a low cost or no cost inspection because rightly so, they realize (or you tell them) that with this building purchase they have another building to care for. People who employ a no fee Advisor-Broker will be given the names of his craftsmen (on a confidential basis, with the understanding that these names will not be given to others. This is in writing). These Craftsmen will probably be delighted to gain another recommended customer. This second inspection method is more time consuming, for you have to make the individual calls, then arrange a mutually convenient time to meet them at the property to be inspected. And also a convenient time to the Seller who will probably have the keys. Ideally, I arrange to meet with all four Craftsmen on the same date, with each appointment spaced about one hour apart so I can tag-along and ask questions and learn more about this building.

If you do not have a source for individual Craftsmen, and you call them "cold" out of the telephone book, they will charge you, but their total cost will probably be less than the $200 combined Inspection, but twice as good, if the Craftsmen you employ are truly Craftsmen.

The important thing about this Inspection Project is NOT to go to the trouble and expense of the Inspection until you have an agreed-to and signed Contract For Sale between you and the Seller. This agreement must contain words to the effect that "this contract is subject to a professional building Inspection regarding the electric, plumbing, roof, structure and foundation, (with termite inspection provided and paid for by the Owner)". And further that, "this contract is automatically cancelled if any serious damage or deterioration is

70

found in these categories amounting to more than $ which must be paid for by the Buyer." You must mutually determine and agree to the amount to be filled in. This will be determined by all of your previous contact with the Seller and his Broker . . . and what kind of price you are agreeing to pay. Probably the Seller and the Broker have told you verbally that everything is OK and in good shape. So, you are simply protecting yourself in consideration of the age old business practice of "caveat emptor." Secondly, if you are getting the building at a very fair price, you may not mind being cooperative by agreeing to a minimum of say $1,000 in found repair needed. But, if you are buying an expensive building, represented to be in A-1 shape, then you probably do not want to agree to any found and needed Inspection problems. Then, if needed repairs were found by your Inspector; you would go back to the Seller, and suggest that the Seller repair his building into A-1 shape as originally represented . . . or No Sale. The Seller will probably make the repairs pronto.

Obviously, if you are making an offer on a "handy man special", and you are getting the building at a very fair price, then, again on your judgment, you probably will agree to $5,000 or even $10,000 in expected repair. But you have already figured that you will do most of this work yourself, as a handy man.

As stated, the Seller will normally provide the termite inspection (when you demand it) and he will give you the termite report from a responsible Termite Company. If termites are found, if you have provided for it in your Contract For Sale, the Seller will have the building "tented and fumigated by a responsible termite company." (At the Seller's expense, of course.) If a termite insurance policy is currently in effect from the Seller, be certain that the current termite contract can be transferred to you, the new owner. If termites are found, and the current policy cannot be transferred, then you must insist that the owner tent and fumigate the building at seller's expense and to provide a new termite policy, in your name. These termite insurance policies cost about $50 to $100 annually and give you continued protection over the years agreed to in the policy.

Now do not look upon Inspections as a lot of work and drudgery. Inspections can help you negotiate a better price on your considered building. For remember, the Seller has "already spent" some or all of his profits from this "sale" to you, which has been duly signed and sealed by a bonafide, Contract For Sale between you the Buyer, and he the Seller. Now perhaps this Inspection uncovers some needed repairs that the owner had not told you about ("caveat emptor"), or perhaps that the Seller and his Selling-Broker did not honestly know existed. Psychologically, and practically, you have the Seller at a disadvantage . . . and your lower offer to cover the repairs will probably be accepted by the Seller. Otherwise, the Seller may insist on doing the repairs himself. But caution here . . . his repairs may be done cheaply . . . scratch that . . . WILL be done cheaply. So you must be satisfied with the Seller's repairs, with bills provided you from the Craftsmen which contain the length of time the repairs are guaranteed to you, the new owner. Example: if the Seller must put on a new roof, for you to close the sale (because the Inspection determined that a new roof was needed), then it behooves you to get the guarantee that goes with the new roof, which will be from five to ten years. And have it in writing, that this guarantee is transferred to you, the new owner.

Here is a good place to firmly say that whenever you employ a Craftsman be certain that you have it in writing (either on the check for payment or the bill for the work) that the work has been "paid in full." Some dishonest Craftsmen can actually put a Lien (Mechanic's Lien) on your building for unpaid for work, which he may be able to prove, because you do not have proof of payment.

Back to your Inspection Project . . . occasionally you will lose a deal, but in the long run you will thank me for this thorough advice, which beginners are not aware of. I remember at my beginning, I made offers on three buildings before the fourth one was accepted. The first two would not accept my lower offer, and the third would not accept my Inspection clauses in the Contract For Sale. I now realize that

I was dealing with a very "shady Real Estate Broker", and he tried his best to intimidate me into an agreement for sale, without an Inspection Clause . . . because, as he said, "we are giving the building away." I held firm, and so did he, so I walked away from that experience even more determined to get some type of Inspection clause protection in any Contract For Sale I ever enter into . . . for again remember what they say and teach in those real estate classes . . . "caveat emptor" . . . "buyer Beware."

These Inspection Areas should be looked at and considered under the Buyer-Seller relationship which is taught to all real estate sales people in State-sanctioned and State Licensed real estate schools. It is openly and often taught so casually that you would think that everyone knew about . . . Caveat Emptor . . . ie, Buyer Beware . . . that is I find that everyone in the real estate business knows about it . . . everyone except the innocent, casual and carefree Buyer, who normally trusts everything told him in a Sales pitch, and requires little to be put down in writing. I have talked to hundreds of Buyers, and when I ask them if they had heard of Caveat Emptor and do they know what it means . . . most of the time, the Buyer is completely ignorant. Rarely, a Buyer remembers from grade school the ancient Latin phrase, "caveat emptor", but even these few do not realize that when they go to a Seller's Broker, the caveat emptor policy is in force. I cannot elaborate on this subject too strongly . . . because this is why this book and why my Service as an Advisor-Broker is available, ie, to advise and to protect the Buyer in a real estate transaction under a fiduciary-trust relationship . . . the kind of relationship you enjoy with your lawyer . . . only our relationship is less complicated . . . and usually at no cost to you.

Caveat Emptor means to you the Buyer that you must protect yourself in this major purchase of an apartment building by providing for your own professional Inspection, because you cannot take the promise of the owner or his Selling Broker, since it is taught in State sanctioned and licensed classes for real estate agents and Brokers that they are not obliged to tell the Buyer about anything relating to the apartment building "except hidden structural details" (these are the words from the real estate class). This means that if you ask about some construction detail that is not readily and easily seen by you without cutting into and damaging the building . . . then it is taught in real estate license schools that you the Buyer are entitled to an honest statement on that "hidden construction detail." You the Buyer are protected in no other way. In other words, the answers you get to your questions from the Seller and the Selling-Broker had better be in writing or you have no recourse later on. A Buyer will ask a Seller or the Selling-Agent, "How's the roof?" The answer, "fine . . . in good condition." If within a short period of Buyer ownership you have a leaky roof and you discover that the roof is thirty years old and you must pay to install a new one . . . you have no legal claim to the Seller or his Agent . . . for they are protected under the ancient principle, now sanctioned in modern real estate law, of Caveat Emptor . . . buyer beware.

How do you prove such false statements as the old roof told to you as "in good condition." By having all statements in writing. And then backed by your own Inspection. For who even wants to go through the hassle of proving damages through misrepresentation. People are just too trusting and too casual when making this major purchase consideration. They normally ask a lot of questions of the Seller and the Selling-Agent . . . but its all verbal . . . which is difficult if not impossible to prove this deception later. If you don't believe this, just spend a few hours some day in your local Small Claims Courtroom, which is open to spectators. You will hear claim after claim from wronged-people telling the Judge "he said this" . . . "he said that" . . . and all the wronged-person will get from the Judge is a sympathetic smile while asking if he has anything "in writing to prove this deception." The answer is usually "no, nothing in writing." And the Judge must dismiss the case on the grounds of "no proof."

Conclusion: Get all statements about the building in writing in your Contract For Sale. You'll lose some deals . . . but you will not get "stung."

I have been noticing some new "snake talk" lately by some Real Estate "Professionals" . . . "that Caveat Emptor is no longer in effect" . . . and that the Buyer CAN trust the Selling Broker." . . . To this I not only use my standard exclamation, "baloney" . . . but I'll add a second for emphasis . . . "nuts."

It is simply good and basic business to get ANY important business agreement IN WRITING. I don't understand these "smoke screens" from some people in the Real Estate Business. Do you think a business man would transact an important transaction without all important details put in writing? Even in those dusty old Real Estate law books they have it in writing that "THE BROKER MAY PUFF AND EXAGGERATE THE VALUE AND PROSPECTS OF THE PROPERTY . . ." (I call that "Selling"). Folks let's not be naive and foolish, like little lambs on the way to the slaughter house . . . get it in writing . . . you are transacting a large business deal . . . maybe YOUR largest . . . doesn't it just make good sense to act in a business like manner? In fact these new illusions of total honesty, to me, are dishonest and deceitful, and could induce knowing-people, to trust when they should not trust. Back to old English law, on which all of our law is based . . . "you cannot serve two Masters" . . . so how can a Selling Broker, who was EMPLOYED by the Seller to sell his Property for the price agreed to . . . how can this Broker, now turn around (put on his other hat) . . . and be totally honest with you, the Buyer. They try to get you and me to believe that, dear folks, but do not be led into the slaughter house . . . good old common, Mid-West horse sense tells me . . . "It stinks the house out." (This phrase recently made popular all over again, by famous radio Personality, Craig Worthing).

And especially, when you now know that you have a "secret-weapon" . . . your no-cost, Advisor Broker . . . why do you even want to consider relying on the Selling Broker in the transaction . . . after all he is "selling" . . . correct? He is sometimes pawned-off as some miracle-worker . . . who is all things to all people. Baloney . . . he is a human being, with a family to support . . . and subject to all frailties of humanity.

Basically, he is honest, as all of us are basically, honest . . . but it is a business deal, and he is selling . . . so you should be business-like also . . . N'EST CE PAS?

CHAPTER SEVEN

LOCATION IS IMPORTANT

That multi-millionaire Statesman and Advisor to Presidents, Bernard Baruch is credited with being the originator of the statement often used in the real estate business that there are three considerations to make in the purchase of real estate. They are: location . . . l o c a t i o n . . . and LOCATION. This premise says, pay the extra that is demanded for location and you will never regret it. If your are considering two buildings . . . with No. 1 priced at $100,000 and No. 2 priced at $115,000 . . . with everything similar except location . . . I would pay the extra $15,000 for the superior location . . . and this extra payment will come back to you ten-fold over the years, in higher rentals, less vacancies, and a quicker re-sale whenever you wish to sell out at a handsome profit.

Now, as to how much higher to pay for the superior location is strictly personal judgement and ability to pay. I gave the above example in terms of a 15% premium . . . to me that would almost be automatic. But if it were a 25% difference for location . . . I would compare and analyze the figures closely. I do not think that I would buy at a 50% difference for location, because it would take too long for that location premium to pay off, while these better neighborhoods do change these days, and some even deteriorate in the long period of time. A big location premium is really for the wealthy person, who is more concerned with stability than with a quicker and higher return on investment.

PRIME LOCATION CONSIDERATIONS
AND OBSERVATIONS:

• The chic areas of our town. In Miami, the best are Key Biscayne, Coral Gables/Coconut Grove, Northeast, Bal Harbour, and Southwest (when rapid transit gets there in the early 1980's).

- Central enough to major shopping centers, transportation, and important points of interest and attractions, like the Beach, Airport, Amusement.
- Near Public or preferably mass-transit which will become increasingly important with the expected energy shortage and crisis in the 1980's.
- Quick 24 hour convenience shopping nearby.
- Attractive immediate street area and attractive area upon arrival to the area of your considered apartment building. Trees and foliage are important for looks. A "bare area" is more difficult to rent to good tenants.

However, in Bernard Baruch's day, there was no such thing as good areas but now run-down by blight, population decentralization, etc., so the fourth location principle is "former location" which will come back again as does anything good . . . the cycle returns. So, besides just the current chic area of town, there is probably a slightly shabby but intriguing area in a central part of town where the hoi paloi used to reside, but is now out of popularity, but shows signs of returning to popularity. So, not following the 3 location principle can sometimes add up to a good and growingly good purchase. As said before, do not be rigid in the real estate business . . . or in any kind of business . . . be flexible.

So, if the street or area is not in first class condition; but the area is central (more and more important as the energy crunch gets worse), convenient to shopping, transportation and attractions, etc. I would consider this property, depending on how "the numbers" shape up on the property offered for sale. I would also investigate and consider run down areas which have an active "Improvement Association" of resident property owners in that area. Attend one of their meetings. Listen to the progress they report . . . listen to their plans for further area improvement. Then it must be your judgment as to if you believe that this run down area will come-back.

New York City is full of such former central and run down area where fortunes were made in "redeveloping areas." The most recent one in New York is "Soho" (which means South Houston St.), just South of Greenwich Village.

It contained block after block of uninteresting three and four story loft warehouses. Then a few artists discovered this area where space was the big incentive. Then some of the "beautiful people" began to buy in Soho. It literally took this area only a year or two for values to skyrocket. Today, buildings are going for ten times what they were just a few years ago. So look for trends in areas, and active improvement associations and just a "good common sense area" where the cycle will return, and values will increase.

Drive around in central areas, near water, near attractions, near shopping and transportation. Be observant and in some of these partially run-down areas you will notice activity by others like yourself, "who got there first". Don't be disappointed to hear that these "new pioneers" paid one half what it is worth today . . . for there will be continuing property increases in such an older but central redeveloping attractive area. You will find such areas in every City in the USA. As an example, in South St. Louis, surrounding the World Headquarter Budweiser Beer Plant, you will see restoration going on that you would not believe. All these old houses and apartments, some very run down, have now been repurchased, and soon, this central location will be more chic, and more valuable than the chic suburbs which surround St. Louis and have a National reputation.

Ask your real estate man about such areas of redeveloping activity and growth in your City or town. This idea isn't for everyone, but everyone should realize that there are two sides to the location principle . . . current prime location . . . and future prime location.

On the other hand, I do not think that I would ever buy an apartment building in a bad area, in the boondocks that is not central. That could be too much against you. A just average central area can become more of an attraction magnet for tenants as well as apartment building buyers as we approach the energy crisis in the 1980's.

I have a prediction to make about a major transfer of population in the USA within the next few years. I made this prediction three years ago, well ahead of last years (1978) severe Winter in the North. I feel that within five years, as the energy crisis gets more severe, and the Winters get more severe up North, I predict a panic to develop up North (just like the panic amongst a large group of people, like when that night club fire burst out in New England). I predict the cold to be so severe, and the fuel in so short a supply (and maybe none at all), that the Northerners will panic and be jammed up on the highways going out of these Northern Cities . . . all of them trying to make their way to the sunshine in Florida. Of course the panic will be too severe, autos will stall out on the highways after they run out of gasoline. A few lucky one's with larger fuel tanks installed will run people off the highway in their eager sense of self preservation to get to the warmth and sunshine in Florida.

For the past several years, I have half in jest, but also seriously, kidded my Northern friends and relatives to "keep a load of coal in the backyard for emergencies in a severe Winter, when normal fuel supplies become exhausted." Many northern homes are heated by gas fuel, transported via pipelines from Texas and Oklahoma. Don't you think it possible in time of cold panic and a desire for self preservation that Texas and Oklahoma (who also have cold Winters) may just cut off the gas supply to the North and save this heating fuel for their own self-preservation? If these States don't do it first, I can see other States closer to Texas, cutting of this heating fuel from going further North and into New England.

This terrible prediction will on the positive side make sunbelt apartment buildings in great demand, with rentals leaping skyhigh, as in Alaska where during the recent boom there, even a closet rented for $100 per week.

Regardless of weather my prediction comes true or not . . . you will see a gradual buildup of a population swing to the South from the colder North. I already talk to new people who have moved here from the North to avoid the terrible cold Northern Winters. Many people have migrated to Florida just this year from Buffalo, New York which went through a very severe Winter. The past few years Census updates Nationally, already show Florida in the top growth in population, ranking from number one to number three from among all fifty US States. And remember Florida is not a polluted and Industrial State like some of the other population growth States that are growing because of Industry (like the Carolinas, Georgia, etc.). But now, light Industry is beginning to come to Florida, so we will continue to grow . . . because of light, non-pollutant industry . . . and because of the Florida sunshine, when the majority of the rest of the Country is freezing.

Geographically, it may interest you to know that South Florida (which encompasses the "goldcoast", consisting of Palm Beach, Ft. Lauderdale, Miami, and Key West), is the only sub-Tropical area in the USA. Sub-tropic means not-Tropic . . . but on the fringe of the Tropics. This is the warmest area in the USA in the Winter . . . even North Florida, even Mickey Mouse in Orlando does get freezes . . . but never in South Florida. And yet in Summer, it is hotter in Northern Cities than in Miami. Check your weather maps for a period of time and you will see that when its 85 in Miami in Summer, it is often 90 or 95 or 100 degrees in St. Louis, Chicago, Cleveland, Philadelphia, New York, and Boston. Well that is enough of my sincere public relations for South Florida. As a recent "transplant" from the North, I love it here, but in general, if you relocate, GO SUN-BELT!

One other favorite thought of mine in the consideration of buying real estate for an investment, is what that sage old humorist, Will Rogers said way back in the 1930's . . . he said . . . "buy real estate, they're not making it anymore." It's true, is it not? Then add the extra potential of four apartment units on that piece of property (with expenses not much more than that for your private home), and you can begin to see the multiplying benefits derived from owning an apartment building . . . and these benefits are just the beginning . . . you have great tax deductions, great building depreciation for more tax savings . . . you have the ever increasing worth of your building, as inflation continues to spiral. With inflation you are valid in increasing rents, which increase the value of your building more (rent multiple rule in another Chapter), and instead of your paying rent, you are collecting the rent checks, which are paying off the mortgage.

With all this you are living rent-free. That's a pretty sweet incentive to get into apartment building ownership . . . is it not?

The real name
for this book should be:

"HOW TO LIVE RENT FREE
AND NOT PAY
ANY INCOME TAX EITHER . . .

AS APPROVED BY THE I.R.S."

Back to location, recently on a talk-radio program I did (with popular radio personality, Mitch Sandler, who is the originator of "trivia.") . . . no comments, please . . . a caller called in, said he was familiar with Miami, and would I please give him some examples of redeveloping-locations. I countered, that it would be more meaningful to the entire radio audience, if I would give him location tips in a general way. I said, "go for "magnets" that will appreciate your Property continuously . . . buy near parks . . . near water . . . for sure near public transportation (energy crisis) . . . a nice quiet and pretty neighborhood, but in walking distance to shopping is a "magnet" to make you money over the years . . . every city has such redeveloping areas. I read in an architectural trade magazine recently that there are about 50 such redeveloping areas in the New York city area . . . in a top 10 or top 20 city like Atlanta . . . there are perhaps 12 redeveloping areas . . . in a city the size of Colombus, Ohio, there should be about 5 redeveloping areas to search out . . . in a city the size of Hattiesburg, Miss. perhaps only 2 or 3 . . .", I continued to answer this radio-caller; "the most famous of all redeveloping areas is Georgetown, in our Nations Capitol. Formerly this was the stable area and the slave quarters to Washington, D.C. . . . today, Georgetown is for the very chic . . . the Kennedy's live there . . . how much chicer can you get?" Then after that windy dissertation, the caller quietly but excitedly answered: "after your fine general explanation of where to

look for a redeveloping area that will make me money ... I
KNOW JUST WHERE TO GO IN MY OWN HOME
TOWN ... AND I'M NOT EVEN GOING TO SAY IT OVER
THE AIR." To this fine compliment, I replied: "Yes, you are
all excited tonight ... but will you be tomorrow? My main
concern, Mr. Caller, is ... will you do it, or will you procrastinate?" That is why, when I autograph my book for a purchaser in a bookstore, I always put the date below my
name ... then I look the purchaser in the eye, and say:
"Now if you come across this book on your shelf in the
1980's and you realize that you have not acted on living rent
free ... let us state it right now ... that you should then
know that you are a procrastinator. (Please don't think I am
too harsh in dealing with procrastinators dear readers ... for
it is a disease, like alcoholism, and must be dealt with forth-
rightly ... and it can be cured ... after we admit that we
have this disease.)

This location premise of mine of buying in or near Central
redeveloping areas to make money faster has the same
meaning around the World. Recently I was in Paris, to revise
this book, in its third printing, for the World market, and also
to arrange for the printing of your book in French, German
and Spanish. For not only are foreign investors more easily
able to invest in USA Property these days ... these foreign
countries also have had a love affair with those little rose
covered millstones (the home) for even a longer period than
in our younger country ... but financial survival can also be
had for the European, the Asian, the South American ...
even the Tahitian (as I said before) ... you can live rent free
anywhere in the world, using this Quad-Plex or Duplex
theory of ownership.

Now back to Paris (redeveloping areas) ... on a Sunday
afternoon, we were invited to visit the new "Centre Georges
Pompidou" ... a new architectural monstrosity in the center
of old-Paris, built on the site of the old market center ... the
famous "Les Halle". Picture this new gigantic building in a
center area, surrounded by 300 to 400 year old magnificent
townhouse type buildings. These old buildings are now being
restored. Even so quickly as the past several years most of

these very old neighboring buildings have already been restored on the outside . . . and you must look and look very carefully to find a very old one not yet restored, so you can see what this entire area looked like just several years ago. You don't have to be a financial genius to know that these buildings increased in price ten to 20 to perhaps 50 times in just a few years because THEY ARE LOCATED NEAR A NEW "MAGNET" . . . THE CENTRE GEORGES POM-PIDOU, IN PARIS. So you see; people, places and ideas are really the same, World wide. While in Europe, I learned that the Quad-Plex is very popular in Germany . . . and why not . . . the Germans are very smart people . . . just look at how many VW "Beetless" they sold us Americans.

But as I say to anyone who has also discovered the general-ly overlooked Quad-Plex/Duplex ownership lifestyle World-wide . . . although I am not selling my book, just as a general warning . . . EVEN IF YOU HAVE JUST ONE DUPLEX . . . AND YOU HAVE JUST ONE TENANT LIVING IN YOUR OTHER DUPLEX APARTMENT . . . YOU CAN HAVE A BED OF ROSES . . . OR A CROWN OF THORNS . . . for that tenant can either be a star-tenant . . . or that tenant can drive you crazy . . . its up to you; and I am sorry to say that in talking to many people about tenants . . . most owners just don't know how to "screen new tenant applicants" . . . how to talk to them in arriving at a mutual understanding of the tenant/owner relationship . . . and then to have all of this IN WRITING (see my long Chapters on this important subject).

* * *

Another bigger idea on buying in a redeveloping central area . . . recently an architect approached me after my lecture at the Diplomat Hotel and asked about some old and run-down area in downtown Ft. Lauderdale (I give this as an example only, and there are situations like this one in every city large or small . . . in the world) . . . from what he de-scribed, I pictured a pretty run down area, something too big for the average person . . . but here is the advice I gave to this architect . . . "As an architect, in business and knowing many other professionals in the building-industry . . . why not get a few people together that you know . . . don't go into a partnership (which I am basically against in property ownership, since most of the time one person does far too much of the management, while the other partner? does nothing) . . . but just get a few people "together", with a MUTUAL AIM OF REDEVELOPING A BLOCK OR AN ENTIRE STREET of a redeveloping area. This method allows you to guide your own destiny in a very big and profitable way. For the entire block or street will quickly take on a new look with greatly increased property values. And here is how to work this with say three dependable people in a one block area. Each person puts a down payment on one block area. Each person puts a down payment on one or two buildings (sometimes you can get very cheap Government loans in areas the Government encourages redevelopment, as in "Soulard" in St. Louis); then simultaneously, all three persons get options on 2 or 3 other run-down buildings on this same block . . . pay money for these options if necessary . . . for the big profit you will make in one year or more will greatly offset any option investment. Then you three begin your very own "Urban Renewal" . . . you each begin to restore your two buildings . . . that makes six scattered buildings being restored on one "interesting" but very run down block. There are many others that will be interested in investing in this same block . . . after you start the ball rolling . . . you will be surprised at the investor interest in your "block." In fact, some investors will search you out, to buy your optioned buildings (putting a select for-sale sign discreetly on one or two of the 15 buildings you three control on the bloc, will help Commerce along.) This example of Citizen-Urban-Renewal is not a Mass Idea as is most of this book, but I think it good for all of us to see a next bigger step forward if we really get into the business of investment in a central redeveloping location. At least, YOU may be one of the ones that saw the discreet for-sale sign . . . and bought just one of the 15 buildings optioned out by the three people in the example above. Don't despair, when some smarty-friend tells you that what you paid $20,000 for . . . was bought for $10,000 the year before. These kinds of comments, I find, usually come from the "dreamers" ... its good "bar talk" ... (where the biggest dreamers usually hang out) ... your replay to this "Dreamer" can be ... "fine, and what I paid $20,000 for today, will be worth $50,000 in a year or two ... AND ... I AM DOING SOMETHING ... YOU MY FRIEND ARE A "DREAMER" ... WHO JUST TALKS A LOT ... BUT DOES LITTLE."

FLASH: PARIS EDITION, HERALD TRIBUNE, Mon. June 12, 1978. As I sit here in old Paris, near where Van Gogh and Monet lived, painted, and died ... and as I write in a beautiful little French salon ... looking out a large old French window, into a garden with roses blooming profusely, a huge cherry tree filled with fruit (that I hope ripens in the next two weeks) ... I think: "What an inspirational setting ... no wonder Van Gogh painted such masterpieces here ... what inspiration ... I feel the same; writing here." Anyway, as I sit here writing about redeveloping-Central-areas around the World; my French maid brings in my cafe' and croissant and the morning Paris edition Herald Tribune ... and there is a big, front page story (just like my book hitting the front page as it also deals with "shelter" and the changing modes of living) dealing with Central redeveloping areas throughout Europe. It is too much of a coincidence not to quote a few passages from this front page feature story.

FROM AMSTERDAM, HOLLAND. "Municipal officials, who issued dire predictions of the decay of the City 20 years ago, are now congratulating themselves because the inner City has now been preserved in its historical aura, along with an enviable mixture of MIDDLE CLASS RESIDENTIAL, and business life. In ten years it is predicted the number of affluent people in the City Center may overwhelm and push out the last remnants of the working class."

(... or as I put it in this Chapter ... the smart people are getting rid of that box in the boondocks ... and are investing in a Quad or Duplex in or near the Central City.)

(More from this Paris Tribune story)... "The exodus of workers has overtaken a number of Western European Cities, and in some cases it means a large TRANSFER OF POORER PEOPLE TO SUBURBAN AREA ... AND THIS TRANSFER PERIOD CAN LEAD TO SOCIAL TENSIONS BETWEEN BLUE COLLAR AND MIDDLE CLASS RESIDENTS." (So help me Hannah ... that is what it says ... you have the newspaper and date if you wish to verify ... that THE CHIC SUBURBS ARE TURNING INTO SLUMS ... AND THE INNER-CITY FORMER-ELEGANT SLUMS ARE NOW BEING RESTORED BY THE MIDDLE CLASS AS THEIR HOMES. So you see, what I wrote in the past several years is coming to pass, even sooner than I expected ... so sell your little millstone in the boondocks, you "doers" and buy your Quad in a central redeveloping area. Soon, the remaining "boxes in the boondocks" may even drop in value with the above type social change plus my original comments that you won't be able to afford the $2 per gallon of gasoline to drive out there.)

(More from the Paris Tribune story)... "Paris has lost half a million working class people to the suburbs"... "in one section of Paris, hundreds of blue-collar families have banded together in a so-called "defense-Committee," seeking legal and political aid against the entry of the more affluent who now wish to live there, and the ensuing real estate price rise which is certain to follow, and which the blue-collar families will not be able to afford, and will have to move out to the suburbs."
... Want more?... "London is losing 100,000 worker residents per year, searching for cheaper housing in the suburbs, with the middle-class moving into former blue-collar strongholds. "THIS INFLUX ... KNOWN DEROGATORILY AS "GENTRIFICATION"... HAS PRODUCED IMPRESSIVE RENOVATION OF DECAYED STRUCTURES, BUT IT HAS ALSO SPARKED WORKING CLASS RESENTMENT BECAUSE THE NEWER MIDDLE CLASS RESIDENTS TEND TO TAKE UP MORE LIVING SPACE AND DRIVE UP THE COST OF HOUSING ... WITH

LANDLORDS GREATLY INCREASING THE RENTS BEYOND THE REACH OF BLUE COLLAR FAMILIES."

So, what is happening the past few years in Europe, will happen in the USA also . . . it sometimes takes us a little longer for a social type change. People are basically the same all over the World, and there are obviously good people everywhere that want to get back to the "roots" of their existence by living in a more central and possibly historical area, closer to work, avoiding the traffic jams to work, the $2 per gallon gasoline (I just heard that it is $3 per gallon in Jamaica, right now!) . . . and you dear wives will keep hubby from the tension of a heart attack . . . he will live as long as you . . . and you won't be a long term widow . . . so think it over . . . there are many changes in store for us in the 1980's . . . and I seem to be the only one giving some sensible solutions to the people.

* * *

Now as a sequel to my fantasy about those Northern "snow-bunnies" mass exodus to the sunbelt after not too many more freezing winters . . . I have saved a few clippings that show it is getting colder and colder up North . . . in fact I recently heard the CBS Network meteorologist (he has about the best National reputation for accuracy) predict that we are in for ten more years of very cold Northern winters. So, read these stories, and figure it out . . . is it worth ten more winters of your life . . . go to the Sun Belt if you can and enjoy life. There is more opportunity in the Sun Belt also . . . A recent Government study showed that ALL TEN of the top-ten growth cities are in the SunBelt. Think it over folks . . . its your life and your money.

Giant Snowstorm Paralyzes East

Saturday, January 21, 1978

A bitter shroud of snow and ice buried the East Friday.

A blizzard — sometimes piling up snow at the rate of an inch every hour — halted travel, marooned thousands, turned cities into ghost towns and turned everyone into a pioneer.

THE STORM afflicted Philadelphia, Pittsburgh, Washington and Baltimore. More than a foot of snow fell overnight from Maryland to Maine and inland to Ohio and Kentucky.

Cincinnati had a record 16 inches in 24 hours.

The National Weather Service predicted the snow would turn to sleet and freezing rain and continue into the weekend. Flooding was feared.

Many Marooned, Travel Halted

Saturday, January 28, 1978

SIXTY PASSENGERS and crewmen were stranded aboard the Miami-bound Floridian when the train stalled in a snowdrift in western Indiana and froze to the rails.

Blizzard Buries East Coast

Tuesday, February 7, 1978

New York, Baltimore Declare Emergencies

The Associated Press

Heavy snow driven by high winds rampaged from Virginia to New England Monday, crippling road, rail and air traffic and bringing business and government to a near standstill for the second time in 17 days.

Offices closed early and workers struggled to fight their way home. Snow emergencies were declared in New York City, Baltimore and dozens of other cities and towns.

Govs. Milton Shapp of Pennsylvania and J. Joseph Garrahy of Rhode Island declared emergencies that allowed them to call out National Guard units to help stranded motorists and road-clearing crews. Pennsylvania's Civil Defense headquarters was activated.

Blamed for at least 36 deaths, most of them either heart-attack victims who were stricken while shoveling snow or motorists who were asphyxiated while trying to stay warm in snowbound cars.

Boston also suffered a power blackout early Tuesday, with service cut off to 75,000 Boston Edison Company customers from 1:40 to 8 a.m.

Tufts-New England Medical Center, one of the city's largest hospitals, was without heat. Nurses passed out extra blankets to help the 400 patients keep warm in 50-degree temperatures.

Looting ensued in some parts of Boston and 43 persons were arrested in the Roxbury and Dorchester neighborhoods.

90

Abandoned Autos Clog Main Highway, I-95

Sunday, Feb. 12, 1978

THEY WOULD be trapped, victims of the worst catastrophe in this state's history, a disaster more brutal than even the hurricane of 1938 which sent water into the second floors of Providence stores.

By the week's end, hundreds still had not found their way home through the yard-deep snow which paralyzed entire cities; stranded more than 3,000 automobiles, caused at least 16 deaths, and staggered the state's economy.

MASSIVE TRAFFIC jams developed around the icy ramps of I-95 and I-195, the main expressways that criss-cross the heart of Providence, a city of 167,000.

Hundreds of cars and trucks are still buried where they stood. Most of the drivers fled to shelter. Some could not, or did not.

George Plante, 46, was trapped throughout the night in his car. He is crippled with a muscular disease and can't walk.

Policeman William Green, trudging from car to car ordering people out before they froze to death or were asphyxiated, spotted Plante,

With police immobilized like everyone else, looters sacked stores at will and broke into abandoned

About 2,500 jammed into the Marriott, which has only 250 rooms. They organized "chain gangs" to shuttle needed food from delivery trucks stalled on the highway.

"This is like something you see in a science fiction movie, the Poseidon Adventure or Towering Inferno or something," said the attractive blonde woman of about 40. "I'm in a room with four other women and an undertaker. Me and the undertaker sleep on the floor.

Saturday, Feb.18, 1978

Climatologists Don't Think Our Cities Will Ice Over Soon

... but Hudson River scene from last year gave people worries

NOTES & QUESTIONS

JIM ANDERSON'S "HOW TO LIVE RENT FREE" BOOK

CHAPTER EIGHT

APARTMENT BUILDINGS CAN BECOME
"YOUR OIL WELL"
FOR TAX DEDUCTIONS . . . AND MUCH SAFER

Many people purchase apartments only because they are superior tax deductions. Uncle Sam, in his great wisdom has a belief in a more stable citizenry through an increased number of citizens who become property owners in this great Country of ours. So, to increase the number of property owners, Uncle Sam has declared a great number of tax incentives to property owners to increase and encourage more citizens to invest in real estate and buildings here. You can truthfully consider your apartment building just as beneficial as your very own oil well (as far as beneficial tax deductions) . . . only not near as risky.

Against your total rental income you can deduct the interest that you pay on your building's mortgage, you can deduct a significant amount for depreciation to your building (although Uncle Sam knows quite well that buildings really appreciate, and rarely really depreciate). You can deduct property improvement expenses (which will eventually make you more money since improvement will increase the building's value). Also, your improvement of the building will allow you to increase rents which will give you more immediate income, and will also increase the sales worth of your building. For as I have said before: If you manage to double you rents (through improvement, better tenants, etc.) your apartment building is now worth double what you paid for it.

Mortgage Interest. Say you have a $60,000, 20 year mortgage. At 12% interest your annual mortgage payment is about $8,000 per year. And any home owner knows that during the first five to ten years of a mortgage payment results in the payment of mainly interest. Then after ten years, you begin to pay off more of the Principal with each

93

monthly payment. Therefore, in the beginning years of your apartment building ownership you will have a nice annual tax deduction of the interest portion of these mortgage payments, right off the top of your total income, of about $6,000 in the above example.

Depreciation on your apartment building is another great tax deduction. Lets say that you have your tax man set up depreciation on your newly bought apartment building that cost you $100,000, and lets say that you decide to depreciate it on a "straight line basis" (there are other accelerated methods that can interest high current income purchasers). Therefore, this $100,000 building, depreciated by you over a twenty year period, "straight line" (which means the same amount, each year), this gives you another $5,000 tax deduction, right off the top of your total income. Therefore, already, with just these two deductions, you have been able to deduct $11,000 right off the top of your total income for the year on which you pay no taxes.

Many buyers sell their buildings after the tax deductions and tax advantages wear down, through the acceleration of these tax deductions. So then the next buyer who probably will pay you $150,000 for this building (if you have improved it, and increased the rent rates) and he now begins to depreciate it all over again at the higher rate of sale. So the new owners depreciation over twenty years, straight-line-method, will become a $7500 annual tax deduction, where yours was $5,000.

To the uninitiated, "depreciation" does not mean what it says. The building does not really depreciate. This one building can be depreciated over and over again, by each new owner. It is merely one of Uncle Sam's incentives to encourage you to "invest in America."

And this depreciation gimmick, created and approved a long time ago by the US Government, and wisely so to promote and encourage property ownership in this great USA, and is one good reason why there are always some exceptional apartment values on the Market. Because, the current owner has merely used up at least the good years of his depreciation for tax purposes, and now must sell the building to someone new so the new buyer can begin the depreciation cycle all over again on this same building.

You have probably heard of the big tax breaks in the risky oil well business? Well now you as a US citizen and taxpayer can rationalize that apartment buildings are your very own "oil well situation" . . . only without the oil well risks.

Another deduction for you are all those property improvements I hope you make, that I will discuss in another Chapter. Improvements are not only a good way to improve your property to make it more valuable in resale; but these same improvements almost immediately increase rents which gives you additional current revenue through the corresponding rent increases. And remember the big payoff . . . if you double the rents of your apartments you automatically double the book value of your apartment building. Now lets get back to these property improvements as more tax deductions. They are also deductible right off the top of your total annual income. If your maintenance and improvement costs over a year were $5,000 . . . you have another $5,000 tax deduction. Sometimes it is not advantageous to deduct all improvements in one year, because you may already have all the tax deduction help you need in this one year. So, Uncle Sam, in his great wisdom, and in his interest to help and to protect the property owner (the backbone of this Nation), you are allowed to amortize (deduct just a portion each year) many of these improvement expenses over a period of years, from three years for some improvement expenses to five or ten years for others. Your tax man can tell you before you spend your improvement money, what may be more beneficial for you, depending if your total income will be increasing or decreasing over the next few years. A roof may be amortized over ten years; a paint job over five years.

Regarding tax consultants . . . if your tax man is getting a bit too big for his britches (this means his fees are going way up) I have a suggestion you may want to investigate. In the beginning with my first building, I was recommended a tax man by my lawyer as a "fair and reasonable tax office." I was charged $150 in a combination fee for my personal return and my apartment. However, they did not do a great job.

95

They were poor communicators with the facts, and in general I was unimpressed. Then I was recommended to a local franchised office of the National Company, H. & R. Block. May I say that they have been sensational. They save me more money and their fee is less. They know all the latest and ever changing tax rules and loopholes. And they advise me on future tax procedures that will benefit me and my apartments. And what had cost me $150 at the first tax accountant firm, now only costs me about $50 at H. & R. Block Co. You may want to give them a try. However, for Commercial tax returns on income property, Block has told me to call in advance for an appointment with one of their senior tax consultants. If you get the "brush off" from the little chickie who answers the phone, and who tells you "just come on in" (and wait) . . . ask to speak to the Manager, and explain the situation to him. I understand that the procedure varies at the different Block tax offices, but by talking to the Office Manager, you should insist on getting an appointment with a senior tax consultant who is versed in your apartment building situation.

In conclusion on tax deductions, you can get from $19,000 to $25,000 in tax deductions off this $100,000 apartment building. At least I do, and it can probably be bettered by someone with a sharper tax consultant and by one who needs more tax deductions than I.

And so now you know that the ownership of apartment buildings is really a tax haven . . . a tax bonanza for you . . . so jump on the wagon . . . what are you waiting for. You get mortgage interest deductions . . . depreciation deductions . . . improvement expense deductions . . . and all operational expense deductions.

There are many many more very sophisticated property procedures from a tax point of view; but at this stage it would probably only confuse you. If you have digested all the opportunities available to you in this Chapter so far, you will be acomplishing much.

However, if you wish to read about how the "high rollers" use income property in an unbelievable number of tax rule advantages, read a book that is devoted exclusively to this

APARTMENT BUILDINGS CAN BECOME
"YOUR OIL WELL"
FOR TAX DEDUCTIONS . . . AND MUCH SAFER

subject. Among other books you may want to read on this subject, you may consider; "Modern Real Estate Finance" by William Attebury. Published by Grid Inc., Ninth Printing in 1972. This book is current study material for the Florida Real Estate Broker Course and Examination.

Your head will "swim" with "real estate maneuvers" as worked by the big boys. But one word of caution. Many of those "big boys" got done-in recently by overextending themselves in the recent recessive economy. Don't let this happen to you. Do not overextend. Keep a reserve of money for the unexpected, and you will be secure.

One last observation on you old time owners that proudly say, "I own my home free and clear." From the lessons described above, you can see all the money you are losing. You have no depreciation left. You have no mortgage interest deductions. If building owners sell out when depreciation runs out, maybe that is a good reason alone to consider it when your home runs out of depreciation tax credits.

What I am really talking about as a tax deduction on your Quadplex . . . is the bandied investment term "tax shelter." In my travels, in lectures, on radio and TV talk-programs, I constantly ask the people "how many of you have tax shelters?" . . . Very few have them . . . would you believe . . . maybe 5% have? I say to these audiences (in a conscious-raising fashion) . . . "Your Doctor has a tax shelter . . . why don't you? (No answers, so I continue to tell them why) . . . You are frightened to death that with a tax shelter in an unfamiliar field . . . that soon you will loose your investment capital . . . and have nothing left to "shelter" . . . and you were correct, when you refused all the "shelter gimmicks" in recent years that were "the fashion" and "the vogue" to lose more money. They were the "Cattle tax shelters" . . . "the farm tax shelters" . . . all losers in my estimation, because the only ones that made the money on these were the big investment operators who sold these deals to the public. How-ever . . . now let us conscious-raise more and deeper into You . . . Through all these years of playing the "stock game" plus an investment through "a big tip from the local tav-ern" . . . your best investment, 9 out of 10 times, has been your home . . . but you know what? . . . don't take any credit for being a financial genius on your home as an investment . . . lets face it . . . you, like all of us "needed a roof over your head" . . . and the little woman nagged and nagged until you bought the home, the dream of every red-blooded American girl. Now, however, this "home buying experience" has shown you clearly that your best investment has been your home . . . so? . . . if that is true . . . why not do it again . . . only "times four" . . . by a Quad Plex!

Next, I always get a question about paying property taxes. My answer is that I do not pay the taxes . . . or the mortgage and its interest . . . and the insurance . . . and the property upkeep . . . MY TENANTS DO . . . AND MY TENANTS ALSO PAY MY RENT . . . AND I AM ALLOWED TO KEEP MORE OF MY SALARIED INCOME (less income tax) BECAUSE I CAN DEDUCT BUILDING DEPRECIATION AND THESE EXPENSES THAT MY TENANTS ACTUALLY PAY . . . YET I CAN DEDUCT THESE EXPENSES OFF MY SALARIED INCOME TAX. IT HARDLY SEEMS FAIR TO THE RENTERS . . . HUH? Well my challenge to some of the renters (the "doers") . . . become a Property Owner . . . AND STOP PAYING RENT . . . START COLLECTING RENT. And to some of you renters who don't have the down payment . . . see the section in this book entitled . . . HOW TO OWN YOUR OWN DUPLEX EVEN IF YOU DON'T HAVE THE DOWN PAYMENT . . . AND SOON LIVE THERE RENT FREE . . . AND PAY LESS INCOME TAX ALSO . . . AS APPROVED BY UNCLE SAM.

So you can see from the above that Property Taxes really don't bother me, although I am thrilled to see that "Section 13" Tax Bill pass in California . . . and I predict that it will sweep the Nation . . . because one of the big inflationary pressures is bureaucratic waste . . . for when the Mayor Beame of wasteful New York City has a government pension plan that gives the former Mayor Beame MORE INCOME NOW THAT HE IS RETIRED THAN WHEN HE WAS MAYOR . . . SOMETHING IS WRONG WITH THAT GOVERNMENT . . . AND THEY MUST TIGHTEN THEIR FAT BUREAUCRATIC BELTS.

APARTMENT BUILDINGS CAN BECOME
"YOUR OIL WELL"
FOR TAX DEDUCTIONS . . . AND MUCH SAFER

Do you know that YOU WORK FROM JANUARY 1 UNTIL ABOUT MAY 11 JUST FOR YOUR GOVERNMENT . . . THEN THE REST OF THE YEAR YOU WORK FOR YOURSELF . . . THIS TO ME IS FRAUD . . . and the tax-revolt will cut our Property Taxes . . . but my Tenants pay for them anyway . . . but I am delighted to see this tax revolt. It will be good for the Country . . . and have you noticed that when opposers to this tax reduction in California (like Governor Brown) talk against it . . . he looks like a villain with a kiss of death on his cheek. The voter is saying, YOU ARE SPEAKING AGAINST THIS MASS TAX REVOLT AND WE WILL NOT RE-ELECT YOU. As popular as Governor Brown was (before his opposition to this tax Proposal 13), he was even looking good as Presential timber . . . I predict, that unless he "skirts this issue" . . . that he will not be re-elected Governor of California. Somehow, he will have to change and become a champion for Proposal 13, or he will be doomed. Since most politicians talk out of both sides of their mouth . . . lets watch Brown's "footwork" . . . (or his "mouthwork").

So Property Taxes? Don't worry about them . . . your tenants pay them, but it will even "better" a good situation by having this Property Tax Revolt.

99

HOW TO LIVE RENT FREE . . . By James W. Anderson

Revealing the "tax bite" off $10,000 in profits from investments in: STOCKS . . . versus, TAX FREE BONDS . . . versus, RENTAL INCOME PROFIT.

PICK YOUR TAX BRACKET:	$10,000 INTEREST OFF STOCKS	$10,000 INTEREST OFF TAX FREE BONDS	$10,000 PROFIT OFF RENTALS
OFF EACH $10,000 YOU WILL PAY AN INCOME TAX OF:			
25%	$2,500	ZERO TAX, NO PLUSES	ZERO TAX, BIG PLUS*
35%	$3,500	ZERO TAX, NO PLUSES	ZERO TAX, BIG PLUS*
45%	$4,500	ZERO TAX, NO PLUSES	ZERO TAX, BIG PLUS*

* Additionally, your apartment building should increase in value, as good investment and well managed income properties have done over the past 50 years . . . bonds do not appreciate in value.

* Additionally, the rents (return) will usually increase over the years to keep pace with inflation and salary increases, when you own good investment property, well managed. You can't increase the interest (return) on tax free bonds, can you?

HOW TO LIVE RENT FREE . . . By James W. Anderson

As you see in the chart (preceeding page), rental income normally pays no income tax (the same as tax free bonds), if you can offset your rental income against the tax shelters provided to apartment building owners by Uncle Sam to encourage property ownership. These "shelters" include: building depreciation; the interest portion of your mortgage payments; building improvement and repair costs, maintenance cost, plus Real Estate taxes, yearly insurance payments and other building expenses.

In my case, besides living tax free, plus an income; my tax shelter on three Properties totals about $25,000 per year (with a $7,500 tax shelter just off the five unit building where I live) . . . so, tax shelter is a big plus with income property, for this tax shelter CAN ALSO BE APPLIED AGAINST YOUR SALARIED JOB . . . so maybe where you paid $7,500 in income tax before . . . with your apartment building, YOU NOW, NOT ONLY LIVE RENT FREE . . . BUT YOU PAY LESS, OR NO INCOME TAX ON YOUR SALARIED JOB . . . what a sweet deal?

Why do you think your prosperous Doctor is so concerned about tax shelters? He probably owns big tax shelters so he can keep more of his earnings. He would keep very little of his large income if he did not have a tax shelter. You can do this very same thing . . . even if on a smaller scale.

So although tax free bonds and rental income (as defined above) pay no income tax . . . the tax free bonds do not increase in value as income properties (properly bought and operated) usually do . . . with tax free bonds, what you see is what you get . . . and not a penny more. Stocks can increase in value (but on a much more erratic set of standards than a substantial piece of income property), but you must pay income tax (see chart) on stock income . . . you will pay no tax on most of your apartment rental income, and will probably save paying income tax on your salaried income, for now you have a tax shelter with your apartment building.

(These two pages checked and verified by H & R BLOCK INC., Marilyn Fey, MGR., Miami, Fl. 33010.)

101

NOTES & QUESTIONS

CHAPTER NINE

THE "CONTRACT FOR SALE"
IS YOUR DEAL . . .

I remember when I was looking for my first apartment building three years ago, that I had made several low offers on my own (without legal help) on buildings, via the Contract For Sale form (eagerly supplied to me by the selling Broker), but these offers were not accepted by the Sellers.

Then I could have gotten a little sloppy and careless and easily could have not given respect to all the stipulations on my next Contract For Sale.

Here is where your Advisor Broker really earns his no-fee from you. This Contract For Sale is your deal, and all the promises and statements as to the building's condition, plus all your negotiated terms of your offering should be clearly stated in detail. Your Advisor-Broker will go over your notes of Seller statements, and if you have not made many notes, your Advisor Broker will do the best he can by talking to the Seller and the Selling Agent to question them in a general way regarding the normal points that should be in writing in your Contract. Then you should take this document to your lawyer for final, legal, approval.

But back to my story. Finally one Seller accepted my offer, and only then did I call my lawyer. He calmly told me that I had "already made the deal with the mutually agreed to Contract For Sale document," and further, that the lawyers services at the "closing" "were merely a formality to enforce what we, the Buyer and Seller (with only the Seller's Broker helping both of us) had already agreed to in writing and bound by my earnest money." I gulped hard, for I could have just made the monumental error of my life, but luckily (and being detail minded) I had put in that Contract For Sale all of my required and desired protections and Seller promises and Seller statements regarding this apartment building. Luckily, I had made notes during the Inspection and Negotiations . . . and I used them in my Contract For Sale. Then, in fact, my lawyer did just enact all the points that we two Parties (the Buyer and the Seller, and the Seller's Broker) had agreed to . . . without a lawyer or Advisor Broker to protect me. This method is done all the time by Buyers not realizing that they should have someone on their side, concerned for their better interests. Its really a dangerous way to conduct big business . . . and it is done many times every day by unknowing Buyers that do not know or realize that they can have the no-cost help of a professional Advisor-Broker to look out for their interests in the negotiations and in the most important Contract For Sale.

I was just plain lucky with my first Contract For Sale, and I will never do that again. There are just too many little points that are automatic with a lawyer, but are not automatic with me, because I do not examine Contracts For Sale almost every day, or for sure every week, like my lawyer does, for I have been extremely fortunate to do a little better than one per year.

May I say here, not to rely completely on your lawyer to draw up the Contract For Sale. This will take too much of your lawyer's time, and therefore it is too expensive (for every Contract is not accepted) . . . and believe it or not, I do not want a lawyer writing up my deal, because I have been the major investigator in this deal, I know more about this building than my lawyer would ever know (and he was not involved in the Inspection or Negotiations), so how can I expect my lawyer to write up my Contract For Sale. I as the Buyer (or as the Advisor Broker) will write up the Contract For Sale (with my Buyer's help and information) then we will pass it over the desk of the Buyers lawyer or mine for approval, and to be certain that I or my Buyer is legally protected.

If you are fortunate enough to know a lawyer, versed in apartment buildings, who will not "complicate", or "puff up", or "confuse" your Contract For Sale, to the point where your lawyer can kill your intended purchase with your Seller just walking away from the deal in disgust . . . then you are fortunate and by all means use this lawyer. You will save

THE "CONTRACT FOR SALE"
IS YOUR DEAL . . .

a lot of peace of mind, and perhaps a chunk of your fortune, just because of some stupid mistake you made, which we are all capable of doing when we "stray out of our field."

As a sidelight, my lawyer tells me that unknowing Buyers are "lead into a Contract For Sale by the Sellers Broker frequently and without the Buyer having the benefit of an Advisor or a lawyer." My lawyer says "the Selling Broker infers that the Contract For Sale is only an offer," and further infers to the Buyer "that the Contract For Sale is just a casual document along the way to making a deal . . . but not the primary instrument." Now I know this is true, because it happened to me on my first purchase. Fortunately, I was detail minded, and I made notes, and I knew what I wanted in that first Contract For Sale . . . but I say again . . . I was lucky.

Today, I use a first class, Miami legal firm, versed in Florida real estate law. And even with my personal unusual ownership stipulations that requires additional legal documents not normally used in a closing . . . my total legal fee is around $500 per apartment building. That included looking over the all important Contract For Sale (that I have prepared) with proper legal suggestions of any important omissions that I may have made. The lawyer does the important title search (in Florida you don't want some Indian taking posession of your Property). The lawyer handles and computes all the money transactions at the "closing," and they then prepare all the many legal documents and later send them to me in one complete package with a neat ribbon around it, for filing. Also your lawyer is there to protect you on any extraneous circumstance that may arise wherein you may be taken advantage of, since my lawyer has much real estate experience, he has been through about every conceivable real estate transactions, and can be a distinct help to me when the unexpected arises. For all this work of a technical as well as of a legal nature . . . and for my own peace of mind . . . I feel this is a necessary and a reasonable expense.

Additionally, in case my Contract For Sale is not accepted by the Seller (and I feel that is a 50/50 chance, the way I like to "deal"), then I have made an arrangement with my legal firm wherein they charge me a small flat fee ($25 to $50) for checking over and typing up my Contract For Sale. I really like this system, which doesn't prevent you from using your lawyer on even a marginal deal, where you feel the Seller probably will not accept your offer. I will not mind spending a few bucks to pass such an important and expensive instrument across my lawyers desk.

I am reminded about two stories about offers years ago which have always impressed me. The first was about my boss at a radio station where I worked when I was first out of College. He didn't make much money either, and he had a wife and several kids, and he was looking for a house to buy at a bargain price, which was all that he could afford. I'll bet he made fifty "low ball" (that's really low) offers to Sellers . . . finally one accepted, and he had bought himself a house at a bargain price. I tell this, not to advise you to overdo the low offer technique, because you can also just waste everybodys' time, patience and money on unrealistically low offers that everyone knows will not be accepted. So practice moderation, and again though . . . don't be rigid on either side of the "offering fence."

My second story was a few years later. I had a friend who was a real estate Broker and he suggested that we go 50/50 on a Country House purchase. I was willing, and just as we were about to make the deal, my Broker friend announced that he knew the property and was going to save money by not using a lawyer. I backed out of the deal, although I had not a lot of buying experience, except for several houses I had bought to live in. But through the years, I guess I had heard from family and friends that a title search and a lawyer are important. I stand on what I said originally . . . I do not think professionalism and peace of mind should be sacrificed for a $500 legal fee* for this. Maybe my sharpie Broker "almost my partner" really knew what he was doing. Maybe he is the smart one. But I feel a $500 fee to Close on a valuable apartment building is in line with reason. Oh yes,

* Legal fee includes Title Insurance.

years later now my sharpie Broker is floundering and out the real estate business. My first boss who made all those home offers is running a company, and is doing very well. There's a lesson there. (Read it again.)

Another Closing tip.   Request and demand in the Contract For Sale that the Seller provide you with "take over information from each tenant and signed by Seller and Tenant." All this information to be put on a reproduced form that you prepare. This form will list and inventory the Sellers (and soon your's) property in each apartment from the frig or stove, to air conditioners, rugs, furniture, et al. You will want the condition mentioned by each appliance like, "in good working order." Also on this form will be a place to list any Security payment held by the Seller, which must be turned over to you at Closing. (This alone can save you thousands of dollars on some future deal). Have a space to list any special deals or arrangements between the Tenant and the Seller. For you don't want a tenant to tell you right after you take possession that "the former owner had promised him a new refrigerator." This form filled out and signed by Tenant and Seller is a must and will protect you from many many future problems with existing Tenants. You must go with the Seller when he makes the calls on each Tenant. (It's also a good way to meet and be introduced to your take-over Tenants.) You are there and you are a witness as to what was put down on the form, and what was said and agreed to by Seller and Tenant. With this there are no surprises at the Closing, at least we hope not, and you are off on your adventure to fame and fortune as the owner of your first apartment building.

"THE HOW TO LIVE RENT FREE BOOK" by J. ANDERSON

(Actual form used. Not made up)
(Similar form should be used when you
go around with the seller, and have tenants sign)
Takeover confirmation of tenant rights.

Miami, Fla.

Aug 9 19____
(date)

FOLD BLDG
FOUR EAST

This will confirm that I am occupying Apt. # 1 _____ at the

_____IRIS_____ Apts. at _____N.E. Street_____ Miami, Fla.
                        (street)

I (do...do not) have a lease, and I agree to give a thirty

day notice should I plan to move. NUMBER OF OCCUPANTS ONE

My rent is payable on the ___1st___ day of each month in the

amount of $ 165.00 per month, plus _____
                                      (anything else)

2nd

utilities. My lease termination date is _December 31 - 1976_

I (have...have not) paid a Security Deposit of $ 165.00

said deposit is being held by _____
                                (landlord/agent)

108

My rent is paid up to ___Aug 31___, and there have been
(date)

no other advance payments. There are noother agreements

between me and the landlord.   **("Takeover",bottom half.Actual form)**

Property of the Landlord in my apartment includes: Refrigerator,

Stove, Air Conditioner, Water Heater, (list and itemize furniture)

[signatures]

I agree that my apartment is in good and working condition with
plumbing, electric, walls, ceiling, floors,etc.in good condition, with
the exception of ___All in Good WORKING ORDER.___.

"THE HOW TO LIVE RENT FREE BOOK" by J. ANDERSON

Signed ___

tenant in apt.# ___

109

Author Tells Way To Get Financing

Six ways to finance your house

©1979, New York Times News Service

In these days of skyrocketing interest rated for real estate mortgages and predictions that 80 percent of Americans will no longer be eligible to finance a home, a best selling author and real estate expert offers six ways to get no-frills financing to buy a dream home or investment property.

"The real estate industry was waiting for me to come along and to solve their problems," says Jim Anderson, who has made a million dollars investing in real estate in the past two years, and has written a book, now in its 5th printing, "How To Live Rent Free" (Brun Press, N.Y.).

One chapter of that book discusses six easy ways to finance real estate, which are often overlooked by the professionals and buyers.

• The purchase money mortgage (P.M.M.). With this method, the seller is the banker. The buyer can show the seller how, by holding the mortgage himself, the seller can save paying big income taxes on his profitable sale, plus get 2½ times more for his sold property through becoming banker and accepting a P.M.M.

• Existing mortgage takeover (assuming the current mortgage). Anderson says: The first thing I ask a seller is 'Do you have an existing mortgage and is it assumable?' I recently helped a buyer take over a $50,000 mortgage at 7½ percent. They are all over if you look. All of my properties are on 'assumables' plus PMMs.' They are around. Just search. A low interest assumable mortgage is an asset worth going after."

• "Wrap-around-mortgage." "This frightening-sounding term commonly used by tycoons," says Anderson, "is something that can also be used by the home buyers. Simply, it allows you to 'take over' a low interest existing mortgage when the bank says that this mortgage cannot be 'taken over'." The seller simply keeps paying the bank while the buyer pays the seller. A "wrap-around mortgage," Anderson says, is

• VA loans. There are almost 20 million veterans who have never used their no-down-payment, "G.I. loan privilege," mainly because of lack of knowledge or misinformation about this bonanza, Anderson says. Brokers also discouraged their use over the past 30 years because of the extra paper-work. Says Anderson: "I am using my VA no-down-payment loan to purchase another property. The VA loan is a big asset that should be used. There are also another 10 million veterans who have the possibility of getting a second no-down-payment property loan through the Veterans Administration, but these 10 million vets don't even know that they still qualify."

• F.H.A. loans. These loans have been ignored by most brokers who over the years always recommended a "conventional bank loan" (because they are faster and easier), Anderson says. Now the brokers are beginning to suggest FHA as a way to buy property.

• Second mortgage. In the states where this is allowed (they are allowed in Maryland), Anderson says, "I tell the two out of every three family units in this nation you are sitting on an oil well and don't even know it. Your house has gone up in value $10,000 to $50,000 and more in just the past several years . . . get a second mortage on your home (but don't squander it on a mink coat or vacation). Put this money into a piece of small income property and make inflation your partner instead of you enemy and you will have lifetime of peace and prosperity. I did it three times in the past three years without any previous experience, and you can too."

CHAPTER TEN

NO-FRILLS FINANCING

There are complete books written on this subject which would be good for you to read if you are so inclined and if you can understand the terminology.

Several suggested books on real estate finance which are currently used in the Florida Real Estate Broker Classes as required study for examination are:

"THE REAL ESTATE ACQUISITION HANDBOOK" by Wm. T. Tappan, Jr. 1979. Prentice-Hall $7.95.

"TWO YEARS FOR FREEDOM". By Bill Greene $16.00 (order from Brun Press, Box 370034, Miami, Fl. 33137)

However in this Chapter, I will give you some of the basics to help you purchase your first apartment building, and in everyday words and terms.

There are many ways of financing a building. However, on your first venture and even later on, I would not suggest that you get too fancy. Real Estate is a stable type investment (unlike stocks and retail businesses) and your financing should also be stable and not overextended as people tend to want to do. My only reason to suggest stability in financing is to have a backup position for the unexpected . . . be it your health, the economy, etc. Be stable, don't overextend like so many quick-rich types do, and they usually end up on the bottom of the heap. There is plenty of time. You have selected the most proven and solid form of investment. Have you ever truly run into a poor property owner? I have certainly run into a lot of poor people who trade in the Stock Market.

And don't get too fancy with your finance plans like the big Developers of large real estate projects do. (Its all in the first book above however, if you are curious). These Developers are very, very creative, and in many instances I feel that their creative financing borders on genius . . . but on the other hand, this same creative financing genius got them in a lot of trouble recently, because they just over extended themselves too far and spread themselves out too far . . . then a slack period developed, and like covering stock margins in a declining Market, these Developers lost a lot of money and property. Don't let this happen to you. At least be conservative on your first apartment building, and you will not get in trouble in this business.

In building financing, this is one of those times when you can draw from some of your past experience in financing a home . . . and you may plan to live in this apartment building anyway. But again, I suggest that you be conservative on your first apartment building venture.

I remember three years ago when I began looking at many apartment buildings before I bought the first one. Along came a Seller's real estate Agent (caveat emptor) who explained how I could buy a ten unit building instead of the five unit I knew I could afford, "by arranging for a balloon mortgage." I'll tell you what I think of that now, but then just on a hunch that I didn't like the sound of it, I turned down this balloon mortgage idea. Its really for greedy people, who extend themselves beyond their real financial capabilities as they are today. It's all predicated on a hope that your income will improve to take care of the gradually increased mortgage payments. Isn't that suicide, when you are planning such a serious and important plan as the happiness and your own long term future? What an irresponsible recommendation by that Seller's Broker, who knew that this was my first venture in this field of buying apartment buildings. I am sure that this same Agent got other Buyers to take out balloon mortgages, and I heard about a lot of these people that went broke because they could not make their escalated mortgage payments. That Agent incidentally is a million dollar producer annually.

Remember why such an irresponsible recommendation can happen. The real estate agents are taught caveat emptor (buyer beware) in their real estate classes sanctioned by the State of Florida. The Agent obviously can say and recommend what they feel at the moment to sell the property . . . it was up to me (with no advisor at hand) to sense the danger of this balloon mortgage and to refuse this greedy notion. So if your friendly real estate agent (Seller' Agent) is your friendly helper . . . who needs enemies? You should have a friend when in such a spot and that is where your no-cost Advisor Broker can help you.

Of course the majority of real estate Agents want to be fair, they mean well, but they are guided by the influence to sell you to earn another commission. They want to be friendly and sincere, but it irks and frightens me to think that if I had taken that real estate agent's balloon-mortgage suggestion, I could have overextended myself too soon, and could have been wiped out financially. Further, I would not own the three buildings and eighteen units I own today, and I definitely would not be writing this book. Responsibility can be taken so lightly by some.

Also remember that most selling agents that you deal with do not own and operate their own apartment buildings; so everything they tell you and suggest to you (like balloon mortgages) is hear-say, and not experience they have had on the firing line managing their own buildings. As the great Packard automobile used to say in their ads . . . ASK THE MAN WHO OWNS ONE . . . that statement is one hundred times truer when it comes to seeking advice on buying an apartment building.

Now, more on financing the easy way. Many times there is an "existing mortgage" on the building that interests you, at a low interest rate from maybe five years ago, when the interest rates were 8% & 9%. If there is such an existing mortgage on your intended building, include it in the Contract For Sale that you want "the right to take over the payments on this existing mortgage (and spell it out) at X%, for the next X years, at $X payment per month, this existing mortgage balance being $X." Further try to get an agreement to be able to transfer this existing mortgage to any future person that you sell the building to. This may be difficult,

113

but get in the habit of asking, since you always want to have as attractive package as possible for the next buyer.

Secondly, try to get the Seller to take back a Second Mortgage, for the difference between your agreed-to, down payment plus the existing mortgage . . . and the agreed to selling price. Here is an example. $100,000 agreed to selling price. $20,000 agreed to down payment. $50,000 existing mortgage at 8% for 15 years remaining, which you can take over. (Banks agree to a transfer and take-over of a mortgage today, normally only because the Seller wisely had this clause originally put in his mortgage agreement, ie, that it could be transferred. Today, banks do not readily, or hardly ever, give out transferrable mortgages. . .), so, the balance that you still need to be financed is the $30,000 remainder. This $30,000 is what you request the Seller to take back on a Second Mortgage, (terms negotiable and depending on how badly you believe the Seller wants to sell), but try perhaps for about 11% for 20 years (this being written in 1980) . . . the seller may counter at 12% for 15 years, since holders of second mortgages usually do not like even this long a term for a second mortgage, but a seller who owns the building will. Remember though. It's all negotiable.

An alternate idea coming into more use and can be used when the seller is leery about taking back a long term second mortgage, is to suggest that the seller create a "wrap-around-mortgage." This is one stable but creative form of financing that sells a lot of apartment buildings and is not bad or risky for either the seller or the buyer. All the wrap-around mortgage involves is that the seller holds his current $50,000 mortgage (instead of your taking it over), and he makes those payments from your total mortgage payment to him monthly which will be a total for both the first and the second mortgage. This wrap-around mortgage is at one package interest rate, which of course is the current higher rate. So the Seller gets his pot sweetened a little bit for going along with a longer term second mortgage . . . and you have $80,000 financing, long term, on a $100,000 building, with a $20,000 down payment. Now, if the operating-dollars shape up where you see a good situation to make the mortgage payments, pay the operating expenses and come out with a profit, or to live there rent free . . . you have a nice first investment. (It may take a year of inflation to do it.)

Incidentally, never kill a good purchase possibility in a haggle over one interest point. People take too much concern over the interest rate instead of looking broadly over the entire package as to its profitability. The difference between a $50,000, 20 year mortgage at 12%, versus the same mortgage at 11% is about $35 per month. (That's only one or two rent increases.) And if the building is really a good money making deal for you (which should be your primary concern), I would not kill a deal because of one interest point. And many buyers and sellers haggle over a 1/2 interest point, or a 1/4 point. Look at the total deal. If it is nicely profitable, negotiate. Maybe that is why this property has stayed on the Market . . . because everyone haggled over one interest point.

The Purchase Money Mortgage, normally called a PMM. In half of all deals the Seller will be your banker, indebting you directly to the Seller at about 4% points less interest. (You try the PMM where there is no transferrable take over mortgage on the building). Also your chances for a PMM is greater when the seller really wants to sell . . . and/or . . . does not need all the cash payment right away, and he will be getting almost 3x's the sum of the loan over the 20 year term The PMM is another way the seller can sweeten the pot for the buyer for with a PMM you pay no "closing costs" or "bank loan points" which can cost you $3,000 to $5,000 at a bank when they give you a loan. (I've gotten 3 P.M.M'S.)

Regardless of who holds your mortgage (the owner, the bank, or third party friend or relative), try to get a clause in the Contract For Sale stating that you can "prepay all or part of the mortgage balance at any time and without a prepay penalty." This is a protection to you, so that if and when the interest rates decline substantially below what you are paying, then with this clause, you may borrow money elsewhere at the now lower interest rate and pay off the higher interest rate old mortgage. Also try always to get a clause included in your mortgage that it is transferrable to anyone you may sell the property to in the future. Gives you great flexibility, and makes your property easier to resell.

Another fact of financing to know and remember . . . the bigger your cash down payment . . . the bigger is your leverage to negotiate for a lower total price . . . and for better terms . . . and for a lower interest rate.

When you get down to the Contract For Sale have your Advisor Broker work very closely with you on your offer to buy. He can help you on negotiating terms. Also have him go over with you all the personal notes you made from answers to your questions that you got from the Seller and his Agent. Your Advisor Broker will scrutinize their statements to you very carefully and probably will call the Seller or Agent to verify their statements before he puts them in the Contract. Remember . . . caveat emptor (buyer beware) . . . you must put down in writing on the Contract these Seller's statements that have convinced you to purchase this particular apartment building. If these seller-statements are not in your Contract For Sale . . . then forget they were ever stated, for you have no legal proof that they were ever made.

Every Contract For Sale will have different facets . . . no two are alike . . . and your Advisor-Broker can save you substantial money on your offer and the negotiations and the protection you need in this Contract to be insured that you are buying exactly what you thought you were buying. It is therefore extremely important that you bring in an Advisor Broker to help your side of the cause at this critical time . . . THE CONTRACT FOR SALE.

I have discovered that there are 30 million veterans that can qualify for (up to) a $100,000 no money down Quad-Plex and they don't even know it. (Get full details from your nearest VA office). Even World War II G.I.'s who bought their first home with a G.I. Loan CAN NOW QUALIFY FOR A SECOND G.I. NO MONEY DOWN LOAN.

F.H.A. has been "rediscovered" by the Brokers as a good way to help you get your Quadplex for a very small cash down payment.

Second Mortgages on your existing house (even at high interest rates) are another way to buy this productive investment.

116

CHAPTER ELEVEN

HOW YOU CAN GET THE MOST
OUT OF THIS BOOK

Have you ever heard of a book hitting the front page regularly? Most writers say they have seen it happen "once in maybe 25 years." This book did it the first three consecutive times.

While most authors must be content with a few short paragraphs about their book in the book review column way in the back section of the newspaper . . . James W. Anderson's HOW TO LIVE RENT FREE book regularly hits the front page along with other local and World news events. Of perhaps 500 news stories a news editor reads daily, he has put this book among the most newsworthy. In fact, the very first three consecutive articles on this book . . . ALL HIT THE FRONT PAGE, and they are reprinted herein this THIRD PRINTING with the news media's consent.

These feature stories (of about 1,200 words) report on Anderson's "overlooked but simple plan of living rent free; which will change America's living habits in the next five years, as we go into the inflationary spiral of the 1980's." And Anderson hastens to add, "this is not another get-quick-rich-book."

Some critics said that the people would never pay the $25 price. They obviously have as this book has become a best-seller in its first 90 day introduction period and is now in the third printing. As Anderson figured it: "I am selling 30 to 50 years of happiness and I am very willing to share my secrets discovered in doing this thing 3 times in 3 consecutive years without any previous experience . . . and you can do it too. The young, the mids, the old. The students just starting work, women alone . . . are all candidates among our Nations 120,000,000 workers who wish to live rent free and pay less income tax." He continued: "Buy the $20 cookbook or the $20 book on sports, and maybe have 30 to 50 years of grief . . . or buy this $25 REFERENCE BOOK and get on the road to financial freedom. You are at the crossroads of your life, and the choice is yours."

Secondly, readers are now reporting-in that they have read this book; they report that they understood this clearly written book; they report that they trusted the authors experience and common sense methods; they report that they acted upon the authors motivation; and now they also live rent free. This is the biggest reward.

Thirdly, Anderson's talking-book, off "live" radio and television programs, make it so easy for you to learn his successful techniques. In the first 3 month introduction period of this book, the author appeared on 50 hours of radio and television (never has there been such a demand for an author to speak). The listening audiences called-in their own personal questions to problems they felt they may have with Anderson's rent-free & tax-free solutions. You will find that these audience questions are the same ones you would ask . . . and so was born Anderson's innovative talking-book; three hours of stimulating question and answer discussion . . . three hours of simple instruction, on easy-to-learn, instructional tape cassettes. The tapes are called: THE BEST OF JIM ANDERSON'S HOW TO LIVE RENT FREE BOOK, OFF 'LIVE' RADIO AND TELEVISION.

Author Anderson suggests that you sit down and relax and listen to the instructional tape cassettes. Play the tapes daily or weekly, until you are totally familiar with the contents (its your life's savings we are talking about. True?) Then read the book, and make notes of questions you wish to ask the Author, via the mails. Then as you get into this project of living rent free, plus an income . . . plus paying less taxes on your salary; your trusty reference book and the tapes will be at your side whenever the slightest problem arises. Remember, your Author did this project THREE CONSECUTIVE TIMES, IN THREE CONSECUTIVE YEARS, WITHOUT ANY PREVIOUS EXPERIENCE. And he spent two years in writing this book to tell you his secrets and solutions to problems BEFORE they arise. Anderson will show you how to prevent problems from arising in the first place. Anderson predicts 1,000,000 people will follow his lead in the next year. Since you have discovered this book . . . YOU CAN BE AMONG THE FIRST TO DO IT!

AN AUTHOR'S CONFESSION . . . AND A TRIBUTE TO THE PRESS

WHILE THE AUTHOR HONESTLY ADMITS THAT THESE FIRST FEW LETTERS AND EXHIBITS FROM PROFESSIONALS FROM HIS CONFIDENTIAL FILE ACCLAIMING THIS BOOK MAY SELL A FEW BOOKS . . .

. . . THE AUTHOR STRONGLY DEMANDED THAT THEY BE INCLUDED IN THIS THIRD PRINTING, REVISED WORLD EDITION; FOR TWO VERY GOOD REASONS. 1) THESE THIRD PARTY, VERY INDEPENDENT PROFESSIONALS HEREBY LET THE PUBLIC KNOW THAT "LIVING RENT FREE" AS CONCEIVED AND WRITTEN BY MR. ANDERSON IS ACCLAIMED AND ACKNOWLEDGED BY THE PRESS AND OTHER PROFESSIONALS . . . AS A DISTINCT POSSIBILITY. 2) THESE THIRD PARTY OBSERVATIONS WILL ACTUALLY INSTRUCT THE READER FROM ANOTHER WRITERS POINT OF VIEW.

IT IS THE RESPONSIBILITY OF THE PRESS TO "PUNCH HOLES" IN ANY NEW OR DRAMATIC IDEA (OR "SCHEME") . . . CERTAINLY, "LIVING RENT FREE AND PAYING LESS INCOME TAX" HAD TO BE LOOKED AT VERY CLOSELY. THE PRESS ANALYZED ANDERSON'S TEXT AND PROPOSALS, AND THEN HONESTLY REPORTED THEM AS THE PRESS SAW THEM . . . AND IN A VERY POSITIVE WAY.

. . . TO THOSE THEN, WHO SAY THAT THE PRESS ONLY REPORTS THE BAD NEWS . . . "BECAUSE GOOD NEWS IS NO NEWS" . . . LET THEM LOOK UPON THESE FEATURE AND HEADLINE NEWSPAPER STORIES TO PROVE THAT . . . THE PRESS REPORTS THE GOOD STORIES AS WELL AS THE BAD.

The Miami News

A Cox Newspaper

Friday Afternoon, May 26, 1978

56 Pages

Friday

(BLUE STREAK)

15¢

Carter proposes five-year freeze on nuclear tests

Story below

How to live rent free

Story, Lifestyle

(this front page photo is reduced
to half size to fit on this page)

James Anderson outside the quadplex that allows him to live rent free

The Miami News · BILL REINKE

Live rent free

Homes, condominiums are 'millstones'; buy a quadplex, says Miami author

BILL von MAURER
Miami News Entertainment Editor

As far as James W. Anderson is concerned, you can take that old framed cross stitch that says "Home Sweet Home," made so lovingly by Grandma and hung so carefully in the parlor by Gramps, and bounce it into the trash.

And as for that vine-covered cottage, that split level in the suburbs and that ranch type house out in the project, they are "millstones" around their owners' necks.

Anderson is the author of an enticingly titled book "How To Live Rent Free." With "don't sell the steak, sell the sizzle" zealotry, Anderson pitches the idea of buying a quadplex instead of a single family home. That way, he claims, you'll be living in "your own gushing oil well."

The registered real estate broker and 5-year Miami resident, says that people "have overlooked the solution to their own financial survival as we go into the inflationary spiral of the 1980's that will basically change the living style of Americans over the next five years."

The way to outfox this gloomy prospect, according to Anderson, is to buy a quadplex (four unit apartment building) and live rent free under the blessings of a tax shelter.

"You don't have to have previous experience to do it," he says, adding that its a step anybody can take.

"There are 47 million homeowners in this country. The most important financial step they have ever taken is to buy a home, a roof over their heads. True, it has increased in value since they bought it, but actually it is a millstone around their necks because it is unproductive. It's a box in the boondocks. With the price of gasoline going up, they soon won't be able to commute," he expounds.

"But that house is their biggest resource even though it is all expense and no tax deductions (except mortgage and interest).

"Sell that millstone," he enthuses, "and buy a quadplex."

Anderson says that you can do that with $10,000 down, but he insists on at least $5,000 in reserve to contend with such crises as sickness or other setbacks.

Why a quadplex? Because, according to Anderson, that will keep HUD off your back. He looks upon the giant federal agency as a profligate bureaucracy that recklessly flings around $50 billion a year. If you buy five apartment units or more it opens the door to HUD which can then tell you how, when and who to rent to.

"If you own more than five apartment units, HUD can tell you what to do and frankly I want to reserve the right to discriminate," he explains.

HUD, he says further, has in its possession a publication on tenant-landlord rights that contains "dynamite" information about apartments but that when anybody tries to get a copy "they are always out."

If you decide to follow his advice and buy a quad, Anderson suggests that you go by the rule of thumb of six to eight times the annual rental when trying to arrive at price.

"If the asking price is more than that, negotiate. And before you buy, look at 10 buildings if you have to and remember that every asking price is negotiable.

As for the problem of "handling tenants," a fear expressed by a lot of prospective quad buyers, Anderson says that if you can't do that you are running a business like a candy store.

"I don't accept the first warm body that comes to the door with three or four months rent," Anderson says of the way he rents his apartments. He owns three quads.

"I consider myself a property owner, not a landlord. When someone wants to rent, I look for stability, good job, appearances."

Anderson's book includes advice about how to evict undesirable tenants through a simple application blank. "Most property owners don't even bother to have a prospect fill one out," he says.

As for that other bugaboo, children and pets, Anderson says he's willing to rent to them. He has such tenants sign a tough clause in their leases covering this worry.

"Nine out of 10 mothers won't sign it, but dog owners will," he says philosophically while petting his Russian wolfhound Natasha that he rescued from the pound.

Anderson says that there are from 10 to 15 million renters in this country who possess the $15,000 in assets to qualify for his conditions to buy a quad.

Once they take that step they are home free, so to speak, because now they can live in one unit themselves and let their tenants pay the rising costs of inflation.

"They will have to pay nothing or little on their income tax because of a magic word 'depreciation.' A

$60,000 house, for example, depreciates $3,000 a year for up to 20 years. You can feather your nest even further," Anderson advises, "by putting in new baths and kitchens, for example, and reap the additional depreciation. That way, you will have your own gushing oil well. If you want, you can sell the units in 10 or 12 years and start all over again. It's a game."

Anderson lives in his own "gushing oil well" in the northest section near Biscayne Bay where he occupies the ground floor unit of a four-unit, Spanish style complex with a number of years on it.

What if you are one of the 60 million wage owners, according to Anderson's figures, who don't have $15,000 to invest in a quad?

Buy a duplex, he says.

"There are no mirrors, no magic. You can buy a nice duplex for $2,500 down on a $25,000 unit or even $500 if you shop around. To do that you can get a friendly loan (from a relative) or an unfriendly one (from a mortgage lender). Good heavens! people will borrow that much to buy an automobile but would never think of doing it to purchase a place to live.

"You can live in the duplex and have the loan paid off in 3 years with the rent from the other side; after that it will be paying your mortgage and you will be living rent free. And, he adds, don't forget to try to convince the owner to take back the mortgage. That way you will be avoiding closing costs."

All of Anderson's ideas about living rent free are spelled out in his 190-page book which is published by Brun Press of New York and Paris. The book, on sale locally at book stores, is priced at $14.95 as an introductory offer. It will eventually sell for $24.95.

Isn't that price a little steep? Anderson was asked. "Well, you can buy a cookbook for $40 and have 40 years of grief or you can live rent free for 30 years," he replies.

During Channel 2's recent annual auction, the book went for a bid of $140 and Anderson has a note from the station to prove it.

If you are smarting over Anderson's view of home, sweet single home, ponder his thoughts on condominiums.

"The're even worse than a millstone. You are not even in control of your own destiny. They are a Mickey Mouse investment."

Feel better?

(this front page is reduced in size, to show Author, Anderson on the front page with World Celebrity Tom Jones.)

A Bit Unusual...

PARTICIPANTS WHO WALKED, sloshed and jogged through 18 miles of Kirkwood pavement Saturdays for the Walk for Mankind were greeted by a rather unexpected surprise at the end of their day-long trek. British performer Tom Jones made an appearance at the Kirkwood Park ampetheater to sign autographs and thank the walkers who helped raise money for Project Concern by participating in the event. Jones (above, center) autographed the jacket of Terri Davis, a 15 year old from Chesterfield, while other autograph seekers awaited their turn. Jones was in St. Louis to perform in a concert at the Checkerdome Saturday night.

Journal Staff Photo by Dennis Davito

Tired Of Mortgage Payments? Live 'Rent Free,' Author Says-

By NANCY SOLOMON
Journal Staff Writer

Jim Anderson says he will revolutionize living patterns in the United States within the next five years.

The man who spent his childhood in Webster Groves and now signs his name with two vertical lines through the "s" ($), has hit upon a plan designed to save most people about a quarter of their annual income. He calls it living rent-free.

"People are very casual with their money," Anderson says. "They're like little lambs going ..."

Anderson, himself, says he has mended his wasteful ways, sold his $100,000 box in the suburbs, moved into a Biscayne Bay Spanish villa in Miami, picked up a tax shelter and no longer pays for the roof over his head.

HIS NEIGHBORS — actually his tenants - do.

Anderson purchased the five-unit villa about five years ago and now his tenants are paying off his mortgage.

"I'm trying to get people out of their rut," he says. "I'm interested in helping people do what I did."

His advice, plain and simple. "Sell your millstone in the boon-

docks and buy a quadplex", a four-unit multiple dwelling.

"You did one home, you know it's right. Do it times four," he says. "I live it. I love it."

But what about the folks who don't own a home? Anderson has alternate plans for both renters with some extra cash around for a down payment and those who do not have any savings at all.

Of the 120 million persons in the American work force, Anderson estimates 47 million own homes.

"The one thing they did right they didn't plan. They had a roof over their head. That was a nest egg," he says.

Sell it, Anderson says, "and enjoy it for life."

THE MAN WHO describes himself as a professional problem solver suggests putting down as little money on the property as possible and taking out a huge mortgage. This, he claims, will stop the inflation clock at 1978.

Anderson predicts inflation will continue to skyrocket because of soaring costs of labor, energy and running the government.

"We ain't seen nothing yet," he says.

The real estate broker, formerly general manager of a New York television station, tells all in a 70,000 word book called "How To Live Rent Free"

Super A...
Propose...

By MATT MATTINGLY
Journal Correspondent

Consolidation of all existing committees into one super committee to provide input from the community to the Kirkwood R-7 Board of Education will be a central feature of Superintendent Thomas N. Keating's new management system for the district, if approved by the board May 15.

Keating outlined his proposal — including the central Citizens Advisory Council — in a presentation to the board Monday night.

"I think it is important for the district to establish the sense of direction it wishes to attain," he said.

His proposal aims at infusing "a sense of mission" which Keating feels is at present lacking into the district.

He stressed the importance of definite planning and evaluation on continued positive development of curriculum and staff.

IN THIS RESPECT, Keating noted two projects will be presented May 15 as suggested goals. "Project Excellence" in curriculum development and "Project People" in staff development.

Although he offered no exact cost estimate, Keating said these would probably "cost out at $60-80,000 in year number one."

Curriculum, staff and Board of Education are only two of six proposed "goal" areas for the board's consideration, the other general categories are: students, support services, buildings and finance.

Keating said each of these six areas require short- and long-range goal-setting and the creation of a master plan that would be "reviewed from year to year, changed and updated."

His proposed management system would build on current practices and add definition, Keating said.

"The school system has the responsibility to provide a positive atmosphere, a clear statement of goals and adequate instruction to enable the learner to reach his or her maximum potential," he maintained.

To provide "a continuum of information" with a view to improvement, Keating added, the planning process must include evaluation of individual as well as program performances for schools, the curriculum, staff and students.

THE FIRST STEP in the process would be establishment of short- and long-range goals by the school board. According to Keating's proposed timeline, July 17 would be the deadline for completion of the short-range goals, Oct. 1 for the long-range.

Concurrently, board members, staff and citizens would present goal suggestions to the board for

Crestwood
For New S...

By LINDA HERMANSON
Journal Staff Writer

The Crestwood board of aldermen paved the way for developing a new street maintenance and repair plan at Tuesday's meeting.

Alderman Charles Sisler, aldentative to the ...rd, said the citi... urging the city five-year street ...an in favor of a three-year one and to allocate $1.8 million from the budget to implement the accelerated plan.

126

Live Rent Free

ST. LOUIS, MO., WEDNESDAY, MAY 3, 1978

56th YEAR: NO. 18

Webster author Jim Anderson and his book.

Journal Staff Photo by Gary Brady

By NANCY SOLOMON
Journal Staff Writer

Jim Anderson says he will revolutionize living patterns in the United States within the next five years.

The man who spent his childhood in Webster Groves and now signs his name with two vertical lines through the "s" ($), has hit upon a plan designed to save most people about a quarter of their annual income. He calls it living rent-free.

"People are very casual with their money," Anderson says. "They're like little lambs going to slaughter."

Anderson, himself, says he has mended his wasteful ways, sold his $100,000 box in the suburbs, moved into a Biscayne Bay Spanish villa in Miami, picked up a tax shelter and no longer pays for the roof over his head.

HIS NEIGHBORS -- actually his tenants -- do.

Anderson purchased the five-unit villa about five years ago and now his tenants are paying off his mortgage.

"I'm trying to get people out of their rut," he says. "I'm interested in helping people do what I did.

His advice, plain and simple, "Sell your millstone in the boon-

docks and buy a quadruplex , a four-unit multiple dwelling.

"You did one home, you know it's right. Do it times four," he says. "I live it. I love it."

But what about the folks who don't own a home? Anderson has alternate plans for both renters with some extra cash around for a down payment and those who do not have any savings at all.

Of the 120 million persons in the American work force, Anderson estimates 47 million own homes.

"The one thing they did right they didn't plan. They had a roof over their head. That was a nest egg," he says.

Sell it, Anderson says, "and enjoy it for life".

THE MAN WHO describes himself as a professional problem solver suggests putting down as little money on the property as possible and taking out a huge mortgage. This, he claims, will stop the inflation clock at 1978.

Anderson predicts inflation will continue to skyrocket because of soaring costs of labor, energy and running the government.

"We ain't seen nothing yet," he says.

The real estate broker, formerly general manager of a New York television station, tells it all in a 70,000 word book called "How To Live Rent Free" which will be released nationally this fall.

give the hometown folk a little advance," he says. Anderson presented his book at Webster Groves Library Monday.

The book, a humorous non-fiction, how-to work, does much to dispel the myths surrounding apartment living, Anderson says.

THE AUTHOR says owning a house is no more than "an un-productive millstone" -- a crush-ing, heaving burden.

He says a quadriplex need not resemble a sleazy motel. Interesting multiples are available along a golf course, a park or a river. Tenants can live above, below, in a separate building or right next door.

But what about having neighbors so close?

"Do you want to live in the prairie" with 10 acres around you?" Anderson responds. "Co-exist, my goodness. Are you a cannibal? Can't you coexist with your neighbors?

"It's so absurd to me but it always comes up," he raves.

(Continued from Page 1)

"Look, people buy $50,000 to $100,000 condominiums. What's wrong with having your own condominium and having three others next door?"

128

Tired Of Mortgage Payments?
Live 'Rent Free,' Author Says

The key to getting along with neighbors is having good raw material to work with, in the first place, Anderson says.

"I get Mr. Good Tenant who I turn into Mr. Star Tenant. I want them to nest -- make that a home."

ANDERSON SAYS his plan, which he calls conservative, can work for a person who does not own a home but has $15,000 tucked away. His advice is to spend $10,000 for a down payment on a quadplex, keep $5,000 in reserve, let the tenants pay off the mortgage

Those with no savings can use the same basic approach and eventually stop paying rent.

Eventually?

"You can't expect a rose around your neck if you haven't paid for it," he says.

First, a person must find a $25,000 duplex and arrange to get his hands on $2,500 for a down payment. Anderson suggest obtaining a friendly loan --

known as borrowing money from a friend or relative -- and paying it back with interest.

"They're hardly going to be able to say no," he says.

In case they do, however, Anderson advises people to borrow the cash from a mortgage company and save closing costs by having the seller, not a bank, take back the mortgage.

THE TENANT pays off the $2,500 loan. The new owner buys back the mortgage from the old owners. Within three years, the tenant's rent check goes to the new owner and the new owner has stopped shelling out cash for the roof over his head.

"Stick out your hand, palm up. That shows you can pick up the rent check," the real estate broker quips.

Anderson sees the best way to find a nice place for a reasonable price is to buy in a redeveloping area. Soulard, for example

"That place is going to be very, very big," he says. "Central redevelopment with magnets. That's how to make some money."

A magnet can be a river, park or forest. Anderson says there are probably 12 up-and-coming areas in St. Louis.

Before putting a John Hancock on anything, however, Anderson suggests looking at at least ten buildings. "You should know when you get a bargain. You buy coldly."

HE ALSO SAYS people should find a real estate broker to help hunt for a building. The so-called "secret weapon" will have number one interest with the buyer, not the seller.

Anderson predicts 10 per cent of the people who read his book will heed his advice. "They'll be very happy people -- the doers."

The rest? Well, Anderson calls them the dreamers. Many of whom will make ideal tenants

Business

How to live rent-free

By Edwin Clark

When James W. Anderson moved to Miami in 1975, he put down $15,000 on a five-unit apartment building valued at $64,000. Today he claims the building's worth has climbed to about $120,000 because of some inexpensive improvements and inflationary pressure on property values.

Nice, but only part of the story. Anderson has parlayed the deal into an economic lifestyle philosophy that includes financial stability, excludes paying rent, and gives the Bronx cheer to the American dream of owning a home. True to his innate promotional showmanship (Anderson was once known as "the James Bond of Madison Avenue"), he's written a book promising "peace of mind and prosperity through wise investment."

"It's uneconomical to have one private house on a lot," Anderson says from his Spanish villa-type apartment where he lives with his wife and Russian wolfhound. "Most people buy a house when they should be buying a four-unit apartment building and living rent-free in one of the units. The rent from three of the apartments will pay the mortgage, all expenses and the rent on the owner's apartment."

Anderson now has three buildings in Miami, all doing well, but it's the first one that he calls "an oil well without the risks." It was old and plain, but its structure was sound. Location near the Palm Bay Club along Biscayne Bay ensured an increase in value

. An derson moved into one of the units, fixed the place up, planted some tropical foliage, used clinging vines to adorn the trellis at the entrance and scoured various "junk" sources looking for offbeat items to enhance his property's value. Rent increases followed the improvements until apartments originally going for around $100 now bring $200-225 without utilities. The rentals have paid off the mortgage and are producing extra income.

Next step: two more buildings, purchased for a total of $18,000 down. Following formula, the property has become more attractive, rents have been raised, and the money rolling in. Both buildings have almost doubled in value, Anderson says.

The success story is detailed in *The How To Live Rent Free Book.* For an investment $24.95 ("introductory offer," $14.95), readers can learn that "anyone with $15,000 can buy four units—$10,000 for the building and $5,000 for emergencies...Part of the money for reserve will go for cheap improvements to help you increase rents. My tenants are living better than originally; my rents are lower than market, yet I've doubled them."

Anderson likens owning a single-family house to wearing a "millstone" around one's neck. "There are people with homes who have up to $100,000 or more in equity, and could be putting this into income property. They worry about keeping up the mortgage, and it's one reason people suffer from heart attacks. But if they bought an apartment building instead of a home, they would have done much better. Now the millstone is out of date."

130

Claiming that spiraling inflation will soon
put an end to the dream of owning a private
home, Anderson points out that a medium-
priced house is now $50,000—within the eco-
omic reach of only one-fourth of American
families—and values will quickly soar 70 per
cent. Meanwhile, he says, apartment build-
ngs in developing areas are underpriced.

"The secret weapon is buying right," says
Anderson. "I recommend buying in more cen-
al areas instead of in the boondocks like
outh Miami, Hialeah and Opa Locka. The
ental apartment building market is full of
argains at the present time, especially along
iscayne Bay near the water, from the Omni
l the way up to Ft. Lauderdale. Stick near
e water in older, redeveloping areas; proper-
is cheap and the water will develop the value
ster. People have forgotten about Biscayne
ay...The water is what Miami is all about.
s why I came here. The other part I call
rizona."

One of the main tips in Anderson's book is
employ a qualified broker-advisor to help
gotiate the buy, rather than relying on a sel-
g broker. He says that 99 per cent of all
me and apartment buyers don't realize they
n employ such a broker for a percentage of
 purchase price.

'They buy through ads in the papers or
m 'for sale' signs on property because peo-
 like location and drive around an area they
e," he says. "But it's wrong, because you're
ing to the selling broker who is employed by
 owner, and the selling broker owes his pri-
ry fiduciary to the owner, by law."

The better way, according to Anderson, is
find a broker to represent you just as you
uld if you were selling a home instead of
ying. "You can even get advice on beginner
nagement problems," he says.

If you're buying a home in Coral Gables,
the best real estate broker in Coral Gables
 owns a home [there]. He knows the laws,
zoning problems, taxes, the good and bad
as...If you're buying a condo, buy it from a
ker who owns a condo in the immediate
...and hopefully even in the same building.
knows the by-laws of that building, which
as thick as a phone book in some cases.

"Don't go to Uncle Harry," he says. "It involves your life savings. Talk to the guy who
has the expertise and is successful, because
real estate is a local business. Ask him if he cooperates—that is, will he share in the commission as your broker?"

Once you buy the right building and fix it
up, the rest is easy, Anderson says. "It's only
tough in the beginning, but after there is ap-
preciation of your property through inflation,
and you increase your rents, you'll make a
living because your mortgage payments will
stay the same."

Among the "secrets" in Anderson's book is
establishing a mode of conduct for tenants
which guarantees their "desirability."

"You get a lot of gypsies in here because
we're a transient area," he says. "I don't want
them. That's why I carefully check out all references." He also points out that once you
start raising rents, it becomes routine to attract
good tenants. While inflation skyrockets and
people rush to move to Miami, the landlord's
job gets easier and more lucrative, he says.

Anderson spends only "an hour or two a
day" managing his three buildings. "It's not a
full-time job, nor does it require any sort of
special skill besides a good head for business.
It can very definitely be a job for women, who
are attuned to the real estate business."

For those whose American dreams die hard
and don't relish the thought of continued
apartment life, Anderson recommends living
somewhere else and using rent income to pay
the mortgage. "You don't have to live in that
fourth unit. But my suggestion is, don't be
rigid and in a rut, just because you've lived in a
little box home all your life. An apartment
building that's enabling you to live rent-free is
not a millstone. Sure, you can have a sexy
lemon, if you're buying a building that's too
high-priced, [without] enough rent increase
potential and too high expenses. You have to
buy right, obviously."

As a rule of thumb, Anderson says a building should cost between six and eight years'
rent, depending on the neighborhood. Then,
he claims, if you've made a good investment,
you're in the clear.

"All you need to become a success is to be
able to put out your hand and accept the rent
money...I invite anyone to come see the gushing oil well where I live. Just call first." ∎

READER: READ THIS SCRIPT, FOR AN OVERVIEW, BEFORE READING THE BOOK.

THIS RADIO SCRIPT WAS BROADCAST OVER A 200 STATION RADIO NETWORK ... AND IS JUST THE FIRST OF A SERIES OF MINI-RADIO NETWORK NEWS DOCUMENTARIES ABOUT THE "HOW TO LIVE RENT FREE" BOOK.

THE CONTENTS ARE IMPORTANT FOR YOU THE READER ... BECAUSE THIS CAPSULIZES IN CONCISE NEWS REPORTER FASHION, A GREAT PART OF THE SUBJECT MATTER IN THIS BOOK.

IT IS DEFINITELY RECOMMENDED THAT YOU READ THIS CAREFULLY ... FOR AN OVERVIEW ... BEFORE YOU READ THE BOOK. (Fortunately we have a very similar version taken off a radio station, which is at the beginning of each instructional tape cassette.)

Want to play "Walter Cronkite" and do your own 3 minute news-document-ary with bestselling and dynamic Author, James W. Anderson who just wrote a 100,000 word, 24 Chapter hard cover: HOW TO LIVE RENT FREE... Which Author Anderson says "will change the living habits of the U.S. 120,000,000 working force in the next five years as these people look for financial salvation in the inflationery spiral of the 1980's." Anderson's is a simple and NOT a get-rich-quick plan which will solve this problem, while you also acquire your own, simplified tax-shelter so you pay little or no taxes on your salaried income...while you live rent free...and "give the finger...to inflation."

COMMENTATOR: THIS IS your WORLD NEWS ROUNDUP...............NEWS

AND COMMENT ON AN ITEM OF POSSIBLE INTEREST TO YOU.

I'M _____ REPORTING.

PAYING RENT CAN BE A TRAUMATIC EXPERIENCE EACH MONTH

133

TAKING A SIZABLE BITE OUT OF THAT PAYCHECK...BUT THERE

IS AN ALTERNATIVE...THAT'S THE MESSAGE BEING PUT FORTH

BY, JIM ANDERSON, AUTHOR OF "HOW TO LIVE RENT FREE"...

ANDERSON'S BOOK TELLS HOW TO GET OTHERS TO PAY YOUR RENT,

WHILE YOU BUILD A SOLID TAX SHELTERED INVESTMENT...

AND THE FIRST PIECE OF ADVICE HE GIVES TO THE 47 MILLION

HOMEOWNERS IN THE U.S....IS TO GET RID OF THOSE HOMES...

(CUT #1)

I CALL THE HOME, THE MILLSTONE, BECAUSE AS WE GO INTO THE INFLATIONARY

SPIRAL OF THE 1980'S, YOU'RE GONNA HAVE A REAL FINANCIAL CRISIS ON

YOUR HANDS...WITH THE GAS AND ENERGY CRISIS...THE BUREAUCRATS SPENDING

MORE AND MORE OF OUR MONEY...AND THE UNIONS DEMANDING BIGGER AND

BIGGER WAGE INCREASES...SO YOUR HOME IS UNPRODUCTIVE...IT DOES NOTHING

AND YET IT REPRESENTS YOUR BIGGEST MONEY RESOURSE. ..THROUGH ALL THE

YEARS OF PLAYING THE STOCK-GAME YOUR HOME HAS BECOME YOUR BEST IN-

VESTMENT...SO I RECCOMMEND TO THE 47 MILLION HOME OWNERS OUT THERE...

TO SELL THEIR HOME...AND FOR THIS HOME-EQUITY (BELIEVE IT OR NOT)...

FOR ABOUT $10,000 DOWN...YOU CAN BUY A 4 UNIT APARTMENT BUILDING.

IF YOUR OWN HOME HAS BEEN YOUR BEST INVESTMENT...WHY NOT PLAY IT SAFE

AND JUST DO IT AGAIN...BUT "TIMES FOUR"...BUY A QUAD PLEX.

135

COMMENTATOR: THEN ALL YOU DO IS RENT THE OTHER 3 UNITS AND LET YOUR

TENANTS PAY YOUR MORTGAGE AND ALL OTHER BUILDING EXPENSES.

AND THAT BUILDING PROVIDES YOU WITH A TAX SHELTER FOR

YOUR SALARIED INCOME...THE MORTGAGE COSTS, ANY IMPROVEMENTS

AND YOUR UPKEEP OF THE BUILDING...ARE ALL DEDUCTIBLE...BUT IF YOU

DON'T HAVE THE CASH UP FRONT TO BUY A QUAD-PLEX...WELL, YOU CAN

ALWAYS BUY A DUPLEX...

(CLT #2)

YOU GET A FRIENDLY LOAN OR AN UNFRIENDLY LOAN FOR THE AVERAGE DOWN

PAYMENT NEEDED ON A NICE DUPLEX OF ABOUT $2500...TRY GETTING THIS

LOAN FROM AN UNCLE OR AUNT...MOM OR POP...PAY THEM THE SAME INTEREST

RATE, ITS A 3 YEAR LOAN...OTHERWISE GO TO AN UNFRIENDLY MORTGAGE CO.

...YOU'RE SECURING A BUILDING SO YOU SHOULD HAVE NO PROBLEMS GETTING

A $2500 LOAN FOR THE DOWN PAYMENT ON THE BUILDING...WHICH YOU DON'T

HAVE...MANY PEOPLE BORROW THAT AMOUNT TO FINANCE AN AUTOMOBILE PURCHASE

...SO NOW, YOUR TENANT IN YOUR DUPLEX IS GOING TO BE PAYING OFF YOUR

SHORT TERM, 3 YEAR DOWN PAYMENT LOAN AND DON'T BE DISCOURAGED IN

FINDING SUCH A DEAL...I'VE DONE IT OFTEN...YOUR TENANT'S MONTHLY

RENT WILL EASILY PAY OFF THAT SHORT TERM LOAN ON A MONTHLY BASIS...

...NOW YOUR MONTHLY RENTAL PAYMENT IS NO LONGER RENT...YOU OWN THE

DUPLEX AND YOUR PAYMENTS ARE PAYING OFF YOUR LONG TERM MORTGAGE,

AND I RECCOMMEND THAT YOU SET UP THE MORTGAGE THROUGH THE OWNER

INSTEAD OF T HE BANK...ITS EASIER TO DO...AND YOU SAVE THE BANK

CLOSING COSTS WHICH YOU MAY NOT HAVE EITHER...IF YOU DON'T HAVE THE

DOWN PAYMENT. I DID THIS THREE TIMES ON MY FIRST THREE BUILDINGS...

I CALL IT NO-FRILLS FINANCING...

...AND SO, YOU END UP IN THREE YEARS WITH YOUR DOWN PAYMENT BEING PAID OFF BY YOUR TENANT...NOW YOUR TENANT'S RENT GOES TOWARD YOUR LONG TERM MORTGAGE PAYMENT AND YOU ARE LIVING RENT FREE IN 3 YEARS

...AND YOU OWN A DUPLEX WITHOUT A DOWN PAYMENT...HOW ABOUT THAT?

COMMENTATOR: ...WHICH ALL GOES TO SHOW THAT ANYONE WHO RENTS, IS PAYING OFF SOMEONE ELSE'S MORTGAGE...SO IF YOU FOLLOW ANDERSON'S BOOK AND BECOME A LANDLORD YOU MIGHT BE WORRIED ABOUT RELATIONS WITH THOSE TENANTS...BUT HAVE NO FEAR...ANDERSON ALSO INCLUDES 10 CHAPTERS ON HOW TO RAISE YOUR RENTS AND MAKE YOUR TENANTS HAPPY ABOUT IT.

.. WHEN YOU BEGIN TO LOOK FOR A QUAD-PLEX OR A DUPLEX MAKE SURE TO USE ANDERSON'S "NO COST SECRET WEAPON"...DON'T GO TO THE SELLER'S BROKER...HIS FIRST LOYALTY AND TRUST IS TO THE OWNER WHO EMPLOYED HIM TO SELL IT...SO IF HE CAN GET YOU TO PAY A BUNDLE FOR SOMETHING THAT ISN'T WORTH IT...WELL, HE'S DOING HIS JOB. THE THING TO DO IS TO GO TO A BROKER WHO OWNS APARTMENT BUILDINGS HIMSELF, AND ESTABLISH HIM AS YOUR PURCHASING AGENT...THAT WAY, HIS FIRST LOYALTY WILL BE TO YOU INSTEAD OF THE SELLER...

...THESE ARE JUST A FEW OF THE TIPS OFFERED BY ANDERSON IN HIS NEW 100,000 WORD, 24 CHAPTER "HOW TO

LIVE RENT FREE" BOOK...FOR THE COMPLETE STORY, YOU'LL

HAVE TO SHELL OUT $15 FOR THE BOOK WHICH WILL SOON

COST $25... AND IF NATIONAL SALES ARE ANY MEASURE OF

THE BOOK'S INHERANT WISDOM, IT MIGHT BE NOTED THAT IT

IS THE CURRENT BEST SELLING NON FICTION HARD COVER

IN MIAMI WHERE IT RECENTLY PREMIERED.

COMMENTATOR (OPTIONAL CUTE AND MEANINGFUL ENDINGS), use either or both.

COMMENTATOR: MR.ANDERSON...WHAT IF EVERYBODY SEES GREAT ADVANTAGES TO

YOUR RENT-FREE-WITH-A-TAX-SHELTER PREMISE...THEN THERE

WILL BE NO BUILDINGS REMAINING TO BUY?

(CUT #3 OPTIONAL)

...IMPOSSIBLE FOR TAX DEPRECIATION REASONS AND BECAUSE WE ARE A

NATION OF ONLY 10% "DOERS"...THESE 12 MILLION "DOERS" WILL BUY OR

OR BUILD A QUAD-PLEX OR DUPLEX...LIVE RENT FREE...AND I PREDICT WE

WILL CHANGE AMERICA'S LIVING PATTERNS IN THE NEXT FIVE YEARS AS THE

INFLATION FORCES US INTO AN ALTERNATE LIFE STYLE...THE OTHER 90%

OF THE PEOPLE I AM SORRY TO SAY ARE THE PROCRASTINATORS...SOME OF

WHICH WILL MAKE YOU EXCELLENT TENANTS.

COMMENTATOR: MR. ANDERSON...I UNDERSTAND THAT YOU DID THIS WITHOUT

ANY PREVIOUS EXPERIENCE IN REAL ESTATE...BUT DO YOU

THINK I CAN DO THE SAME?

(CUT #4 OPTIONAL)

...LET'S SEE YOU STICK OUT YOUR HAND PALM UP...AH, THAT'S GOOD...

NOW THAT SHOWS THAT YOU CAN STICK OUT YOUR HAND TO PICK UP THE

RENT CHECKS...MY BOOK DOES THE REST. (AVAILABLE AT YOUR FAVORITE

BOOKSTORE OR SEND $15 to BRUN PRESS, PO BOX 370034, MIAMI,FL.33137.

PROOF TO YOU, THAT ANDERSON'S 3 HOURS OF INSTRUCTIONAL TAPES WILL BE INSTRUCTIVE AND ENTERTAINING.

* * *

NEVER BEFORE HAS THERE BEEN SUCH AN INSTANT DEMAND FOR A "REFERENCE BOOK AUTHOR" FROM RADIO AND TELEVISION PERSONALITIES, TO INVITE THIS AUTHOR "ON THE AIR." AIR-PERSONALITIES ARE INTERESTED IN INTERESTING MATERIAL THAT WILL BE PRESENTED IN AN INTERESTING MANNER. . . THIS. . . THE AUTHOR DOES.

* * *

. . . AND ALL TYPES OF PROFESSIONALS AGREE:
(See some actual letters. . . turn the page)

- CRITICS
- RADIO & TELEVISION PERSONALITIES
- LISTENERS FROM THE AUDIENCE
- BOOK INDUSTRY PROFESSIONALS
- PURCHASER-READERS OF THIS BOOK

. . . THIS THEN IS YOUR GUARANTEE THAT YOU WILL NOT BE BORED, LISTENING TO AUTHOR ANDERSON AND SOME OF HIS CALLERS. . . EVEN FOR THE ENTIRE 3 HOURS. (And we cannot say the same for ALL of the other instructional tapes that we have heard.)

142

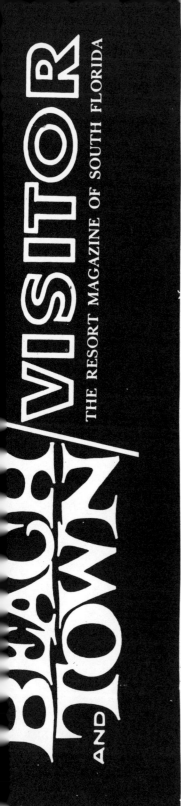

BRUN / VISITOR AND TOWN

THE RESORT MAGAZINE OF SOUTH FLORIDA

How To Live Rent Free Book
By James W. Anderson
Brun Press New York-Paris
$14.98

James W. Anderson is a registered real estate broker and owner of apartment buildings as well as an independent expert available to help you personally in South Florida.

His book really does tell you how to live rent free if you follow his basic rules. He tells you how to buy a four-unit apartment, how to manage and rent out the other apartments and how to shop to keep costs down. I do not doubt a word; only doubt that I could do the same in many instances. He even has a special section on 10 ways to increase rents. By the way, my copy came from the charming people at "Books and Serendipity", 7105 Collins Ave., Miami Beach, but I imagine it's available at many book stores.

Anderson has had many successful careers but now is in building management and brokerage. His book is really a good adv. for his services as Advisor-Broker but is meant to be a "how to" book with chapters on nearly everything you need to know from "how to get the money to buy" to "how to hire cheap but good help." If you are interested in having the pleasures of owning your own place with the advantages of tax shelters and income property, you'll enjoy this book. It may shape your future.

BOOK REVIEW:

MS. JEAN GIRARD
(Herself, the Author
of several books)

WJNO

1230 AM
24 HOURS

A CBS RADIO NETWORK AFFILIATE.

Jan. 31, 1978

Mr. Jim Anderson
Author/"How to Live Rent Free"
Palm Bay Villas
701 NE 67th St.
Miami, Fla. 33138

Dear Jim,

Your 3 hour talk-interview on my program....in a word,
WOW!!!!!

I've never had a bigger reaction to a guest or topic in
all my years conducting talk shows on both Radio & TV.

A Proven
Talk-Show Guest!

CONTACT: Andree Oukhtomsky
(305) 756-6249
Box 370034, Miami, Fl. 33137.

you and our call-in audience... Jim Anderson is going to make YOU a star."

As I told you, "you stay on the air as long as you get calls"...your provocative and incisive answers kept the phones solidly lit upfor the entire 3 hours, and we could have kept going for the rest of the nite into the following morning if the flesh had been willing.

And you recall how you motivated them; one caller raced out and drove 20 minutes to purchase your book. He wasn't just buttering you up as his comments showed he had already digested some of your advice in the book.

You were very gracious, by the way, in agreeing to meet some of the callers later.

You'll have to come back; maybe in addition to chatting about "Rent Free", you'll share with my "Open Line" crowd, some of your TV & advertising experiences.

Well done, Jim, keep in touch. And if it can prove useful you may use this letter as an unqualified endorsement of you and your book. Let the skeptics call me.

My best,

Mitch Sandler

(This was one of the first talk-programs when this book was first being "tested" the media. Thanks Mitch. You gave me encouragement at the start.)

WALTER-WEEKS BROADCASTING, INC.
Box 189 · 1500 N. Flagler Drive · West Palm Beach, Florida · 33402 · Phone 659-1230

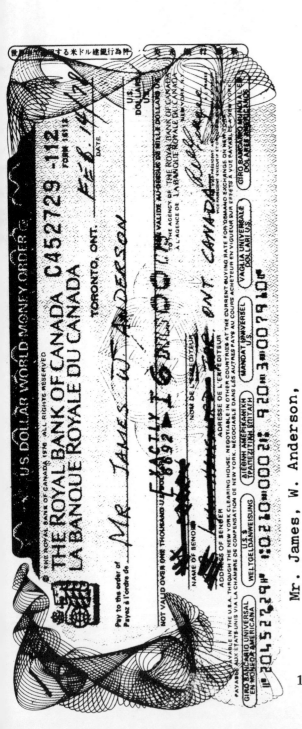

Mr. James, W. Anderson,

701, N.E. 67th Street,

Miami, Florida. 33138

U. S. A.

Dear Mr. Anderson,

My wife and I were on a vacation in Southern Florida last week. On the evening of February 11, we listened to you on WIOD radio station with great interest and respect.

146

You have worked hard to establish your apartment rental business and are now unselfishly sharing your valuable experience and the essence of your success with the public. You have also emphasized that you are a property owner and not a landlord who usually just collects the rent and does nothing else in the interest of the tenants.

You have mentioned on the same radio program that you have published a book titled "How To Live Rent-Free" which at the present time would cost $14.95.

Our vacation has ended on the February 12, and we are now back in Canada.

We would appreciate it very much if you would send us a copy of your book at your earliset convenience.

Enclosed, please find a money order of $16.00 US (included is $1.00 to cover postage.)

We would like very much to study your book first, and hope some time in the future we can meet you in person.

With best wishes.

Yours sincerely,

Miami-Dade Public Library System

Press Release

~~OLGA~~ ~~A.~~ ~~EASON,~~ ~~HEAD~~
COMMUNITY RELATIONS DEPARTMENT
MIAMI-DADE PUBLIC LIBRARY SYSTEM
ONE BISCAYNE BOULEVARD
579-5016

March 15, 1978

A special thank you to the Miami Dade Staff: Director Edward Sintz; Micki Carden, Community Relations, and Sylvia Wahrberg in Publicity. Your support at the very beginning will not be forgotten...and I understand that there is a continual big demand and wait list for the multiple copies that you stock.

FOR IMMEDIATE RELEASE

The Miami-Dade Public Library System is pleased to announce the appearance of Mr. Jim Anderson, author of How To Live Rent Free at their weekly Book Buffet, Tuesday, March 28th at 12 noon in the auditorium at 1 Biscayne Blvd. Mr. Anderson will lecture on his fascinating and informative 70,000 word book and will conduct a question and answer period immediately following his talk. If you ever thought of living rent free, now is the time to speak up and be heard by an expert who is probably the most

knowledgeable person in the country today on this subject. Mr. Anderson's

unique and dynamic presentation will make one sit up and listen with un-

divided attention and the public is invited to attend this exciting event

at no charge. Bring your lunch and enjoy! Coffee and donuts will be available.

Mr. Anderson will also appear on the Miami-Dade Public Library System

radio program on WYOR-FM, Monday, APril 3rd at 1 A.M. to discuss his book with

Ms. Micki Carden , Community Relations Director of the Library System. How

To Live Rent Free will be explored in depth as well as Anderson's experiences

and successes in the apartment ownership and management field. This program

should be of interest to every citizen in this community whether you own or

rent at the present time so become informed on a subject that is of vital

importance and be entertained by a formidable and provocative author.

###

149

THE BOOK OUTLET

MIAMI'S TOTAL DISCOUNT BOOKSTORE

OFFERING THE MOST COMPLETE SELECTION
OF SALE BOOKS

CAUSEWAY PLAZA   DENNIS M. HALKA
N.E. 123RD ST. & BISCAYNE BLVD.   (305) 893-8371

April 3, 1978

Andree Oukhtomsky
BRUN PRESS
701 NE 67 St.
Miami, Fl.33138

Dear Andree,

Your author's new book, HOW TO LIVE RENT FREE is our

single best selling non-fiction hard cover, since we

opened...and the book is building...being a simplified

and humorous, how-to, reference book.

"How To Live Rent Free" is our
best-selling non-fiction hard-cover
book, since we opened.

I believe the author's statement to the 47,000,000 home owners (the millstone as he calls it)...that this book will insure "financial survival in the inflationary spiral of the 1980's"...and..."finally:a simplified tax-shelter for the average man."

Your author also knows how to promote his book and I have been selling books for 10 years; and my book store is one of the bigger book stores in Miami.

Best regards,

Dennis M. Halka

DENNIS M. HALKA
Proprietor
The Book Outlet
Miami, Fl.

151

LAMBERT'S
LITTLE PROFESSOR BOOK CENTER

190 GULF GATE MALL / SARASOTA, FLORIDA 33581 / (813) 922-6758

Brua Press
P.O. Box 370034
Miami, Fla. 33137

Gentlemen:

Last month we had the good fortune to have Jim Anderson (How To Live Rent Free Book) here in Sarasota for a talk show. Afterwards he came to our store and autographed his book for customers. Response to the radio show was excellent. We even had a large group of people waiting for Mr. Anderson here in the store following the broadcast.

I personally listened to the broadcast and was quite impressed with the way Mr. Anderson handles himself. I've heard quite a few speakers and the vitality and assertive tone combined with his vibrant personality ranks Jim Anderson with the best. We would welcome him back anytime.

Cordially,

Kenneth A. Lambert

152

13th Annual Auction

Auction Game
April 2-9

wpbt2

Public Television
Auction Central

Mailing Address:
Channel 2 Auction
P.O. Box 610001
Miami, Florida 33161

CALL:
Dade 949-2241
Broward 467-7399

May 16, 1978

Mr. James Anderson
c/o Bruns Press
701 N.E. 67th Street
Miami, Florida

Dear Jim,

Just wanted to thank you again for your generous support
of our 1978 Public Television Auction. Your donation of
copies of your book "How to Live Rent Free", along with
an hour of personal consultation, were certainly one
of the more unique items we had. We were amazed at the
response we got from our viewing audience. The bidding
was fast and furious, no doubt stimulated by your on
air appearance.

The winning bid on your book was over $140.00, for an
item whose retail value was $24.95, that is an incredible
overbid.

Once again, on behalf of Public Television in South
Florida, I wish to thank you for your contribution.

Very truly yours,

Bernard D. Kamiat
Executive Committee

Due to the tremendous
response of this 6 times
overbid on his book,
Author Anderson realized
that a lot of readers would appreciate some
personalized council regarding their personal
situation, so refer to page 52 for "rent-free
newsletter" order blank; page 308 & 309 for
memberships in related organizations.

153

Ft.Lauderdale, Fl.33315
April 7, 1978

James W. Anderson
PO Box 370034
Miami, Fl. 33137

(this is an exact typed
letter of the hand writ-
ten original letter in
our files.)

Dear Mr. Anderson,

I drove down to Miami to the bookstore where
you had the promotion for your book.(Author appearance). Unfortunately, for me, you were not
scheduled to appear until the afternoon, but
your book has given me a great deal of inspiration as well as an achievable goal.

Some six or seven years ago i had purchased
a triplex and a four-plex. Thanks to your book
I have upgraded (these buildings), raised the
rents and getting them in shape for a critical
buyer.

Rather than an outright sale however, I
would like to trade up, using the equity as
down payment on a larger building.

Of course, now that they are upgraded, the
income is much better and they are a good investment also.

Specifically, this letter is being written
to ask if you will consider working in Broward County, or if you limit yourself to Dade.

I like your philosophy of an Advisor-Broker and certainly feel your approach is fresh
and imaginative.

Sincerely,

Irene M. Brown

Ft.Lauderdale, Fl.33315

154

RECENTLY ON A RADIO INTERVIEW, THE RADIO
PERSONALITY SUGGESTED OF
MY HOW TO LIVE RENT FREE PROJECT . . .
"THAT SEEMS TO BE
NOTHING NEW" . . . TO WHICH I ANSWERED . . .
"CORRECT, IT HAS JUST
BEEN OVERLOOKED, BECAUSE WITH 2 OUT OF 3
FAMILIES OWNING 'MILLSTONES' THAT'S
JUST TO HIGH."

HOWEVER IN THE FRENCH EDITION
OF THE READERS DIGEST MAGAZINE A PROFOUND
ANSWER TO THIS RADIO PERSONALITY'S
COMMENT IS GIVEN BY GOETHE, THE FAMOUS
GERMAN POET-NOVELIST. HE SAID:
"ON A DEJA' PANSE' A TOUT.
LA DIFFICULTE' EST D'Y REPENSER."–GOETHE
(translated into English)
"MAN HAS ALREADY THOUGHT OF EVERYTHING.
THE DIFFICULTY
IS TO THINK ABOUT IT AGAIN."

NOTES & QUESTIONS

JIM ANDERSON'S "HOW TO LIVE RENT FREE" BOOK

CHAPTER TWELVE

INTRODUCTION:
TEN WAYS TO INCREASE RENTS
(I'm not a slum-lord nor a rent-gouger ... I'm a proud-property-owner. As a businessman, if I cleverly improve my apartments, I am entitled to a fair rent increase.)

My theory is ALWAYS IMPROVE YOUR APARTMENTS AHEAD OF A RENT INCREASE. For sure, don't come upon the scene as the new owner, and immediately begin by increasing everyones rents. You may end up with no tenants.

However, take-over in a low key fashion, be nice and polite to all the tenants and keep everything at a status quo. If any tenants ask you if there will be a rent increase (and some of them will ask you), simply say that you do not intend to increase rents at this time. But of course Mr. Tenant, as your pay or Social Security or Interest Checks or Union wages continue to go up ... so do my taxes, my repair costs, my costs to borrow money, my services to the property, etc.

So now, back to the theory above in line one. If you feel that by adding a screened porch to one of your units that it would add value to the unit and therefore more rent ... you are right ... but you must add the screened porch before the current lease is up and before you ask the current tenant for a rent increase.

You will probably find that your tenant will not be complimentary at all to this improvement of your property and improvement to his apartment unit. So as you go on your merry way improving the property ... painting ... planting shrubs, etc., etc., don't expect compliments from your existing tenants ... in fact, they may throw out a critical defense comment about "all the mess caused by your work" ... and their "generosity in ignoring the inconvenience." The tenants may "smell" a rent increase coming and any compliments to you could be the clincher for a rent increase. So don't expect compliments from your tenants as you beautify and improve your property ... that is why you are the property owner, and why they are the tenants.

So then, a month or so after the improvement, probably when the lease is expiring, you have a quiet discussion with the tenant, you tell them that as it now adds up, you cannot make all the increased payments on the property since your costs and mortgage is higher than the previous owners... and that your taxes are going to increase, etc., etc. and you ask the tenant "if a small increase of $15 (or $25 or whatever is required) will be OK with the new lease?"

CAUTION: Do not even mention the improvements that you have done to the apartment and possibly to the entire property. The tenants reply will only be that "it is unnecessary," for the tenant is not concerned like you to improve your property. So totally ignore the improvements, but the tenant will sub-consciously say to himself, "OK, I got a new doohickey put in my apartment... I like the apartment better now... and moving will only cost me more... and where can I get what I have for the same increased rent... so I'll be gracious and pay the increased rent."

I find that if I put the rent increase news to the tenant in a fashion similar to the one above, (in effect I have ASKED his help and cooperation), the tenant will normally reply... "sure, I will help you out." Now you have made the tenant the hero.

On the other hand, if the tenant says he just cannot afford your needed increase... then the tenant will just have to vacate; or you may consider reducing the increase if this tenant is extremely desirable (quiet, prompt rent payment, etc.).

Ten ways to increase your rents will be detailed in the next ten Chapters my dear students because this is one of the most (thought of as) difficult parts of apartment management... how to increase rents. For you want the increased rent... but you also do not want a lot of vacancies. May I humbly say that in the past two years of acquiring 18 apartment units (three buildings) wherein I have greatly increased the rents in all these units from 50% to 150%, that I have never had any serious vacancy rate because of these continuous increases.

Increasing your rents is also very rewarding for WHEN

INTRODUCTION:
TEN WAYS TO INCREASE RENTS

YOU HAVE DOUBLED THE RENTALS OF YOUR APARTMENT BUILDING . . . YOU HAVE DOUBLED THE BOOK VALUE OF YOUR APARTMENT BUILDING. So if you paid $72,000 for your first building as I did, and then proceeded to double the rent rolls in the next eighteen months as I did . . . now that $72,000 apartment building is worth $144,000 . . . and my labors have earned me $72,000 on paper . . . not in cash mind you, because I do not want to sell even if I found a Buyer because this building is a pleasant little money-machine . . . but nevertheless I have doubled the value of this building, since as you recall in another Chapter, I discussed how to figure the fair price for an apartment building. Well, if I had paid six times annual rental for my building . . . then doubled the rents in the next 18 months . . . then today that same apartment building is worth double to what I initially paid for it. Not a bad days work . . . huh?

It isn't always easy to cash in and collect these paper-profits right away for it takes time to sell any building. However, the new value is there and you are collecting double the former rent every month and that is certainly just reward for your labors. Now you are not only living rent free as you had originally figured it out to be . . . but now you have additionally gained another income besides . . . so now you work less at your regular job (maybe even begin to do a little fishing or golf) and you may begin to look at a second apartment building to invest in.

CAUTION: Never give a mass rent increase to everyone in the same month. I methodically and immediately plan to stagger my leases so each tenant lease expires in a different month . . . and I plan my leases to expire WHEN IT IS CONVENIENT TO ME AND NOT NECESSARILY THE TENANT. As example, in Florida, Seasonal rents in the Winter months are about double the annual lease rate, so I plan all my leases to expire in the Winter months when renting on an annual basis is much easier, and I may even desire to pick up a profitable "seasonal tenant" for one unit to help pay some extra bills. My main point however is that as example, if you lease to a new tenant in July 1980. You expire that lease in a Winter month, like October 1981. If the tenant asks why, you say your accountant wants your leases to expire in October. Then the next lease you plan it to expire in November. The next in January. (December is difficult because of Christmas.) Also, if I find a good tenant at a good price in April or May, but he can't sign a lease for one of many good storied reasons), I would consider a no-lease during the Summer months.

Now after that relaxation, you may want to purchase that second apartment building as I did. Now that you know much more than at the beginning of your new career, the second building will come a lot easier. And you will find that there are additional savings by having that second and perhaps third building. Some "professionals" say that "to make a good profit in apartments . . . you must own about fifteen units." I disagree with this to the extent that I have made a good profit on my first five units. However, after adding the second six units . . . and then the third seven units, (all within ten minutes of each other for easy control) . . . I will say that it is just as easy to manage 18 units as 5 units, and there is volume savings on materials and labor and planning time.

Actually my first five units provides me and my wife with free rent in a very realistically priced $450 value apartment, plus a $300 monthly profit income, with the other three apartments paying the mortgage, the utilities, and the taxes. But remember, when I purchased this first five unit apartment building several years ago, it was not that good a deal financially. I used all the advice in the next ten Chapters to improve my property, select the proper tenants and to double the rents.

All my records are available for inspection to show you the progressive improvement of this five unit building over the past two years. Also my records are available to show you on the next two buildings as well.

160

HERE IS AN EXAMPLE OF HOW "SMALL RENT INCREASES BRING YOU TREMENDOUS PROFITS"

$100 IN MONTHLY RENTAL INCREASES GIVES YOU $20,000 IN TEN YEARS (no baloney)

Last week I again increased the rents in my latest (3rd) building by $100 per month (can be verified by existing signed leases), and I am thrilled that I not only will gain this $1200 per year in income (I JUST GAVE MYSELF A $1200 RAISE!) as long as I keep this property; but if I sell the building after ten years (the average) . . . that little $100 rent increase today, will become $19,200 in ten years.

Here's how:

INCOME: $100 per month equals $1200 yr.
                    Average length of owner   x 10

                          Income $12,000

NET WORTH: Now lets say that you sell your apartment building after 10 years. Now, in addition, you will get "six times annual rental" (standard value ratio) on all your increased rentals in the selling price.
                  . . . using this one rent increase
                    (annually) $1200
                  . . . rent-multiplier   x 6

                           $7,200

TOTAL INCOME AND NET WORTH
OFF JUST $100 INCREASED MONTHLY
RENTALS IN TEN YEARS $19,200

I JUST GAVE MYSELF A $1200 RAISE

Now you say that you won't sell your "little gold mine" after ten years? I am with you, why sell? But then you must figure the $1200 annual increased income off the $100 monthly rental increase by 30 years (you and your heirs average ownership). Now you have increased your actual income by $36,000 and not the $19,200 as outlined above.

Better yet . . . figure it anyway you wish. You will see a fantastic multiple for every rent increase dollar you develop.

* * *

I especially compute my profits this way because I am not one of those quick-rich-operators who buy and sell continuously. I plan to keep my Properties at least ten years . . . and maybe a lifetime. Or at least until my depreciation (taxes) runs out in about 20 years) . . . and maybe even for my lifetime.

Selling transactions cost time and money. My Properties are little gold mines. They are "oil wells without the risk." Why sell? (Unless an offer comes along that I simply cannot refuse) I am making good income off the increased rents. And the rents will continue to increase as the economy increases. Also I am not greedy. I want a fair and reasonable return on my investments. But greedy? I am not. (And greed can get you in a whole lot of trouble with all this "leverage baloney, etc.). SO TAKE YOUR $20,000 in ten years for every $100 in rent increases . . . AND BE SATISFIED.

BUILDING EXAMPLE No. 1

* 3 Year Rent Increase History
* 3 Year Value Increase History of
  My First Building Purchased

Building No. 1 — Palm Bay Villas
(tenants pay utilities)

	Purchased 1974	Today 1977	Immed. Poten.
Apt. No. 1 Lg. 2 BR	$250	$450	$450
Apt. No. 2 Lg. 1 BR	$ 90	$250	$250
Apt. No. 3 Sm. 1 BR	$ 90	$175	$175
Apt. No. 4 2 BR	$130	$160	$225*
Apt. No. 5 2 BR	$130	$195	$225*
Mo. Rent Income	$690	$1230	$1325

Firstly, the above shows you that I doubled the rents in three years. Actually I did it in two years.

* Part time Mgr. in Apt. No. 4 gets discount rent. Very good tenant in No. 5 gets his rent held another year.

ABOVE RENT INCOME
ON ANNUAL BASIS   #$8,280   ##$14,760 $15,900

\#   I paid $64,000 for this first apartment building. They initially asked $82,000. This is about 8 x's annual rental, which suited me fine ... elegant owner apartment ... by water and park. Central, foliage. Plus adjacent lot for future building.

\#\# Now, three years later (and $10,000 in property and apt. unit improvements), with almost double the rent roll (potentially —above— more than double), this building is worth about $120,000 today (plus $20,000 more for the vacant lot). This is an $80,000 profit in 3 years.

Maybe I won't get a $120,000 offer tomorrow, and I really don't even want to sell. (Where would we live?) However it is comforting to know that in less than 3 years I have improved my property that much. You can't do that with a home, can you?

What I can bank on, every month and every year ahead is: $500 more per month in rental income, than when I purchased the building or about $6,000 more in income annually.

I live in the elegant old Spanish 2 Bedroom Villa (front) along Biscayne Bay . . . RENT FREE, which beats living in those uninteresting little box-like millstones that many people call luxury-homes.

I lived rent-free from the day of purchase . . . but now, after rent increases I also clear about $300 per month or $3600 per year, after two units pay all the property expenses of: mortgage, taxes, insurance, water, gas, licenses, and fire extinguishers.

The property is now a showplace with beautiful lawns, terraces, trees, awnings, patios, trellises, blooming flowers, birdbaths, new paint, etc. In fact, one good friend who had not visited us in one year, actually passed by our property (not recognizing it) as he was coming to our home for a dinner party. He is in real estate and should be more aware than most. It was just our miraculous-transformation.

Here is the "buy" numbers I looked at when I looked at the offering on building No. 1 . . . would you have bought on these numbers? I doubt it. But today, in just 3 years (actually it only took 2 years) . . . Building No. 1 is a little gold mine.

Here are the "buy" numbers . . .

Asking Price	$82,000
Negotiated Pr.	64,000
Annual Expense	6,000 (inc. Mort.)
Cash Down	15,000
Income off apts.	5,280 (4 units. 1 live in 5th)

There was a difference of $720 annually between income and expenses. So, for $720 the first year ($60 Mo.) I lived in the fifth unit.

As for "return" on this investment if I considered renting all 5 units . . . the profit was about $2,280 off my $15,000 down payment for about a 15% return on investment . . . but I wasn't that concerned about "return" . . . that is for your stock market freak friends . . . they always talk about "return" because that is just about all there is to consider in the stock and bond investment business . . . I was looking at something that had much more to offer than "return" for I was looking at prime real estate . . . apartment buildings . . . which will continue to increase in value over the years as the rents go up with inflation. The rents pay the mortgage monthly . . . but the mortgage stays at the same level, while the rents go up almost on an annual basis. So your rental income continues to give you more and more income each year after you pay the expenses including the mortgage . . . until the mortgage disappears completely (when it is paid up) and then you get all that extra income monthly also.

While all of this is going on, from the beginning of the purchase I am getting about $7,500 in tax shelter annually against my other income . . . and I also get "that return" on investment which is all the Bond Market investor gets . . . maybe.

So have your stock market freaks tell me all about "% return" . . . and maybe that is why the stock-players usually lose and have never gotten into the more substantial business of apartment building investments. I repeat . . . I have seen a lot of poor Stock and Bond investors (and salespeople) . . . but I rarely (if ever) see a poor apartment building owner.

Pardon my sarcasm and disdain for the "Market" boys and girls, but I still see too many of my friends "drugged" on the "hope" the Market still may bring them after they may have lost as much as half of their life's savings. That is a crime and any conscience raising I can do to wake these people up . . . will reward me greatly in knowing so.

Actually I made part of my life's savings in the Stock Market while working in the Television Industry in New York City. And if you are a hard driving young-turk climbing up the Corporate ladder, stock investments is the easy way out. Luckily I got out with some profits before the Mutual Funds began to take over and influence the entire Stock Market. I don't think us little people have much of a chance in the Market . . . but I know that I can "guide my own destiny" as to the success of my apartment buildings. No stock investor under a $1,000,000 can say that about his investments.

But back to looking at the "buy" numbers of my Building No. 1 . . . as you look at them, you will see, as you will see quite often, that the income just about matches expenses most of the time. Through negotiation, and a reasonable down payment to keep the mortgage payments a little lower; you will obtain a reasonable "buy-deal."

As a wise investor once said . . . when you find a good potential apartment building . . . it is not going to have the words "bargain" . . . "bargain" . . . written all over it. It will be up to you and with the possible help of your advisor to realize this "bargain" building.

The end of the story on Building No. 1? (No, not the end, just the happy result after only 3 years of ownership). I now live totally rent-free, pay the $6,000 in annual expense out of the increased rents, and I now also collect $3600 in annual income. Would you have bought it? . . . I found out later that this building had been on-the-Market, and For-Sale, for more than one year, and had many "lookers" who just "over-looked" my "little gushing oil well". . . my building No. 1.

BUILDING EXAMPLE No. 2

* 2 Year Rent Increase History
* 2 Year Value Increase History of
  My Second Building Purchased

BUILDING No. 2 – DON MEJOR VILLAS
(tenants pay utilities)

Mixed neighborhood. Some People say "Black is Beautiful" . . . I say "Black is Golden."

6 Units (2/2BR; 2/1 BR; 2 Efficiencies)

Take over rents inconclusive since 4 of the 6 units were vacant.

SELLING PRICE $20,000 WITH $10,000 DOWN.

Now with $6,000 in improvements (fixed up vacant apartments before renting) . . .

ANNUAL RENTAL INCOME IS $10,000, which I know is more than double the rent when I purchased this building.

POTENTIAL ANNUAL RENTAL INCOME $13,000. But I keep the rents "low" to attract good tenants. Example: My 2 room efficiency has a market value rental of about $135/mo. I rent them for $110/mo.

ACTUAL ANNUAL RENTAL	POTENTIAL AN. R.
$10,000	$13,000
x 5*	x 5*
$50,000 value	$65,000 pot. val.

* Used a low rent-multiplier of "5" because of the mixed neighborhood.

In two years I have again doubled the value of this property should I wish to sell. However, selling "mixed area property" is not that easy truthfully ... but why sell? I have a little black-goldmine here.

I get my $10,000 down, back in rental income EVERY YEAR.

I also get a high return on investment. Off my $16,000 outlay (down payment plus improvements), I profit at about $6,000 annually ($10,000 annual rent).

So I get an unbelievable 30% return off my investment.

Be happy with a 10% return on investment in a better neighborhood ... but Black can be golden.

I don't really gauge a building by % percent return anyway ... (that's for all you stock gamblers and stock losers) ... for unlike the "shell game" ... oops .... I meant stock-market ... besides % return on investment in real estate ... you get depreciation off taxes which will save you thousands annually, you get interest payment tax deductions ... you get property appreciation, more tax deductions for maintenance and improvements ... and all the other "goodies" mentioned throughout this book.

Would you have bought this building? That is really an unfair question, since I would not have either ... If I had not purchased my first one already and had begun to see the great promise in apartment buildings.

But anyway, look at these negative numbers that I looked at in this buy:

$20,000 Selling Price
10,000 Down Payment
4,000 Expenses
2,100 Rental Income from 2 units)
(4 units vacant)

And so I purchased this building whose rentals only covered one half its expenses. But I now realized that I was selling the most saleable of all products . . . "a roof over your head" . . . Food? . . . you eat your food under the roof over your head that I rent . . . what is more basic than owning apartment units?

So I knew that if I could fix up this property quickly (inside and out) . . . and if I could do it reasonably by using all my new knowledge of obtaining low cost materials and low cost Craftsmen . . . then I would have a real money maker.

So would you believe it . . . I asked the existing two tenants to leave so I could go into extensive remodeling of the property. And I actually chopped up one tenants apartment into two more saleable units.

Six weeks after purchase, me and my two Craftsmen working side by side transformed this 6 unit complex into some very nice looking apartments. I have a entire picture book of "before" and "after" photographs to prove this miraculous transformation . . . in fact today I call this property my "Adult Country Club." When I bought it I described it to friends as looking like "a bombed out Vietnam." Also refer to the "Don Mejor Villas" Poster in the advertising Chapter of this book.

Another happy ending to story No. 2? . . . from a $2,000 annual loss at purchase . . . within 2 months after purchase I began to make money which became a $6,000 annual income off the $10,000 cash down plus the $6,000 in improvements.

$6,000 return annually off $16,000 invested? That's a 30% return after the first year's ownership . . . but when I bought this building it delivered a "minus 20% deficit on investment" . . . (if there is such a computation term in the investment business).

All I know is that today I don't say "Black is beautiful" . . . I say . . . "Black is Golden."

BUILDING EXAMPLE No. 3

* 1 Year Rent Increase History
* 1 Year Value increase History of my
  Third Building Purchased

BUILDING No. 3 — BISCAYNE BAY VILLAS
(tenants pay utilities)

	Purchased	Today	Immed. Poten.
Apt. No. 1 1 BR.	$160	$195	$225
Apt. No. 2 1 BR.	$160	$195	$225
Apt. No. 3 1 BR.	$160	$195	$225
Apt. No. 4 1 BR.	$160 (mgr)	$150	$225
Apt. No. 5 1 BR.	$170	$195	$225
Apt. No. 6 Effic.	$ 85	$135	$150
Apt. No. 7 Effic.	$100	$135	$150
Monthly Rental Income	$995	$1200	$1425

With about $3,000 in property and unit improvements, in one year, I have increased the annual rental by about 20%.

The "potential rent increases" in 1979 is not blue-sky-projections of some button pushing man in an ivory tower. I have already put in most of the improvements which will merit these 1979 rentals. (Remember, I suggested to improve-ahead-of-rent-increases?). Additionally, when you consider inflation which continually goes up as Unions increase wages, and Social Security increases, etc., etc. Now I have attracted a much better grade of tenant (I had to "not renew" several leases). That is the third "force" which will make those 1979 pot. rent increases a reality.

**ABOVE RENT INCOME
ON ANNUAL BASIS** $11,940 $14,400 $17,100

I paid $72,000 for this, my third building. They had initially asked $82,000. This is about 7 x's annual rental which is "average", especially when I had to pay only $8,000 down on this emergency-sale. Good neighborhood. Building and apartment units in fair condition. Near water, shopping. Central. Plus two car garage that I have converted into my warehouse for all three properties.

Next year (2 yrs. ownership) I will have increased rents by 50% from takeover, which is tremendous, for I don't want you to believe that you can double the rents of every building you buy, in two years like I did on building No. 1 . . . even if you read this book thoroughly and follow every principle in it. You also must make a proper purchase of a BUILDING WITH POTENTIAL. Every building has a potential for rent increases . . . not every building can be "doubled" in several years. I consider the rent increase history of this No. 3 of 20% in one year, and a strong potential to 50% next year MORE SATISFYING THAN BUILDING No. 1 . . . because the challenge was greater . . . but I had a great incentive on Building No. 3 . . . I purchased it (emergency sale) at ONE HALF the down payment of Building No. 1 ($8,000 and more units than No. 1). So, everything is relative . . . and don't get greedy . . . I am very pleased with the increased performance of this building No. 3.

Now, one year later with $3,000 in improvements, this apartment building has a worth of $100,000 at the same 7 x's annual rental.

This is a $30,000 appreciation profit in just one year. I'll take this any year over the crazy and fluctuating "shell game" . . . oops, I mean stock market. I have seen a lot of poor stock market investors . . . but haven't seen many poor income property owners. Don't you agree?

My biggest problem here was beautification of the front of building and the entrance . . . believe it or not. The apartments were very spacious, livable, tall ceilings and thick walls

172

for perfect tropical living . . . but the front was a tall un-interesting 2 story nothing, with a few scrub shrubs in front, and a bad looking entrance, with a 1 ft. deep garden area.

I immediately put in three of my instant 30 foot tall giant bamboo trees in front to "soften" this cold looking building. Then smaller areca and traveler palms and blooming ixora, with giant philadendra on trellises trained to grow up 40 feet. to the top of this uninteresting building. Then I installed the elegant black and white square tiles in the front and rear public hall ways with a nice chandelier (flea mkt.) in each hallway. Painted the front steps and put down nice looking foot mats. Now a prospect-tenant does not "just drive by" without stopping in. My No. 3 is now inviting and tenants are proud to invite their friends over. Cost? Not more than $150 . . . I did the work enjoyably. So, in one year I clear $5,500 after mortgage, taxes, public utilities, Lic., Fire, Water.

To recap this building . . . $14,400 in annual rentals NOW . . . $9,400 in expenses . . . so I clear about $5,000 in profits annually, NOW, one year after purchase. Next year, with those rent increases already justified and realistic, per market competition; my profits will be $7,000 annually. (Off an $8,000 invest.)

My $8,000 investment is delivering me $5,000 per year with-in one year . . . that's about a 65% return on investment, right? But there are buildings to buy . . . good potential buildings that bring a 5% or an 8% "return" NOW . . . I repeat . . . that "return" baloney is for the stock buyers, who lost most of their hard earned money in the schill-game . . . I mean the stock market . . . and are "limping" into the apart-ment building arena to try to recoup with an intelligent investment. But to equate apartment buildings to "return" like Bonds is ridiculous, because you also get inflation, ap-preciation, depreciation, tax shelter, etc. along with an apart-ment building purchase which for decades has been cared for by Uncle Sam with many "incentives" over the Market-Game.

My future with No. 3? Next year with $7,000 in profit off No. 3 I will be getting a COMPLETE RETURN ON MY ORIGINAL INVESTMENT EVERY YEAR OR SO. I know of no type investment in the World with that kind of return or peace of mind. Apartment buildings remain the single most basic AND NEEDED type of investment there is. Everyone needs a roof over their heads . . . food? ? (restaurants) people can eat in their apartment. So please don't even compare land, stocks, businesses, in the same breath!

Now lets go back to the beginning when I purchased No. 3 one year ago. This building was not that attractive then, but it was still a good buy . . . would you have bought it? (I have since met people who did not.)

Expenses:

Mortgage	$7,000 per yr.
Taxes	720
Common Elec.	860 (1 apt. I pay)
Insurance	270
Licenses	31
Water	432
Fire Exting.	28
Annual Expenses No. 3	**$9,341**

With a rental of $12,000 annually, when all apartments are rented. With the one existing vacancy the income at the time it was offered to me was about $10,000. Also I was not completely certain as to the rental potential of the neighborhood. I had known of this building for sale for one year as I was buying No. 2 . . . I did not buy this one (they asked higher, with more down). But I repeat . . . would you have bought this building, WHICH TODAY IN ONE YEAR IS A LITTLE GOLD MINE . . . but when bought delivered $10,000 to $12,000 in rentals with over $9,000 in expenses. (Even a $2,000 return on $8,000 is 25%). I hesitated . . .

thought I saw a potential . . . and knew one beautiful thing . . . I was buying a 7 unit apartment building in a good neighborhood for only $8,000 cash. I knew that if I could hold on . . . make expenses . . . and fix up . . . raise rents . . . that I would do OK . . . not even considering inflation, appreciation, depreciation, tax shelter and all the rest.

The major secret that you must learn from all these numbers is that HOMES ARE OVERPRICED . . . AND QUADPLEXES ARE UNDERPRICED. Americans are in a blind, mad, misguided rush to purchase the overpriced yet underbuilt single family home which will become extinct like the dinosaur in the 1980's with Quadplexes taking over as the "private" way to live. Those cliffdwellers (even the millionaires) will still have their three ring circus of "crime-noise-pollution" in their very un-private Alcatrz-type large apartment complexes.

Quadplexes on the other hand are underpriced because they are undiscovered by the Masses. There is an old economic Law which says "supply & demand." Demand increases price. Also there are maybe 90% "candy store owners" of existing Quads, where the Tenants "run" the building. These "owners" (who probably inherited the building but not the wisdom of their Parents) advertise as such, "illness forces sale" . . . baloney . . . that's a candy store operator, with a Tenant driving him crazy . . . just "slap in" a $10,00 or $20,000 less than selling price, offer . . . and "steal" a building. (Brokers, Banks & Real Estate Editors who always talk about the high cost of real estate . . . and that "it is impossible for most citizens to buy Property" . . . are merely reporting "from under a rock.'") Get your buy-information from someone "in the trenches" like me. Example: I just bought my fourth Quadplex along beautiful Biscayne Bay. Perfect condition . . . not even "an ugly-duckling" that I usually like to buy (with peeled paint and no shrubs) . . . FOR . . . WOULD YOU BELIEVE $68,000. Also consider that the New York Times reported Fall 1979, "MIAMI'S REAL ESTATE BOOM" (it's booming except for the undiscovered Quadplex).

	No. 1	No. 2	No. 3
PURCHASE PRICE	$64,000	$20,000	$72,000
YEAR PURCHASED	1974	1975	1976
DOWN PAYMENT	$15,000	$10,000	$8,000
IMPROVEMENTS	8,000	6,000	3,000
TAKEOVER RENT	8,280	5,000 E.	11,940
TODAY'S RENT	14,760	10,000	14,400
EXPENSES	6,000	4,000	9,000
ANNUAL PROFIT	9,000	6,000	5,000

Per the above, in the past 3 year period I have amassed over a quarter million dollars in solid apartment building real property from my original cash outlay of $33,000, plus about $17,000 in property and unit improvements. (Improvement money can also come from a bank in the form of a building loan . . . or can come out of rent money profits.)

So in my case, with a $50,000 outlay over three years (it could have been done with the $33,000 down plus bank loans for improvements), I own a quarter million dollars in apartment buildings (18 units) . . . and as inflation is assured to continue to go up as long as the Unions continue to ask and demand wage increases . . . my rents will continue to go . . . up . . . and up some more while my mortgage payments not only stay the same (and get easier and easier to pay) . . . but finally (20 years) the mortgages are paid up, and they stop completely.

After three years, I profit $20,000 annually off that $33,000 outlay in down payments . . . and this is a part time job for me. Now I am a Registered Florida Real Estate Broker and I am beginning to advise others to do the same or better.

CAUTION: I give my "examples" only as a guide and as goals for you to improve upon and to beat. There are many good and potentially good apartment buildings. Further, you can buy them for a fair or even below market price and with good terms that will not hinder your growth. Then feel that you have done a good job with your pre-arranged Advisor-Broker no-fee agreement for owner-council after the sale, and his list of low cost craftsmen.

But what you do after the sale IS UP TO YOU. And whatever you put into this project is returned to you 100 fold . . . and that is no exaggeration (which I know you agree if you have been absorbing this book.)

Just one little staggering statement . . . $100 in monthly rental increases will give you $20,000 in income and worth in ten years. And don't forget . . . we are talking of big returns on investment and big tax shelter in the solid and stable real estate field and not in some quick-rich, Mickey Mouse scheme to make a fortune. I repeat . . . you don't see many rich stock market players around . . . but have you ever met a poor apartment building owner? . . . Oh, one last thought . . . you don't pay those mortgages . . . your tenants do . . . and as those rents go up . . . it takes less and less apartment rentals to pay those mortgages and the rest goes to you.

I want to give you one more reason why Quadplexes will always be available for sale. The smart buyer takes all 20 years "depreciation" (your legal tax dodge) out of the Quad in the first 10 years like your millionaire Senators do. That is called "double declining depreciation." So almost the total Market price of your first building is deducted from your salary in the first ten years . . . so then the smart buyers must "exchange" and buy-up to a more expensive building, and do it all over again like your millionaire Senators. And you paid no income tax on the building that you sold after ten years at a great profit.

NOTES & QUESTIONS

HOW TO INCREASE RENTS . . .
"THE SHUTTER TREATMENT"

Decorator-shutters do miracles for apartments which on the average are devoid of any natural charm. In fact, most units remind me of some cold hotel room or maybe a glorified jail cell.

I have special places to buy my shutters (used) for 10 cents to 50 cents each depending on the size. These cost about $5 each, new. You have to spray paint the new as well as the used. A $1 can of spray paint will cover about four window shutters front and back . . . and don't be sloppy. Do a good job. No runny paint. Work the shutters so they don't stick . . . take pride in your work. Its your apartment isn't it? I buy my shutter doors for closets and area-dividers for $1 to $2 used . . . new they will cost $10 to $20 each. I have personally installed 200 decorator-shutters on windows, doors, cabinets in kitchens and baths . . . almost anywhere there is a normal door or window opening, except where privacy is desired, like the bathroom and bedroom.

Besides shutter giving your drab apartment the glamour-treatment, here in the warm climate area, shutters have a practical value of cooling an apartment and preventing mildew as in closets.

I estimate that when I give one of my units "the shutter-treatment" that I can get a 10% rent increase just off this one improvement.

Shutters, even at the new-store-price can possibly cost you several hundred dollars per unit for window shutters (bottom half only) in six windows (four per window) plus a nice pair of full length shutters to go in the hallway between living room and kitchen.

That unit which was renting for $180, can probably be rented to the next tenant for $195. So, in one year, the rent increase has paid for the shutters (at the new price), and after that first year, you now have an additional $180 income, each year for yourself. And besides all that profit, you have increased the sale value of your property by $1160 (the "six times annual rent multiple" rule).

Can you imagine why shutters are so cheap in the "used stores"? My theory is that most people (including me) do not know how to affix the special "stand off" shutter hinge that allows you to install various sized shutters (ones you find in the junk store are not always the exact window size) on any one window size width. I learned this actually, after one year, by installing some shutters for my Aunt Dorothy in St. Louis. I went to K-Mart to purchase some new shutters (it killed me) and I happened to see this "shutter-model" showing how to mount and install these ingenious "stand off shutter hinges" . . . Because most people do not install shutter hinges the correct way, I feel is the reason they give up . . . and "junk" the hinges. So buy the junk shutters . . . save a lot of decor money, and get your rents up quicker.

Ceiling fans are coming back and they never went out as being very practical in warm climates to move the air and to save valuable and high electric costs with a continually used air conditioner. I buy them on sale at Sears and have them installed for a total of about $100. With this item, I have been successful in getting a good tenant to share the cost with me. It is certainly not expected by a tenant, but he can enjoy and save on his electric bill, so his $50 cost is a bargain. Of course the ceiling fan is your property, should this tenant leave, which is the standard rule. Any item permanently affixed to your property, becomes the property of the owner of the building. I make certain the tenant understands this. This ceiling fan can also be used as a rent-increaser wherein you pay the total amount when you are refurbishing the apartment. I am certain you will get your money back in increased rentals many times over.

CHAPTER THIRTEEN

HOW TO INCREASE RENTS: "PAINT UP" IS MAGIC

A good looking paint job is a must, inside and out, if you wish to achieve optimum rents and have less vacancies than the 5% to 10% average.

The majority of tenants are insecure (that's why they act "that way" once in a while) and they need this "artificial lift" that a nice appearing entrance and apartment will give them and their guests.

When an apartment has been vacated, I carefully look it over and consider whether a complete paint job is needed, or maybe just a touch up.

When you have a good long term tenant who wants a new paint job there are various ways to handle it. With the lease renewal, you can decide to maybe give the paint job as good will for an exceptional tenant. Secondly you can agree to a 50/50 split of the cost. Thirdly, and very popular, you can contribute the paint while the existing tenant does the work. But caution here, most people are sloppy painters and especially a person who does not own the building will not give it possibly the care that you or a professional painter would. So inspect the tenant paint job along the way to insure that is done the way you want it done. And tell the tenant before he begins that you only wish a proper and good job and you will "look in" along the way, to help, advise and inspect. Tell the tenant that if the paint job is not done correctly, that possibly one year later the paint will begin to peel (we've all been through this, right?) and then it is a real trouble to scrap the paint off before painting again. I find that people cooperate and respond, if you take the extra minute to explain your reasoning. Most people just give "orders" without an explanation. The other party doesn't like that, so you get no cooperation. If you communicate, you will get cooperation.

181

Back to the tenant painting his own apartment. If a light sanding job is necessary to take off the gloss and to help the new paint stick properly, before a new coat of enamel is put on doors, windows or in kitchen or bath, be sure that the tenant has done the sanding before you provide the paint. This is just protective and good common sense ... and human nature ... I guarantee you, that if you don't do it in steps as outlined above, your expensive enamel will peel off in about one year, like the skin off a boa-constrictor snake.

Whoever paints, be certain to get the proper guidance, step by step, from a paint supplier or manufacturer. Write down the directions if they confuse you. The first painting projects I did three years ago, some are beginning to peel ... but all the jobs in the past 2-1/2 years are in good shape. Why? Because I finally got it through my thick head that if you are going to do a job ... do it right ... or not at all. This is your building ... take care of it, and do a proper and good job, otherwise it will just stare you in the face again, demanding another paint job in just a year or two. Save all that wasted time, redoing what you have already ... save that time for fishing and boating in all the beautiful surrounding waters.

Also: Investigate, and go to a local paint manufacturer. Remember, you are no longer just a little frumpy owner of an old millstone (your home), you are the owner of an apartment building ... doesn't that sound nice? So you no longer buy paint at your local store, you go to a paint manufacturer. Introduce yourself, maybe set up an account, and they will be happy to advise you on the proper paint and its application in that area. Since I live in the sub-Tropics (Miami), I use a paint manufacturer whose paint is made and tested to withstand mildew and heat. I don't even waste my time with those National Brands of paint that are possibly good for the other ninety per cent of the Country up North and out of this sub-Tropical zone. And I do find that locally manufactured paint is cheaper than those National Brands.

My local manufacturer has tested his paints, in this area, over the past thirty years, to withstand this kind of Tropical weather. I have been extremely happy with this discovery.

HOW TO INCREASE RENTS:
"PAINT UP" IS MAGIC

My paint now costs less and I believe that it does a better job that is more long lasting.

So paint the apartments when they are vacant (much easier then), provide paint for good tenants on some agreed to basis, and paint the outside. Its your building, isn't it? . . . So take care of it. And the "first impression is important in filling up that last vacancy.

OTHER CREATIVE FIX-UP TIPS . . . HOW ABOUT A $100 6 FOOT CHOP BLOCK FOR $10?

The first chop block I had made for our apartment cost me $100. For a rock maple one, six feet long and tailored for our kitchen. I just did one for an efficiency apartment and it only cost $10. The secret? I guess liking my work, and treating these projects as the creative crafts pay off handsomely in personal income . . . they are not a luxurious past time. Want to own a six foot chop block counter top for $10 like I did? First you find in a salvage yard (call around) a TOUGH piece of wood maybe 8 inches wide by 12 feet long (cut in two pieces it becomes a six foot chop block). I use the beautiful (but getting scarce) Dade County Pine that is as tough as "nails". Then I take this old and beat up board to my expensive cabinet maker or "mill" . . . and with my quick plan to save time, and not being indecisive (since it costs $10 per half hour for one man and the milling machines), I have them cut the board . . . beautifully "plane" it down to its original lustrous gloss, then drill holes, and "peg" and glue, and . . . you have a six foot counter top for $10 and I would be happy and proud to have it in my kitchen if I had not already spent the $100 (when I did not know better . . . or did not have my inventive and creative juices flowing). There are so many things like this you can do, if you are interested. These things have become my hobby.

HOW ABOUT A POLISHED AND HAND ENGRAVED ENTRANCE NAME PLATE PLAQUE THAT LOOKS LIKE THE "PLAZA HOTEL"

I have such brass plate signs made at the local engraver where they make these little bowler trophies and other dubious awards. They cost surprisingly little (maybe $15) and you have just added elegance to your entrance, which is very important for tenants to impress their guests. And this elegant sign beats those tacky plastic signs . . . and probably costs less.

HOW ABOUT A "LOVE TUB" FOR THAT SPECIAL APARTMENT?

I have a standard challenge that I will turn any negative into a positive. I just think positively . . . where many people think negatively . . . case in point. I had a particularily attractive and interesting apartment with an old fashioned bathroom which did not have a tub (almost a "must") . . . and there was really no room for a tub. I asked my plumber to create a handmade tub in the shower space, but he said it was impossible. A year later we had a leak in this shower which is above another apartment unit, so we had to work fast. I asked the same plumber again . . . only with more finality . . . Jim, we have GOT to make a tub in that shower area. He looked, studied, considered various ways of rearranging the entire set of bathroom fixtures to accomodate a tub . . . but finally agreed that my way was the ONLY way. We both worked for two days and it cost me about $400 in labor and materials. . . tile all the way up, but with a built-up front where you normally step into a shower. The love tub accomodates two comfortably and since we currently have a lovely Japanese Airline Hostess living in this "Garden Penthouse" . . . we call our creation, "A Japanese Love Tub" (they do like to take baths together in Japan, remember?)

OR HOW ABOUT AN AUTHENTIC ORCHID SLAT HOUSE / $25

I like flowers and encourage flower-loving tenants. Recently I built this slat house after checking the local Fairchild Gardens for an authentic design (its your Property, so do it right . . . right?) . . . now these tenants hang their plants out side in this slat house for regular "airings" and I even sent each tenant a memo, giving them the two Orchid Clubs, where they could attend a meeting, free, and maybe get interested in a profitable new hobby and to meet some interesting new friends. As I said in this memo . . . "most estates don't have their own authentic tropical orchid slat house . . . but you do . . . so enjoy it." And I am no dummy . . . it was about $25 in wood and a fortune worth of pleasure designing it . . . and over the years it can't help but attract some very, very nice tenants.

You say you don't have the time or the desire to learn my new hobby, "Creative Crafts in Apartment Living". Well this again is where your cheap retired Craftsmen can help you. But you must initiate the plan.

NOTES & QUESTIONS

HOW TO INCREASE RENTS: TENANTS GIVE "COLD-SHOULDER" TO HIGHER RENTS IF THERE IS NOT ENOUGH HOT WATER

Fix any electrical repairs as soon as possible after you take possession of your apartment building. If there are any building code electrical violations fix them because if you do have a fire, perhaps your insurance will not properly cover the damage because of the electric code violation. Anyway, your electric inspection will turn up any violations even before you went to your Contract for Sale so there will be no surprises for you in this regard.

My first building had too low an electric voltage input into the property, so that fuses were always "blowing." Never enough hot water. Inconvenience to the tenants. How could the previous owner expect to increase rents with such a bad but easy to fix situation.

Since I was new "at the game," after checking three electrical contractors (they were all about the same cost), I chose one of the best at a cost of $40 per hour because I wanted a good and safe job. This electrical service improvement was one of the major steps that enabled me to increase the rent roll considerably at my first apartment building within the first year.

Also too few electrical outlets in your apartments can cause a fire hazard because if there are not enough electric outlets, the tenant will use cheap extension cords which I prohibit, when I see them.

The end of this first electricians story however, is that today, three years after that first $40 per hour electrical job by a master electrician I now have many electric jobs done in all my 18 units . . . for about $10 per hour. And I believe the work quality is superior.

Why and how?

By talking to a lot of people, asking everyone I meet and by trying some Craftsmen who are not good . . . I have assembled my own group of top quality, but reasonable Craftsmen. You should insist in your Advisor-Broker Agreement that he include giving you the names of Craftsmen for your personal use, together with your written promise that you will not pass along this valuable information, regarding these reasonably priced Craftsmen. . . to your friends.

And I guarantee you, all your friends will want their names and numbers if you discuss it. Just make it YOUR LITTLE BUSINESS MAN'S SECRET. For if we provide too much work for these Craftsmen, then their price will automatically go up, because they will realize that they cannot handle all the requests for work anyway, so they naturally will increase their price.

Continually update and improve your list of low cost Craftsmen, and guard your list with care. It will be a major step along the path to big profits in the apartment business . . . for if you can get maybe four times the work done for the same money. . . you can do a lot more improving . . . which will automatically transfer into increased rents to you.

CHAPTER FIFTEEN

HOW TO INCREASE RENTS:
OFFER MODERN KITCHENS AND BATHS

Plumbing is another way to increase rents, believe it or not . . . but again, with all the projects you may have on the drawing board . . . you will want to find a fair priced master plumber. I provide information on good and reasonable plumbers to my Buyers, demand this service from your A.B.

Three years ago, again at my first building, I decided to put in a commercial washer and dryer for our own use and for the use of our tenants . . . coin operated, of course, so the expense of the machines and their installation (about $1,000) plus upkeep and repair expense; would all be self liquidating.

Again it was $35 per hour for the plumber. It was a good job . . . the best. But what building operater can afford $35 per hour for craftsmen when there are so many projects you want to get done, which will increase the rents with all those corresponding monetary benefits to you. Maybe when you lived in that old millstone (your home) you would pay such expense, but now you have a bigger building and it is important just to not pay through the nose for all the services you need.

Today, three years later, I have two fantastic master plumbers . . . one charge is $10 per hour . . . and if he isn't in or available, I call another one who charges $12.50 per hour. And for a superb work. To my thinking, that is still a pretty fair going-wage. These plumbers are nice, talented, and it seems that they can do just about anything in their field. They will even come on Sunday, if an emergency develops a stopped up pipe . . . and at the same week day price . . . not double or triple time as your stranger-"bandit"-craftsman type will do. My Craftsmen take care of me like my Doctor does . . . only they are a lot cheaper . . . and they will make house-calls. And whenever these Craftsmen get out of line and begin charging me exorbitant prices . . . I have others

standing in line to use for myself . . . and to recommend to
my clients. Find an Owner-Broker who does the same.

.Now back to the Washer-Dryer service. I could not find
a service to handle the installing of their own machines at the
beginning when I was new. The one that almost did it was
not interested in just a five unit building. Today, I have
found a very good washer-dryer service . . . even for a five
unit building. They install the equipment (which in this first
instance I paid for). They also pay for the complete installation. Then, they service these machines at no cost to me . . .
(which is $40 anytime the Sears repair man comes to service
my personal installation). And, this service company cuts me
in on the take. I learned (and not too late) after my first
building, and now I can share these savings and revelations
with you, and you can save the $1,000 installation I put in
my first building. You get a lot more from your no cost
Advisor-Broker than those other Brokers you have used in
the past . . . for now You are using your "Secret Weapon."

One more thing on plumbing to save you a lot of money.
Be sure to use the standard lease form that clearly defines it
as the tenant's expense, to pay for any stopped up toilets or
sinks. This is the law here, so use it. I also, again, print it in
my lease-addendum, to clearly point out that if the tenant
stops up the plumbing . . . he pays for the expense to fix
it . . . and properly, without destruction to my plumbing
pipes.

Of course, good modern plumbing is a necessity in a
rental unit. It is always said that the primary appeal of any
type living quarters . . . home or apartment, is a modern
kitchen and a modern bathroom. This will help you to get
the top rental dollar that your area and your type building
commands. With a reasonable plumber craftsmen, you can
have it, and without absurd charges . . . even if you want to
put in Bidets, it won't cost that much, and with the
fixtures at greatly reduced costs. Go first class if you can . . .
but always on a budget. I bought a few fine oil paintings in
New York City over the years and I would always tell the
gallery that "I like art collecting . . . but I only buy it on a

budget." To me, this is the ultimate savings type story on budget-purchasing.

* * *

ROOFING: I stick roofing here, because it is another craftsman job for which I have found reasonable craftsmen to do the job. However, don't expect any tenant to pay you more rent for a dry roof. This is the one basic-mammal-force that tenants feel they have paid the rent for, ie, a roof over their head. But a roof is tricky in the Tropics. Do you know why you see so many of those beautiful curved Spanish tile roofs in the gold coast area? The curved tile is to give an air space and to protect the normal roof under the tile from our intense Tropical heat a few months out of every year in the Summer. Otherwise, small roofing jobs can be done after a little coaching from A.-B. or your nearest roofing wholesaler supply company . . . otherwise, again, shop around for good roofing experts that are fair, reasonable, and able craftsmen.

MIRRORS. I add a note on mirrors, because by adding mirrors in the bathroom inside the closet door for dressing, perhaps in the hallway, you again are adding value and attractiveness to your apartments. If you are handy, you can salvage mirrors with broken edges from salvage, second hand stores and even find some dandys in alley-ways . . . then you take them home and with an ordinary glass cutter (ONE FIRM CUT . . . don't go back over the cutting-line) you can cut these broken mirrors to fit smaller areas in your apartments. I once tried this in one of my ordinary bathrooms. Yes it was clean, neat . . . but the bathroom lacked showmanship to attract Mr. Good tenant at that higher rent. This bathroom had just one small mirror on the small medicine cabinet. I put a full length mirror ($5 at the Drug chain) on the wall opposite this cabinet mirror to reflect the rear-view while fixing-up. Then with some of my junk-broken-mirrors, I lined the remaining walls with mirror on opposite sides for more reflections. Above all these mirrors, I added a low cost three-bulb "theater make up light fixture." Now Ms. Good Tenant can fantasize that she is about to go on-stage every time she puts on her make up in this bathroom. For a $25 investment, I have added great desirability to this apartment, and I am now doing the same to my other units.

To add substance to this story, which I am certain makes sense to you anyway and you cannot help but agree. Recently, I visited with a mirror manufacturer, where I went to get some special mirror fasteners. He casually mentioned this big builder-developer who for years has had this mirror man put extravagant use of mirrors into all this developers homes. Saying that the mirrors helped greatly in selling these high cost homes and at higher prices.

I remember an old business management story told by my Professor in College where the way a factory slowed down their woman workers from leaving the plant after work so no one would be injured in the rush . . . was to install mirrors along the hallway-exit-area. All these ladies slowed down to "primp" before they left the plant, and this stopped injuries. Mirrors are magic. Don't be cheap with their usage in your units. The cost, regardless of how much you spend for them will be repaid many times over.

Here is as good a time as any to advise you how to find good and low cost Craftsmen, besides the ones your A.-B. (Advisor-Broker) gives you per your package agreement. It is the same method that I advised you before, in a previous Chapter as to how to go about finding your qualified Advisor Broker . . . remember . . . ASK AROUND FOR INFORMATION FROM BUSINESS CONCERNS WITH WHICH YOU EXCHANGE MONEY $ MONEY . . . THAT ALWAYS SEEMS TO BE THE KEY, and it has worked for me. If your Uncle Harry just completed a plumbing course at the YMCA, I pity you if you give him his first job, just because you THINK YOU WILL SAVE a few bucks. You can find the $40 per hour electricians and plumbers for $10 and $15 per hour . . . they are out there. I use them. And I am doing you your first big service in this regard in just letting you know that they are there. Many wasteful shoppers just firstly cannot believe this. Now that you know they are out there, available, and anxious to serve willing, nice and concerned apartment

owners . . . now find them as I have told you how. Secondly.
Do not forget your retired, senior handyman Craftsman . . .
they are all over, they work at a reasonable rate, and I like
their work better, because they still have the older qualitative
values . . . with no modern shortcuts.

HOW TO FIND GOOD AND REASONABLY PRICED CRAFTSMEN AND AN AGREEMENT FORM WHICH IS ADVISABLE, FOR YOUR OWN PROTECTION

Quite often, I used retired Craftsmen who are over 60 or
65 years, and they are honored and delighted that someone
(me) still thinks they can do a day's work.

I pay them anywhere from $3 to $6 per hour, depending
on their skill, and they thank me profusely for giving them
work, and extra income, beyond their Social Security. I have
coined a saying that I believe in: "OLD IS BETTER . . . IN
PEOPLE . . . DOOR KNOBS . . . OR HOUSES." You don't
necessarily have to agree with this, but in my vast experience
I find that a lot of "skilled workers" of today, take short cuts
or just do not know what the older Craftsman knows (or
what he even forgot). Pride in one's work is also rapidly
vanishing . . . so get a retired person, or 2 or 3, for various
jobs and the maintenance problem is greatly resolved.

Where to find them? I always ask someone whom I do
business with and whom with I exchange money, goods or
services. I find these kinds of recommendations much more
safe than "a friend's recommendation" (which could be self
serving, and given you with no feeling of any real responsibility). A friend may say: "Oh, you want an electrician? . . . Uncle
Harry fools around with electric work". Then you'll probably
get a poor job, not done per City regulations . . . and overpriced. Go to your Bank, Service Station, your Grocer, your
Supply or Hardware store . . . and ask them . . . remember . . . you are their Customer whom they do not want to
lose through a poor recommendation. You will find quite a
lot of your Suppliers will not even offer a name, because they

don't have a good one they can trust to recommend to you at the moment . . . so, ask, and ask, until you get what you want.

With such dependable retired Craftsmen, I truthfully do not always get such an agreement as below, signed . . . but I have been lucky and somewhat knowing of possible problems that I have covered before the work. However, I strongly urge any beginner-Property-Owner to get a form of information such as this one below signed. Sometimes a Craftsman "will fluff it off as unnecessary" however, there is an old saying: "An ounce of prevention is worth a pound of cure."

At the beginning, for sure, and then once a year or so to keep a good knowledge of current costs . . . get two or three estimates. Your savings will mount up.

CRAFTSMAN NAME _____

ADDRESS _____

CITY _____ STATE _____ ZIP _____

BUS TEL. No. _____ HOME TEL. No. _____

CRAFTSMAN'S INSURANCE CO. _____

POLICY No. _____ EXPIRATION DATE _____

(look at insurance card, don't take a strangers word.)

CRAFTSMAN'S SUPPLIER REFERENCE _____

(For a plumber, get a Plumbing Supply Co., for and electrician, get an Elec. Sy. Co. call them, get reference as to good work, credit, etc.)

IF PLANS ARE REQUIRED, INSIST THAT YOU OK THEM BEFORE WORK HAS BEGUN. (Of course, all this extra detail will merely add money to the job, as "time is money", but on big jobs especially, you should do all stated herein.

Possibly get names of past customers, and his Bank and talk to them. Check **B.B.B.** if they are good in your area.

JOB DESCRIPTION (in detail)_____

_____

COMPLETION DATE (within a day or two) _____

WORK WILL PASS CITY REGULATIONS?_____

WILL CRAFTSMAN HAUL AWAY DEBRIS?_____

IF PLANS ARE REQUIRED, INSIST THAT YOU OK THEM BEFORE WORK HAS BEGUN. (Of course, all this extra detail will merely add money to the job, as "time is money", but on big jobs especially, you should do all stated herein.

CRAFTSMAN'S SIGNATURE _____
                            (agreed to by)   (date)

PAID IN FULL/DATE/SIGNED BY CRAFTSMAN.

PAID IN FULL/DATE/SIGNED BY CRAFTSMAN.

One last big-tip. If the job is big, and the Craftsman requires some money in advance, or in several stages, before completion (usually they ask for some money for purchasing the materials needed for your job), be certain that THE MONEY OWED IS IN YOUR FAVOR, AND NOT IN HIS . . . THIS WILL INSURE COMPLETION OF THE JOB ON SCHEDULE, AS AGREED TO. If timing is very important, you may even want to place a penalty clause in the agreement for every day the job is late; past the agreed completion date.

TURNING GREENERY INTO GREENBACKS

* I have purposefully left this Chapter intact from the Second Printing of the Florida Edition because I just could not write it again, any better. True, you snow bunnies up North where I came from cannot do many of the tricks I describe in this Chapter . . . but I hope you will fantasize with me through this Chapter . . . and maybe you will even see what you have been missing all these years by living up North.

Read this Chapter, while simultaneously thinking of how you can adapt greenery to your area . . . even if you live in the North Pole I am certain that you have greenery that would delight us tropic-freaks. My main point anyway is in this Chapter . . . THAT ANY KIND OF GREENERY WILL TURN INTO GREENBACKS IF YOU PLANT SOME IN THE DEVOID FRONT YARD OF YOUR APARTMENT BUILDING. Tenants want to come home to an attractive entrance . . . Tenants want their guests to arrive to an attractive front entrance . . . and greenery does this job the best, and at very little cost. Call your US Dept. of Agriculture Office (the "Extension Office") . . . tell them your problems and your desires . . . and they will give you the solutions. They will also send you free pamphlets on just about any type tree, shrub or plant in your area . . . and they even occasionally give away free trees and plants. But don't wait for the freebies . . . GET INTO GREENERY AND YOU WILL HAVE ANOTHER BIG TENANT-LURE THAT WILL HOOK MR. & MRS. STARTENANT . . . THE ONES THAT YOU WANT . . . RIGHT? Now relax and read this Chapter, and fantasize that someday YOU TOO will live in the Sun Belt.

CHAPTER SIXTEEN

HOW TO INCREASE RENTS:
TURNING GREENERY INTO GREENBACKS*

Foliage, shubbery, trees, bushes, flowers, plants . . . whatever you want to mention . . . all add up to turning greenery into greenbacks. People today love greenery more and more it seems, as the environment is being threatened . . . and for sure, you can count on it, that for every green plant you invest in . . . you will get it returned one hundred fold from increased tenant rents.

Again, this is another psychological analysis about tenants. They will never admit that your landscaping has attracted them and they are willing to pay higher rents. But the normal insecure tenant likes to come home to an attractive entrance, and for sure, a guy or a gal takes pleasure in bringing friends to their apartment . . . when the entrance outside is attractive.

I have become an agronomist and a horticulturist because besides being intrigued by Tropical greenery . . . I find that growing tropical foliage produces growing rent rolls.

Now the average "joe" on the street will say that buying these plants is very expensive, and he is right. But there are other ways to buy or raise your greenery. As a famous Lady in Miami lectures . . . "don't cultivate your own plants . . . but cultivate friends who have the plants you wish (for Tropical propagation is soooo easy). I recall my favorite snow-bunny-Aunt, whose eyes popped out of her head, when I showed her how easy it was, to put a plant in the desired spot . . . the way the Floridians do it. First you dig a hole by "swiggling" the running garden hose water pressure . . . then you put one of many tree stalks that you see all over Florida, into this hole . . . then you give it several good kicks of your heel around the new tree-plant, to "gently" solidify it in its new environment . . . and voila, you have the start of a new blooming and colorful tree that would cost you $20 at the

nursery or department store . . . but instead, you did it yourself with the running garden hose and your shoe heel. My dear
Mother, who is Champion gardener up North, never told me
how much fun gardening could be. I thought it would entail a
lot of work.

Would you believe that in one hour, one afternoon that I
planted seven tree stalks (Frangi Pani blooming trees), and
they all survived and all bloomed the first year. My cost was
zero, because my neighbor was cutting back his big Frangi-
Pani tree and he was happy for me to haul away the tree limb
cuttings . . . the nursery cost would have been at least $7 a
piece or a total of $49.

There are other ways to save money on expensive plants
and trees which will improve the value of your property . . .
and your rents. I will show you where to buy your plants at
wholesale, way below the nursery cost. And do you know
that there is a Government Agency in Miami that sells plants
flowers, trees and shrubbery at greatly reduced prices? Last
year, I had this Government Agency, truck in about 20
palms, plants, bushes, fruit trees to my second apartment
building which was devoid of greenery (in fact it looked like
a bombed out Vietnam when I bought it). My cost was about
$50 . . . at your friendly nursery my cost would have been
$200 to $300.

While on the Government-subject, do not overlook the
US "Extension Service" if you are a snow-bunny with no
Tropical green thumb experience. My Champion gardening
Mother can not help me here in the Tropics for every thing is
different here. The care of your greenery is different here . . .
so just relax and enjoy it, and you will also find that it is
much easier and more fun to grow things here in Florida.

I encourage my tenants to participate in my tropical-
green-thumb activities and I offer a regular "plant distribu-
tion" to tenants. I regularly put plant cuttings by the mail
boxes (from normal garden trimming instead of throwing the
cuttings in the trash) with easy instructions to my tenants on
the "easy care" . . . simple notes like "stick a pencil in the
soil . . . remove pencil and insert plant stem . . . keep moist
AND STAND BACK (that's a rare Tropical joke inferring

that if you don't stand back that the plants rapid growth will hit you in the face).

Now my tenant has a new hobby which will save him money for the next rent increase. I am terrible am I not . . . but have you ever seen what ridiculous things tenants waste their money on? I would rather that it contribute to the continuous beautification of my premises . . . and their home.

Also, an almost forgotten tropic-technique is that foliage around your buildings can conserve energy waste for you and your tenants by shielding the apartments from direct sun heat. And a bush to protect your outside exposed air conditioning is a must. I recall that when we purchased our first building, the owner couple took us through their apartment and all the air conditioners were going full speed. We thought it a little odd because it was November. Now, after several years of letting the Hibiscus and other bushes around the house grow . . . their insulation from direct sun beams has greatly reduced our need for continuous air conditioning.

Tropic flora and fauna is fun and easy . . . get into it to turn greenery into greenbacks through increased rents via property improvement. Up North it was a drag for me and my Mother could never get me interested. But here in the Tropics I am intrigued by the ease of planting, and the many varieties from which to choose. Do you know that there are about 2000 varieties of Palm Trees? Take a tour in Fairchild Tropical Garden where they have the second largest collection of palm trees including about 1200 of the 2000 varieties. While at Fairchild, observe and make notes of the various and beautiful plants that you want on your property. Forget your roses and other Yankee plants down here . . . go native . . . go Tropic . . . and enjoy greenery without a lot of expensive care. Bromiliads to me are one of the most beautiful of all blooming tropical plants . . . blooms and grows wild in the Everglades (and will do the same in your garden) . . . so why import roses, which don't belong here in this environment.

Also get into the many flowering   trees that Dr. Menninger, Stuart, Fl. can tell you more about. He has several books on this that you can get at the library. Why

199

settle for the drab up-North type trees, when you can plant trees that bloom all or most of the year here. One of my favorites that I encourage you to plant is the Royal Poinciana tree. A magnificent tree, and huge if you have the room and space. It blooms a red or white bloom allover its huge sillouette around June. Drive down S. Miami Avenue (just West of Brickell Ave.) in June and revel in a rare tropical and beauteous sight. Get "into" fruit trees. Join a Club and learn the Tropical way, and again forget everything you ever learned up North. It's different here, but twice the fun. And your newly planted fruit trees will be a long-term joy. Don't be cheap here. Buy the best fruit trees you can find, from an accepted expert. I harvest annually 500 grapefruit, 300 key limes, 1600 oranges, 200 avocadoes, and 500 mangoes. We have regular "fruit-distribution to the tenants." Again, it saves them money for the next rent increase.

I have now discovered bamboo which is practically unseen around Florida buildings, but is such an attractive tree to look at. Almost overnight you can plant thirty foot tall bamboo trees to miraculously transform an unappealing building into a charming one to which tenants will enjoy coming home . . . . and again at increased rents. I have my own relatively unknown supplier of thirty foot tall bamboo trees that cost me only $15 each (usually 3 tree trunks) any building in town would pay $100 each for such tall trees to immediately transform an uninteresting apartment building front into a charming one.

I also recommend tall trellises. This again is instant transformation from a dingy or uninteresting building "look", to a charming building that will command more rent. There are many types of tropical vines to grow on your trellises. I have just planted some monster-philodendron below my trellises. It looks great.

Here is a funny story about me and greenery three years ago when I first came down here from the North. While we were getting oriented in Florida and living in an apartment, one afternoon I saw an old black man (building gardener) dragging a six foot stalk with beautiful sword-like leaves on it out to the dump on the street. I had just begun to fix up my terrace with tropical plants, so I stopped this gardener, and asked him what it was he was throwing out . . . and could I make it grow. He told me that it was a Spanish Sword Plant . . . and regarding it growing he said "you can't kill it". I dragged home this plant, and "couldn't kill it" on my terrace . . . and today I have transplanted it to my rear yard and it is prospering. Annually it has foot-high white cascades of blooms, and later I found that these plants are good property security since if anyone runs into one at night, they would do themselves great harm.

Also I have met many social ladies in Miami who delight in stopping at a trash dump after Mothers Day or any time of the year to pick out a gift plant that looks withered but will transform and continue to give years of beauty, just by cutting back the plant, and planting it in the yard.

The U.S. Extension Service in Florida is very strong, active and helpful here. The first year I was learning about tropical greenery, I was on the telephone to the Extension Service at least once a week. Use this service, your taxes are paying to support it.

Using tropical plants to increase the rent is a natural, and expected by most tenants, but undiscovered by so many unknowing property owners.

As you drive around inspecting apartment buildings you will find a lot of better buys among the ones that don't look too good from the front. That is the ones that have no foliage and trees, etc. in front, on the property. Historically, in talking to a lot of Miami natives, believe it or not, most of them think palm trees or any kind of tree or bush is a pain in the neck and all they complain about is "they are dirty," which translates to mean that once a week or so, they have to carry a branch, a palm frond, or some small part of the tree to the trash pile. These people are just spoiled and lazy. Secondly, these same old-timers believe, today, the old-wives-tale, that if you beautify and plant things, the Tax Assessor his next trip by will increase your property assessment. I have confronted the tax men with this tale, and they laugh (I hope not at me), and regardless I will never stop my beautification with greenery just because of this old gossipy tale. In fact my rent increases through beautification will far out weigh any increased property assessment one hundred fold. And I don't believe it anyway. But I want you to know the background of this thought and it should help you pick up a defoliated building which can be transformed into something of beauty through greenery in a few short months. A tip: Do heavy planting in around April (before the rainy season) and by Fall you won't believe the size of your plants and trees. My first year as an owner I did this. I planted about thirty trees plants, bushes, shrubs, fruit trees . . . you name it. Then once a week, throughout the rainy season I went out in the yard in the beautiful Florida morn with my log book and tape measure, and weekly I measured each piece of greenery . . . its height and the circumference at its base. You will be amazed and educated about Tropical nature if you do this. Want to know my record growth in one week? You won't believe it . . . my poinciana tree grew over two feet (26 inches) in just one week. I thought I had a mistaken "entry" until I carefully rechecked. This blooming tree, when mature is the King of beautiful blooming Tropical trees. Enjoy Florida . . . enjoy nature . . . and you will turn your greenery into greenbacks.

CHAPTER SEVENTEEN

HOW TO INCREASE RENTS:
"COSMETIZE" YOUR PROPERTY

Architectural improvements can be relatively simple and inexpensive and can greatly improve the value of your property . . . and increase the rent.

I had a rear building at my first apartment purchase that had no charm at all. In fact it looked like a "store front in a desert town off a Hollywood movie set." (I have "before" and "after" pictures to prove it.) The buildings were Spanish style so I designed and built a sturdy trellis of 4" x 4" and 2" x 2" wooden beams all along the front of this unattractive buildings' twenty foot long, first floor front. Today two years later over the top of this twenty foot trellis I have grown the beautiful "flaming vine" like you have seen in all their golden red-blooming-glory at the beautiful Hialeah Race Track. You can also see the flaming vines in Fairchild Tropical Garden and learn about a lot of other trees, vines and plants that you want around your property.

So now, what formerly was a so-so uninteresting "2 bedroom, rear apartment" is now a "garden villa" with a rent of $225. (At take over, $125.)

I did the work myself one week end at a cost in materials of about $50. However with the rental potential increase that I will receive over the next twenty years . . . and the buildings appreciation in value, you can see that even if you hire the work out to a retired reasonable craftsmen, that the cost-to the potential is certainly there.

Awnings, decks for sunning and relaxing and screened porches are all an important part of tropical living, but are too often ignored by most "native" owners of apartment buildings. Decks and awnings, up North pay off too.

AWNINGS

I have heard all the native arguments . . . that they don't last.

I buy canvas awnings with bonded plastic on both sides from my special supplier and I believe I will get ten years or more out of the modest cost involved . . . which transforms a building from a dull facade . . . to "the Country Club look." I have an apartment with an uninteresting nice size porch entrance on the second floor (about 15' x 10'). However this porch was never used other than to walk across to get in the front door. I designed and installed a lovely yellow awning (pole structure and canvass cost about $125. Today, I have given that apartment "another room" where the tenant enjoys week end brunch and spends many enjoyable hours there. This apartment rented for $100 when I took over . . . today I get $195 which is a steal . . . and the next tenant will pay $250 (for which I had a bonified offer, but could not accept because of my current lease). This apartment I will admit had unusual potential. But there are others around.

ROOF DECKS

Roof Decks transform uninteresting roofs into sunning areas for your tenants, and the decks protect your roof from people's shoes. Again it is the "country club look" for maybe $25 in lumber. Tip: Always purchase "pressure-treated" lumber in the Tropics. This lumber is injected with a chemical preservative to guard against termites, and will last indefinitely without paint which I recommend against for wooden decks. If you buy "green" lumber in the Tropics, your deck will maybe last one year. My way, it will last indefinitely and with no painting upkeep.

SCREENED PORCHES

Again too often among the vanishing species. We are in the Tropics where there are many pleasant days and evenings when you don't want or need the air conditioning. And there are plenty of tenants that let me know that they would like to save on their electric bill which is mainly the airconditioner. That is why I have gone in "on a cooperative basis" with any tenant who want to share in the cost and installation of a ceiling fan which has always been perfect in the Tropics to "move the air". These fans cost a little over $100 installed, the tenant pays $50 (and will save that on his electric bill very quickly). And the tenant has "nested" a little deeper in my nice unit which will probably preclude him from moving very quickly, even with a needed small rent increase next year.

Gazebos, bird feeders, patio furniture, lounge chairs . . . all give a nice ambience to the surroundings. I put most of these items into my garden area, and I know that my tenants rarely use them because they are too busy with day to day activities . . . but I know they know that.is nice that all these attractive things are on the property . . . and again it does impress their visitors.

Dark areas between buildings or hallways must be lighted. This stops crime, and it is important to protect you from a negligence law suit in case of an accident.

I put pink bulbs in my entrance and hallway lights instead of those stark white bulbs that can make you feel like you are in a police lineup.

If you have taken my advice and searched out your own qualified Advisor-Broker . . . one who owns apartments and believes in this business as you and I do . . . then it behooves you to put in your exclusive agreement to buy, with him, that he will give you advice after the sale on how to cosmetologize and beautify your building with little time and money. To us who have done it, it seems to come quite easy. We know what the tenant wants. We know what materials are the best, and which are the bargains, and which will withstand tenant treatment. So get it agreed that your A.-B. will give you tips on Property Improvement as you look at buildings together, and then after the sale for more help on the building that you purchase. Secondly, get your A.-B.'s confidential list of his low cost craftsmen & suppliers that he agreed to give you, as per your original agreement.

CHAPTER EIGHTEEN

HOW TO INCREASE RENTS:
SIT-TIGHT FOR MR. GOOD-TENANT

Apartment owner "strength" in not accepting just so-so tenants is very verry important.

Your natural "survival" tendency is to accept the first warm body that has the rent money in hand. But this practice can cause many problems during the tenure of the lease. "Seedy" tenants bring down your property value, and other nice tenants will leave. And you will not be able to attract other nice new tenants, at higher rentals, with "Mr. Seedy" on the premises.

Just "bite the bullet" (that means "sit tight and don't act"), let Mr. Seedy's lease application sit in the drawer . . . and lo and behold, normally the next week (if not in the next day) . . . Mr. Good-Tenant will come along. He is the ideal tenant. Good job; not too far away for his own convenience. Quiet living habits. Clean and neat appearing. Good personal and work references . . . therefore a no-problem tenant.

One time, I recall, three bachelor men applied for my two bedroom vacancy. I prefer one or two people in a two bedroom or any apartment because its less wear and tear on the property. Less coming and going traffic. Less noise. Just less of everything when you have less tenants on the property. Well these three bachelors were insistent, liked the property and the apartment and they offered me $225 monthly for this apartment for which I was asking $195. I will tell you it was a temptation but I said no. And wisely so, because the environment of this nice little five unit property would have been hurt if I would have allowed in these three bachelors, and all that would have gone along with these three people. The happy end to this story was that several days later, ONE bachelor took the apartment, on the spot. He is a newspaper writer, quiet. You hardly ever see him. He is gone a lot at work and play, and he wants to come home to a quiet and restful place, instead of those loud screaming "jungles" that some folks call "luxury apartments." I have just increased the value of my property in many ways, with this new Mr. Good-tenant. Mr. Good-Tenant will not only accept your desire to a reference check, but he will probably relish it. Good people are proud of their reputation and are happy to be checked out. In fact when I call a tenant's employer and get a good report, I know that the employer will mention it to Mr. Good-Tenant and this tenant will feel proud in front of his boss that he is handling his life in a first-class way. Therefore, when you get references be sure to call them, otherwise your new tenant will think less of you and of the property.

I always get at least two references: Employer and how long. Next of kin. A lot of people say that reference checks are a waste of time, and I will agree to a great extent. I have gotten some glowing references on tenants who have not turned out to be Mr. Good Tenant, but I have discovered some things that these all-knowing apartment owners have overlooked.

1. When I have the proper employment information. I know where to go if ever we get into litigation and I must take the tenant to small claims court. This is rare, but necessary that you know where he works.

2. Whether we realize it or not . . . we live in a violent world today and maybe one out of a hundred tenants will just disappear. What are you going to do with his belongings. It can delay you re-renting the property. Do you store his junk at more expense? All this is solved if you have "next of kin". Simply call the kin, explain, and request that they pick up the belongings pronto (after they pay any rent due).

I also get the tenant applicant's Drivers License number, from what State, and when expired. Next I get his Social Security number. With these four bits of information, you are more in control. Also, this question is needed by your lawyer in case of eviction. Military Service? Yes or No? If the applicant is new in town, first of all, I rarely will accept a tenant without a job. If he is new in town, I want him to have a job. Then since this employer reference is worthless, I get his former employer in the past city where he lived and worked, and I send this employer a short form, explaining the situation, with fill-in blanks and a self-addressed envelope. Then on the lease, I include: "Subject to verified and good job reference in former city where tenant resided."

Once in a while, with just these four reference questions, I have found that several applicants just did not return. Why? They had given me false information or they did not want the property owner to know all this information about Mr. Bad Tenant. So don't feel sorry, when an applicant who maybe you liked and thought would be a good addition as a tenant, only to never hear from him again. You have just saved yourself a lot of future headaches from a potential Mr. Bad Tenant.

Whenever a scarcity of vacant apartments hits your area, obviously it is in your best interests, as owner, NOT to give a year lease; but to issue only a "30 day lease" (see Exhibit in this book). Then if a tenant breaks your "Golden-Rules" of living on your premises all it takes is a note from you 15 to 30 days in advance; asking "Mr. & Mrs. Bad-Tenant" to "vacate the premises." In many states, if they don't move out landlord-tenant law entitles you to DOUBLE-RENT. Read the Landlord-tenant law (at the Public Library) in your state to know your owner rights. I find most owners do not know owner-rights; instead they listen to misinformation from the guy "on the next bar stool."

"THE HOW TO LIVE RENT FREE BOOK" by J. ANDERSON

REFERENCE CHECK.

(Actual form. Not made up
just for this book)

_____
(date)

To: _____

_____

_____

Mr./Mrs./Ms. _____ has given your

name as a business/personal reference, in application to rent an

apartment.

Please fill out.   Send by return mail. Thank you.

YEARS KNOWN _____

210

(Reference form, bottom half)

RELATIONSHIP _____ (friend, business, relative)

	Good	Average	Fair
CHARACTER (check one)	___	___	___
HONESTY (check one)	___	___	___
DEPENDABILITY (check one)	___	___	___
LIVING HABITS. (check one)	___	___	___
ADDITIONAL REMARKS			

_____

"THE HOW TO LIVE RENT FREE BOOK" by J. ANDERSON

Sincerely, _____

Andree Oukhtomsky
BAY VILLAS
N.E. ███th St.
Miami, Fla. 331██

211

TENANT APPLICATION FOR APARTMENT

NAME(s)_____

_____

VETERAN OF MILITARY SERVICE? YES____ NO____
NUMBER OF PERSONS AUTHORIZED IN APT.____

EMPLOYER(s)_____

_____

ADDRESS(es)_____

_____

HOW LONG WORKING THERE_____TYPE WORK____

WORK SUPERVISOR_____TEL.#_____

SOCIAL SECURITY #'S_____,_____

DRIVE LIC.#_____,_____

LIC.STATE_____,_____EXP.DATE____,__

NEXT OF KIN (in emergency)Relationship____

NAME_____ADDRESS_____

CITY_____STATE____ZIP___TEL#_____

RENT REQUIRED MONTHLY_____LEASE_____

SECURITY DEPOSIT_____

COMMENTS_____

(ACTUAL FORM USED...NOT MADE UP JUST FOR THIS BOOK)

(Don't think you are being nosey when you
ask this information.Mr.Bad-Tenant will re-
fuse.You are turning over a valuable apt.
PROTECT YOURSELF. KNOW A LITTLE ABOUT TENANT

CHAPTER NINETEEN

HOW TO INCREASE RENTS:
PROPER PROMOTION
CAN HELP FILL VACANCIES

I use For-Rent Ads . . . Hand Bills . . . and Apartment Building Brochure to reach Mr. Good Tenant and to keep my apartments filled.

During the most recent recession and even now to some extent, I hear about other apartment building owners with vacancy problems. I never seem to have these problems and all the knowledge to do likewise is herein contained in this book, not just in this Chapter. Successful management is a "Total thing" containing many elements. That reminds me of a good story to make my point. Vince Lombardi that great football coach of the Green Bay Packers was once asked, how did he "take a low ranking team and make them the first Super Bowl Champions in just a year or two?" Coach Lombardi's answer was somber, serious but simple . . . he said, "hundreds of little things." That is the same in any business I feel. If you like your business. If it interests you. And if you are concerned and aware about every little facet and detail of your business . . . then you too can say a couple of years from now, when someone asks you "how did you manage to buy that apartment building, live there rent free, and have an income from it to boot due to your rent increases?" Your answer too, like the great Coach Vince Lombardi's will be a somber, serious but simple, "It took hundreds of little things."

Here then below are three more of those "hundreds of little things" listed in this book.

NEWSPAPER ADS

I find that advertising in the top newspaper in town is the least expensive way in the longrun. If you say "but the ad is too expensive," then you just don't understand the principles of advertising. All advertising media is "is how many people you reach for your money." Some little radio stations will say they sell spots for "a dollar a holler" and that's just about how many people you would reach, and you actually would be wasting your money at what would sound like a terrific deal at "a dollar a holler." Try the biggest newspaper, and try various ads that you keep on file as you try various ways to positively and simply describe your apartment and area. Keep track. When you get better results off an ad, keep it for next time. But sometimes the biggest newspaper might just not reach your tenant-market, but maybe a local regional suburban newspaper will do better for you. The cost is relatively small and your stakes are high if you have vacant apartments without collecting rents. So experiment at first and you will quickly, if you observe, find out which newspaper is best for you.

Only use a two line ad when possible, which is 100% in my experience. Keep the ad in the newspaper daily, and not on just Sunday as some small-thinkers will do. Usually your 7 day rate becomes about half price on the daily-volume basis . . . and it only takes one Mr. Good-Tenant to fill that last vacancy. Talk to the newspaper. Have them explain various savings on ad insertion. I also use a local newspaper ad gimmick that I always schedule my ad for the thirty day rate, but I can cancel after ten (when the apartment is rented) and I still get the thirty time rate. So, investigate carefully, not casually, because you will be putting ads in the newspaper on an irregular basis but with enough volume that a savings can be important to you. Keep this ad daily in your proven newspaper until you have a new and checked out . . . Mr. Good Tenant.

I find that "price" in the ad is a good time saver for both you and the prospect-tenant, regardless whether the rent is high, medium or low. Also list ONE OR TWO POSITIVE ADVANTAGES OF THE APARTMENT. Like "extra large one bedroom" or "large screened porch" or "new bath", "patio", "garden", "cozy", "high ceiling", "thick walls", "for flower lover's", "low rent", "a jewel"

HOW TO INCREASE RENTS:
PROPER PROMOTION
CAN HELP FILL VACANCIES

"three exposures", "swimming pool", "near shops and buses", etc., etc.... Again though... SOMETHING POSITIVE.

Remember these tenants are basically suspicious (of the Landlord image) so when you get "cute" in your ad, you just cause problems, confusion and the vacancies go up ... because you are not properly communicating with tenant-prospects, in your ads.

I remember three years ago when I began, I had a beautiful one bedroom apartment for rent with three terraces, and a lot of other extras. I thought I would describe all of this apartment's glamour with one word ... "unusual". All the phone inquiries asked negatively, "what's wrong with the apartment that makes it unusual?" If I had used the extra positive few words, "quiet one bedroom apartment with three terraces" it would have sold immediately to the first qualified applicant that I would accept. The next time this apartment is for rent, I will use these words and simultaneously up the rent another 15%, and I will rent it easily.

Now with more experience I try to glamorize my ads for rent, like that oleo-margarine TV commercial where when the person eats the margarine ... a crown sprouts upon his head. Analyze why has this TV commercial had a record breaking run on TV for over fifteen years, when most TV commercials last six months at the most? BECAUSE IT DRAMATIZES THE SITUATION IN AN INTERESTING WAY ... WITH A TOUCH OF FANTASY.

So, among all the drab, me-too type ads you normally see in the newspaper, you will see my ads which contain a little drama ... a little fantasy, but never any misrepresentation because this accomplishes nothing and wastes your time with an applicant-tenant who comes over to look at something that is not really there.

Recently at my third building, I had a one bedroom apartment standing alone on the second floor of the rear building. I put up trellises on the two side porches ... a few brass fittings (at very special low prices) my regular decorator shutter-treatment in just a few windows, not throughout.

This apartment was renting for $170 . . . I now priced it a $195 (about a 15% increase) and advertised it as a "Garden Penthouse", which it is in every respect. The local main newspaper's garden editor even checked out this apartment to see what was a "Garden Penthouse". I was just dramatizing what was there. I got a nice older woman who had a lot of flowers and she is totally happy in my "garden penthouse".

If you don't feel capable to do the same with your ad copy . . . just sit down in the apartment with a creative or clever or funny friend or two and have what corporate hierarchy calls a "think tank." I guarantee that after the second drink that you will also come up with A GOOD POSITIVE DESCRIPTION OF YOUR VACANCY, WITH A LITTLE FANTASY ADDED, which will allow your ad to "stand out from the rest", which will attract a better class of applying tenants, with corresponding potential future rent increases.

I remember that my second apartment looked outside like a "bombed out Vietnam." There was no grass, plants, nothing. With autos parked in the yard. I put up a fence to keep out the autos, saying that my yard was for the people . . . then I planted a truck load of trees, fruit trees, plants, shrubs (at a very low cost from a special place I mentioned before). I put in two patio umbrellas, two picnic tables and chairs, lounge chairs, stepping stones. All of this cost me just several hundred dollars, the way I buy. Now I advertise this place, whenever I have a vacancy, as an "Adult Country Club" . . . we were flooded with inquiries and of course rented the vacancy right away to a good tenant. This was no misrepresentation. Just a little fantasy. And it was a lot better than just putting another bland ad in the newspaper for a "2 bedroom, etc., etc.

If your ad does not "pull" (no inquiries) . . . then change the copy after you have tested it about one week, including a Sunday when you should get the most "action" . . . obviously your ad had something missing. Also, look over these drab ads in the newspaper to get competitive ideas. When you see a good ad for a few days . . . then it drops out . . . that ad worked. I have gotten many ideas of items to include by looking at my competitive ads in the same newspaper column.

HAND BILLS

I usually try to put out a one-sheeter. Preferably on regular 8-1/2 x 11 paper listing my apartment value in big, big letters. I ask my local neighborhood merchants to "help their customer to rent a nice apartment" (that's me). I put my handbill in the bank, in the supermarket, in the deli, in the restaurants, IN THE NEIGHBORHOOD. This may sound like a bad idea to you at first, but when you think it out, you will realize that it is genius. Most people are attracted to "an area". If they move . . . they would probably really like to stay in that same area. So, by putting up hand-bills in your immediate area you are reaching YOUR PRIMEST OF ALL TENANT PROSPECTS.

Hand Bill copy reads in big bold type which you can hand-set yourself after a little demonstration by your local friendly stationary store manager. (Else the charge is one dollar per word.) See Handbill in the Exhibit Section of this book, along with other handy and helpful exhibits to you in apartment building management.

You may choose to make up a nice handbill and then take it to your neighborhood printer where you can have 100 copies run off "on offset" for $3.50. That's a lot better than it costing 25 cents per photo copy.

BROCHURE

If you have a large complex that merits the time trouble and the small expense, you may produce a brochure as I have done. I did it even for my first five unit, because I have a very special warm feeling for this first acquisition, and it really is fun to do, that is to put down in a nice form, all the positive advantages of living here. So, I produced eight pages (four pages on each side). I give the prospect tenant all his advantages of "his new life style at the Palm Bay Villas" (that is the name of my first place). I outline shopping, attractions

217

tenant conveniences and amenities on the property. I go into the rich history of this area (Lemon City), which was the first town in Dade County (even before Coconut Grove). The entire eight pages cost me about $25 for the printing. I did all the writing and production and I include a copy of mine as a guide if you choose to do the same. (Exhibit Section)

This brochure is my insurance of "nailing down" that perfect Mr. Good-Tenant that any property owner would like to have. The tenant that other competitors will even discount the rent to snag. After Mr. Good-Tenant inspects the apartment, he may say that he likes it but he has others he has promised to see. Usually that is not a good indication that he wants your apartment, but in some of these cases, by giving him my eight page brochure and he takes it home to read at his leisure, or perhaps shows it to someone at work who begins to rave about "what a perfect place to live." I have gotten calls back from these ideal tenants saying that they want that apartment.

Secondly, this brochure is just a nice tenant-service to help the new tenant get quickly acclimated as to the rules of the property, and where all the shops he needs are located in the area. Some of these items he would never know, or may take a year . . . my brochure is an "instant communicator" for the tenants convenience at his new address. A happy tenant is a good tenant who won't mind an increase in the future.

What's in a name? , someone said. I think names that describe the apartment building or the area are very good. Too often the owners ego takes over, and you inherit names like "Iris Apartments" (probably named in honor of dear old Aunt Iris who loaned a past owner to buy the building?). That building today under my ownership and management is the "Biscayne Bay Villas." Its surprising that that name is still available, isn't it? Yes, I filed it at City Hall . . . and its mine. This building is near the Bay, its Spanish style . . . so why not . . . Biscayne Bay Villas. I can hear my tenants tell their friends, "I live at the Biscayne Bay Villas." What's in a name? I believe a properly descriptive and glamorous name for an apartment is very important.

After reading the preceeding Chapter, you should have no difficulty in finding my ad (above).

I rented this difficult to rent apartment (shower only), off this ad, the first day . . . and, to my chosen applicant.

(Detailed apartment brochure, 8 pg's

Bay Villas

(Actual form used. Not professionally reproduced for this book)

TELEPHONE
305/756-6249

N.E. STREET
MIAMI, FLORIDA 331

YOUR NEW LIFESTYLE AT THE PALM BAY VILLAS

Your new apartment is nestled in a rare stand of giant live-oak trees, covered with monster philodendron vines. There are also twenty varied fruit trees and many species of exotic tropical flora and fauna on the property. We encourage your indoor gardening, and free cuttings are available just for the asking. We also occasionally distribute fruit, when in Season.

Your new apartment is set in a bird sanctuary-natureland, where squirrels eat out of our hands and where occasionally you will see a Mother racoon and her family, in a row, walking by. Quite often, sea-gulls circle the property after they feed in Biscayne Bay, just two houses away. Auto horns and their engines and loud radios don't awaken you here...but a tropical Whippoor-will may. We are sorry to say that for the convenience of your neighbors and the sanitary condition of the property, that no dogs and cats are allowed; nor are children ...this is an adults'-paradise. You will enjoy the quiet solitude here.

Your new apartment is on a quiet and private street in historic Lemon City, which was the first City in Dade County, and was even established before Coconut Grove and Miami; way back in the mid-1800's, when the only other three Florida Cities were Key West, Juno and Jacksonville. These pioneers traveled between these Cities and Lemon City by huge sailboats, up and down beautiful and breezy Biscayne Bay. (Refer to Dr.Thelma Peters new book,"Lemon City-Pioneering on Biscayne Bay. 1850 to 1925" Published by Banyan Books, 1976)

Nearby historic points of interest include the "Ogden Tee House" which has been converted and enlarged into your very own $5,000,000 City Parks Recreation Center; which is just two houses from your apartment in what is today, Legion Park on Biscayne Bay. At the turn of the Century, Mr.Ogden (of the Armour Meat Packing fortune in Chicago) enlarged the "old Brown House" into the shape of a "t" and covered the facade with fancy coral rock (still there today). It became the showplace where the Rockafellers, Henry Ford and other notables visited and vacationed. Mr. Ogden's paramour was a concert singer of some note, and their grand parties were usually followed by skinny-dipping at sunrise in Biscayne Bay.(This was frowned on by the neighbors). However, when Mr.Ogden was not drinking, he planted and operated a famous nursery on these grounds (todays Legion Park) of mainly grapefruit, and Ogden is said to be the first in the area to ship citrus fruit to the North in the Winter. The citrus trees surrounding your apartment are said to be on part of what was Ogden's Tee House Nursery. You can picnic in beautiful Legion Park under today's huge Banyan treeswhich were planted by school children when the property became a Park. You can play shuffleboard on its 20 Courts right on the watersedge. Thursday evenings there is a public dance, and even free lunches for Seniors. Recently, two Bocchi Courts (ancient Italian roo-the-ball-game) have also been built at Bayside. At Legion Park you can learn pottery, ceramics, yoga, languages, etc.and even join others there who sign up for their many bargain group-packaged-trips to DisneyWorld, Cruises, etc. But the best part you can enjoy anytime isto stroll over to this huge and uninterrupted expanse of water front park land right on Biscayne Bay. In front of your eyes is a stupendous view of Miami Beach in the distance, while pleasure yachts, boats and sailboats cruise past you. Directly across, with binoculars, you can see along the Miami Beach skyline those World-Famous luxury hotels. The Fontaine-bleau Hotel and the Eden Roc Hotel are directly across and a little South. Also in Legion Park there is a Bar and restaurant with very reasonable prices and a rare waterfront view. Their week end dinner-dances are popular.

Your apartment is just two houses from one of the most prestigious yacht and tennis clubs in the World...the quiet and discreet ████ Club. Millionaires and the famous belong. During the Winter Season, from the front of our property you can view some of the largest ocean going yachts in their marina. Suggestion: when someone asks you where you live, everyone understands the location when you say; "I live by the ████ Club, along Biscayne Bay."

Your apartment is uniquely situated in a quiet residential area, instead of tl usual congested apartment building areas, surrounded by large and impersonal barracks-style buildings with all their accompanying noise, pollution, crime and congestion. Your apartment at the ███ Bay Villas (only two duplexes here eliminates most of this unpleasant apartment environment. The Palm Bay Villas is for individuals that think for themselves and do not compromise.

THE MOST CONVENIENT LOCATION IN MIAMI

Here you live centrally, surrounded by Miami Beach, the chic NorthEast Miami, I-95 Expressway, Airport, Downtown Miami, New Omni Super Shopping Center, witl direct and speedy access to Miami Beach over the spectacular, toll-free 79th Street Causeway (12 blocks to the North), and the equally spectacular toll-free Julia Tuttle Causeway just five minutes to the South. Your own natureland beaches on the Atlantic Ocean have been recently completed by the City at a cost of over $5,000,000 (79 St.Cswy. to Collins/10 blks.N.). Here, instead of the continuous hotel after hotel that line most of the Ocean's Beaches, you will see only palm trees, picnic areas, and an elaborate wooden elevated walk-way system, from the street to the beach. A five minute drive tc the docks at "Miamirina" at noon or at 4:30PM will get you a fresh fish for supper, just off the boat, and at budget saving prices. While there, cross the bridge, to Dodge Island, to view the World's largest luxury cruise ship port. Saturday AM is a good day to view the many ships usually in Port

223

(Detailed apt. brochure. Actual form) #5

You have a bus-stop at our corner of Biscayne Blvd. and 67th Street. (Check the MTA for the bus schedule). Many shops and stores line Biscayne Blvd. to the North and the South of us. Just down the Boulevard in the 50's is the most stylish Publix Super Market and Eckard Super Drug Store. Next door is a large Florist and Bank. The 79th St. Shopping Center has over 100 stores, including a Pantry Pride Super Market (open Sun./great Deli-Counter), a Wal-green Drug and Restaurant, discount gasoline (USA)) discount liquor (Big Daddy) and a new proto-type McDonald's Restaurant (second only to the first in Chicago)

Just around the corner you have a 24 hour convenience store and a great-earthy Italian restaurant (67th/Bisc.Bl.) Up the street several blocks is a Kentucky Fried Chicken, and boat dockage marinas (Little River). Down the street (ten minutes) is the fabulous, just opened, OMNI SHOPPING CENTER at 16th St./Bisc.Bl. which is the largest multi-million dollar now on the Gold Coast. It includes 150 stores and shops and the only new downtown luxury hotel in Miami in 25 years (550 rooms and Convention Center Complex), also six theaters, four rest-aurants, and a large J.C.Penny's Dept.store. Also many small specialty shops as well as famous named stores from the French Riviera (like Hermes). There is a six story free parking garage behind Omni. Next to Omni is Jordan-Marsh, Sears, and Jefferson's (Montgomery-Ward) which makes Omni (just ten minutes away) the biggest and best shopping center on the Gold Coast.

224

(Detailed apt. brochure. Actual form) #6

You have two convenient boat ramps (79th St. Causeway & Morningside Park). There is also swimming and tennis at Morningside Park, and more tennis and the historic Lemon City Library at 61 St. andthe railroad tracks. And don't miss Mike Gordon's "Fish Shack"(just opened) on 79 St./near Bay. Only fresh fish is served...dinner for two, about $10.

You are living on one of the highest points above sea level in Florida (a staggering 10 feet abovesea level), downtown Miami and Coconut Grove are at sea level. That is why we are cooler in Lemon City as we get an almost constant Biscayne Bay Sea breeze...open your windows and doors and let in the Bay Breeze...you'll save money on air conditioning, andyou will be a lot healthier.

SERVICES...TO MAKE THE "LIVIN' EASY"

On the premises for your convenience is a very reasonably priced automatic washer and dryer. Please cooperate in keeping this area neat and clean for your neighbor. After using, please close the wooden laundry doors to prevent machinery corrosion. Clean the Dryer filter BEFORE using to insure a hot-dry and you money's worth. There is a clothes line for sun-dried-freaks, but please don't let clothes out on this line overnight (it looks tacky).

Your mailboxes are under the front circular stairway. We are happy to receive your deliveries when we are here. You can arrange to have our McArthur Dairy milkman deliver you milk and other dairy products right to your door step.

225

(Detailed apt. brochure. Actual form) #7

As a security measure we have very good lighting on the premises. A strong FPL Mercury light is in the front, and we have installed another mercury light by the Patio Building.

You have your very own electric and gas meter, and we pay for your hot water and your regular water consumption. We provide for all general maintenance and repair (without tenant negligence) as we intend to keep this property in perfect condition. We believe in "preventative maintenance" so advise us when something looks like it will become faulty. Unlike many owners, it won't take us forever to fix it.

We maintain general plumbing repair, not caused by your negligence in clogging up the pipes (as noted in most standard Florida lease forms). A tip: watch hair which clogs plumbing. Also food scraps and cooking grease will cost you.

There are several Hibachi's available for your Bar B Q. We only ask that you clean up afterwards and return the equipment to its place, upsidedown to prevent rust.

We provide reserved off-street parking, plus other parking places for guests.

There is a patio available for your use, with umbrella, tables,chairs,lounges.

(Detailed apt. brochure. Actual form) #8

Garbage cans are in the rear of the property, beyond the parking area, behind the privacy fence. Please put garbage in plastic bags and close the lid, for Sanitation purposes. There is one separate large garbage can for newspapers and magazines (so marked). Large junk and boxes can be put at our proper street entrance point on MONDAY'S , for Tuesday morning pick up.

The Orkin Man services your apartment every month. Leave a note in our mailbox whenever you see bugs, or whenever you have any other problem for us to fix.

We ask that you play your TV and radio at a normal volume, for your own quiet surroundings, for your neighbors pleasure, and so we do not disturb the ecological-serenity at the ▉ Bay Villas.

We have had the pleasure to restore this historic homestead property, near the original Lemon City Harbor and Dock, back to the old elegance of Key West. We call this period..."Hemingway-esque". If you enjoy this kind of quiet, relaxed and convenient lifestyle...join us at the ▉ BAY VILLAS.

227

JIM ANDERSON'S "HOW TO LIVE RENT FREE" BOOK

BISCAYNE BAY VILLAS

■ N.E. ■ St.,
Miami, Fla. 33138

Charming area. ■ St., near Biscayne Bay. Close to shops and buses.
Spacious apartment floor plan. Ideal for one or two adults.
No children and no pets, please.

The AREA: Quiet living on a private and beautiful tree-lined residential
street. East of Biscayne Blvd., but in walking distance to
shopping (100 stores"), and to Biscayne Bay. Several blocks
from the toll-free "79th St. Causeway" for quick acess to Miami
Beach; or to "Little River Parkway" for quick access to toll-
free I-95 with direct routing to Palm Beach or Key West.

The BUILDING: Restored, breezy Floridian white stucco architecture.
This is not a "concrete-jungle" of noisy apartment units.
WE ARE THE ONLY APARTMENT HOUSE ON THIS BEAUTIFUL STREET, and
we have only seven (7) apartments on this property.

The APARTMENT: SPACIOUS. Bedroom is as large as the living room. Separate dining area. Modern kitchen and bath. Three exposures.
Furnished or un-furnished. Washer/Dryer and clothes line for
those who prefer to dry things in the Florida sun. Umbrella
picnic table on flowered patio with Bar-B-Q; and lounge area
in the sun. Off-street parking.

228

FRONT BUILDING (Simple apt. brochure, bottom half. Actual form, not made up) and FLOOR PLAN; Four units. Two up. Two down. Each a two BR Convertible. AVAILABLE: _____ Upper. _____ Lower. Rent _____ . Plus Utilities.

For further information:

Jim **Anderson**, or
Andree Oukhtomsky

Tel: 305/756-6249

(inquire in English,
French or Spanish)

LIVING Room 11 x 14

KITCHEN 8x7

DINING
Room
8 x 7

BATH

CLOSET
2½x4½

CLOSET
2½x4½

BEDROOM 11 x 14

ONE BLOCK FROM: the 79th Street shopping Plaza (100 stores), including Pantry Pride Super Market; Walgreen Drug & Liquor; Lindsley Hardware; Eagle Discout Store; Big Daddy Discount Liqour; Discount gasoline; I.H.O.P.(fast food); Burger King; Banks; Fashion Stores; Savings Banks; Marinas; Restaurants (including Mike Gordon's Seafood Restaurant, down our street, on the Bay, said by many to be one of the best sea-food restaurants in Miami); and a newspaper-stand that sells newspapers from all over.

TEN MINUTES FROM: the Atlantic Ocean and Miami Beach over toll-free 79th St. Causeway... the huge new OMNI INTERNATIONAL SHOPPING

APARTMENT FOR RENT
(This is another simple apt. brochure...IN TWO LANGUAGES. Adding French to this)
DISCOUNT RENTS TO CLEAN AND NEAT ADULTS
WITH GOOD REFERENCES. NO KIDS; NO PETS.

AVAILABLE

Newly decorated. Nice quiet, clean block.
LOCATION: Near garment-district.
Close to buses on Miami Av.& 29th St.

Only six units total.	Value	Discount price.
STUDIO (two rooms)	$150.00	
ONE BEDROOM (3 rooms)	$175.00	
TWO BEDROOM (4 rooms)	$190.00	
PENTHOUSE	$190.00	

New tile floors; newly painted walls and ceilings; remodeled kitchens and bathrooms. Air-conditioning available.

New landscaping (grass, fruit trees, shrubs, flowers) in a fenced-in natureland, with several patios for your leisure. Laundry facilities. Night security light.

SE ALQUILAN' APARTAMENTOS
IN TWO LANGUAGES. Adding French to this)
ALQUILAMOS APARTAMENTOS PARA ADULTOS
SIN NINOS NI ANIMALES.
SE REQUIEREN REFERENCIAS.

DISPONIBLE

Recientemente decorado. Bonito. Silencioso,limpic
LOCALIZACION: Cerca "garment-district" con facilidad de transporte de buses en Miami Ave.

Seis en Total	Precio Regular	Descuento
STUDIO (2 cuartos)	$150.00	
UNA ALCOHOBA (3 cuartos)	$175.00	
DCS ALCOHOBA (4 cuartos)	$190.00	
PENTHOUSE (3 cuartos)	$190.00	

Nuevo pisos; Recientemente pintados sus paredes y techo. Cocina y cuartor recien remodelados. Aire acondicionado a gusto.

Nuevos jardines (arboles, zonas verdes flores) Varios patios cercados. Facilidad de lavanderia' y luz noctura de seguridad.

tored to their original newness. If you are
an INDIVIDUAL, who is not interested in living in those noisey, and impersonal, and crowd-
ed, modren concrete-barracks-type apartments
...then you will like DON MEJOR VILLAS.
"look for the brand new security-fence.

(Bottom half, simple, two language apt.brochure. Actual one used. Not made up.)

...restauradas recientemente para mayor comfort.
Si ud. es una persona que le gusta el silencio
y la privacidad de nuestros apartamentos que
no son fabricados en serie .Ud.debia' visitar.
Tenemos cerca nueva en el terreno.
El dueno esta' accesible.

130 N.W.27th Street

TWO BR	TWO BR
STUDIO	STUDIO
ONE BR-up-	ONE BR-down

DON MEJOR VILLAS   N.W. STREET, MIAMI 33
(owner-supervised daily for your greater comfort)

(Andree speaks Spanish,French)

Call owner telephone first... 7 AM to 10 PM...
Owners Home Telephone: 756-6249. Jim or Andree.

La Casa Del Dueno, TELEFONO: 756-6249(Jim/Andree

SECURITY MONEY AND REFERENCES REQUIRED.

SEGURO Y REFERENCIAS REQUERIDAS

231

APARTMENT *FOR* RENT

(Actual form used...not made up just for this book)...
This is the for-rent poster example...to post in neighborhood shops.

QUIET & PRIVATE

BY BAY-CENTRAL

756-6249

232

(Neighborhood For-Rent Poster) Actual Poster...not made up.)

NEW PAINT INSIDE AND OUT...NEW ROOF...NEW VINYL TILE FLOORS
GAS STOVE SAVES YOU MONEY...REFRIGERATOR...NEW AIR CONDITIONERS IN FIVE UNITS
OUTSIDE: TWO UMBRELLA PATIOS AND PICNIC TABLES...LOUNGE CHAIRS...BAR B Q.
WASHER AND DRYER AND CLOTHES LINE.
PLANTS AND FLOWERS GALORE...EVEN FRUIT TREES.
$1,000 chain link fence surrounds the property. Security light in rear.

DON MEJOR VILLAS
N.W. ST. MIAMI FL. 33

for info. or appt. call Mr. or Mrs. Anderson

(FROM A NATIONAL NEWSWIRE SERVICE)

AUTHOR/INVESTOR LISTS SIX COMMON MISTAKES
MADE BY BEGINNERS IN REAL ESTATE INVESTMENT

MIAMI, Dec. 18 — Jim Anderson, a Real Estate investor and author of the book "HOW TO LIVE RENT FREE" (Brun Press, New York Paris), says his advice can help anyone — homeowner or renter — live rent-free in a "quadplex", but he warns of six mistakes commonly made by beginners in real estate investment.

"I constantly get calls from investors who go through all six of these mistakes in just one short telephone call," says Anderson. "Remember It's your life savings and you can have a lifetime of happiness if you don't goof."

These are the six mistakes beginners make.

1. Having partners. "I find that one partner does all the work while the other partner gets half the profit. And the dead-beat partner never seems to want to sell. Would you if you got a free ride?"

2. Using the selling broker. "Would you ask your wife's lawyer for advice in your divorce? Well, 99 percent of the people ask the selling broker for advice on their purchase. Instead, get a no-cost, advisor broker to act as your purchasing agent. He gets half the commission from the seller. It costs you nothing . . . and you have become one of the smart one percent who buys property the right way."

3. Getting greedy and overextending after you see what you have been missing after you buy your first quad. "Be patient. Save on your job and your income tax shelter . . . then buy quad No. 2."

4. Buying vacant land. "That is a crap game played by the high flying speculators and tycoons. Wait and do that later; after you have made your fortune. Also land will become your second non-productive investment together with your non-productive home. I believe land and the home payments put more men six feet under than anything and give the Nation a bevy of long term widows. With all the pressure involved and needed to make the money to make those monthly payments on these two non-productive investments."

5. Building your first quadplex. "It seems we all have the mother instinct to 'give birth.'" Forget it. It is risky. Your total cost cannot be predicted with rising costs; nor can your income be figured correctly. Buy an existing quadplex on a cold calculating business like basis of six to eight times annual rental, and you will not go broke by building and you will not end up with a sexy-lemon (a poor buy)."

6. Being an absentee owner. "I constantly hear 'I rented my house Florida and went to New York, and my house was ruined.' The owner was too casual. The owner did not select a proper tenant, nor did the owner draw up a proper lease with the proper security money guarantee. And finally, the owner rented the property, and then left town. I live within five minutes of all my property's along beautiful Biscayne Bay, and I want to drive by regularly just to see what's going on. I own the building, remember. And only my concern will properly continue my property values to go up."

Q How many Americans today can really afford that rose-covered cottage we all used to dream about?

(Reprinted with the permission of the Miami Herald)

— MICHELLE REON FOX / Miami Herald Staff

THIS FRONT PAGE CARTOON IN THE MIAMI HERALD IS TYPICAL OF COAST TO COAST NEWS REPORTS, RESEARCHING THE FACT THAT THE SINGLE FAMILY HOME (THAT FORMERLY POPULAR ROSE COVERED "MILLSTONE") HAS NOW BEEN PRICED OUT OF BUDGET OF THE AVERAGE FAMILY . . . BUT WHY BE CONCERNED . . . YOU CAN OWN A QUAD-PLEX OR A DUPLEX . . . AND LIVE THERE RENT FREE, AND PAY LESS INCOME TAX ON YOUR SALARY. YOU WILL HAVE A MORE SECURE AND HAPPY LIFE, WITHOUT HAVING TO SUPPORT THAT UNPRODUCTIVE MILLSTONE AROUND YOUR NECK.

A Using the formula that the purchase price should be no more than double the buyer's income, recent estimates show that fewer than three out of 10 families could afford a median-priced new home last year. In 1950, the figure was seven out of 10 American families.

235

NOTES & QUESTIONS

CHAPTER TWENTY

HOW TO INCREASE RENTS:
PUT IN A FEW AMENITIES

Condominiums have gained great acceptance and success by adding nice conveniences and luxuries to their property. Why shouldn't us apartment owners do it, but on a smaller scale? Immediately, when I purchase a building I put in a substantial patio area in the garden. It looks nice to the new prospect tenant, regardless of whether the tenants use it at all. I put in an umbrella table with benches (I use the round concrete table with benches, they are durable and attractive enough), lounge chairs, Bar-B-Q, bird bath, bird feeder . . . a little park nature land, regardless of what size you are working with. This entire set up cost me about $150, and I have put an entirely new atmosphere into the apartment complex.

I am basically against swimming pools (when I don't have them) and I explain to the tenant prospect that pools create a lot of noise, and can be unsanitary if any kids use the pool. I like to provide a private sun deck area, with a lounge or two. Also possibly a table and a beach umbrella, and you and your tenants have the best of both Worlds . . . you have a nice area in the garden to sunbathe . . . and without the pool noise. We, as owners have even built our own private garden area.

Another needed amenity is an automatic coin operated washer and dryer. At my first building, the tenants had to go to the nearby "laundromat" with their soiled clothing . . . what a bore, and you can't up-rents with such ill regard for tenant necessities. I immediately put in a nice washer and dryer that we use too. The coins will pay it off plus the repairs. However, now I use a washer service, whereby they furnish the washer and dryer at no charge, take off a service charge, then divide the remainder with me. I have this service

JIM ANDERSON'S "HOW TO LIVE RENT FREE" BOOK

at my second and third buildings and prefer it to buying and servicing my own. My first investment in the total washer dryer area was about $1,000. Perhaps in a larger complex, this way would pay off handsomely. Its all in "the numbers" to chose which way is best for you.

I suggest, always try to have a clothes line. Preferably hidden and out of the way, in the far back area of the property. Because no matter how you approach it, some tacky tenant will leave clothes on the line overnight, and that does not improve the property's appearance.

NIGHT SECURITY LIGHTS

Night security lights are a must. Regardless of how nice the neighborhood is where your apartment building is located . . . they all "get hit" occasionally. Police will tell you that the best CRIME DETERRENT IS PLENTY OF LIGHT. One discovery of mine is that you can install a 150 watt Mercury light, which throws off about four times the 150 watt candlepower (600 watts) for the energy cost of 150 watts. To me when I discovered this, I felt it a bargain, and I installed them.

Two more ideas on the Police. First, when you first get your building, call the Police, have them come over to give your property an inspection as to how safe your apartments are against crime. They may advise new locks for the future, etc., etc. The service is free. You pay for it as a taxpayer. Similarily, have the Fire Department over to inspect your building for fire hazards. Secondly get to know some of the officers at Police headquarters. I am very serious. You as a new apartment owner owe your tenants protection, and you want your own property to be protected by the Police. But as I said in an earlier Chapter . . . we live in a violent age, and the Police are overworked with crime in any city in the Country. So, some night when you or your tenant needs immediate Police assistance . . . you will wonder why it took them thirty minutes to get to your apartment . . . or why you had to make three phone calls before you got any action

HOW TO INCREASE RENTS:
PUT IN A FEW AMENITIES

from the Police. They are merely overworked, and they go where they feel is the priority. So, call and get to know a Lieutenant or a Major (maybe, over lunch or a drink). You explain to them that you are a new apartment owner in the area. That you want to meet the Police and to get any suggestions as to how you can run a more crime free area around your apartment. He will be delighted that you are planning ahead. He will help you, and he will become your friend, even to the possibility that he will give you his home telephone number for special emergencies. My new Lieutenant friend did this for me, and I consider him a real new friend and an asset to me as a new property owner. Just a simple example, say one of your tenants or a neighbor continually is making too much noise at night, and the tenants can not get the Police there to stop it. You make your call when all else fails to your Police friend, and you get the noise stopped, which has been depreciating your property, and even possibly jeopardizing your no-vacancy rate. Tenants will move out if there is continuous noise . . . that is good tenants will.

If your apartment is near a park or other nice bicycling area, try to install a bicycle rack with shelter, where your tenants can chain up a bicycle. It is not convenient in the apartment, to store bicycles. Help make a tenant happy and you will have a Mr. Good Tenant.

Tenants always need more storage. If you have some public area on the property that you can convert into storage lockers by all means do it and you will get better and happier tenants. You can even charge a small rental fee, which will pay for the lockers construction. And you will be adding value and future higher priced rentals to your property.

Keep a good attitude that you want to make it as nice and pleasant for your tenants as possible. The old style "landlord" tried to get away with the "leastest" . . . that is the short-term attitude, that will not appreciate your property to the degree that I have done or to the degree that you wish to attain. The little money involved will always return to you TEN FOLD.

"THE PALM BEACH PRIVACY COMPOUND" — Some Millstone owners fear of a "loss of privacy" when they live in their quad-plex. I answered a Dallas talk-radio host recently when he asked me that, "if you were really paronoid about PRIVACY ... the best solution could be a 100 acre ranch." Secondly: many millionaires live in 100 unit buildings in a condo costing up to $500,000. I know a person in Miami who is selling her $500,000 condo-penthouse because the management does not control the Grandchildren skate boarding down the halls and lobbies.

I am master of my domain in my Quadplex. If anyone makes noise or in general breaks my laws of living on my Property (remember they have signed a strong agreement, backed up by two months security which is automatically forfeited if they break their agreement)... this lawbreaking Tenant is simply told to leave (30 day lease), or is evicted in the minor few cases where necessary. I just don't have such problems as the candy-store-owners tell you; or the person on the "next bar stool" OR your "friendly Seller-Broker" who usually does not own rental Property (he also believes all the old wivestales). So, actually, I become Lord & Master of my domain AND I ACTUALLY CONTROL MY ENVIRONMENT that even the millionaires cannot control in those fancy Condos. Lastly, I have created the "Palm Beach Privacy Compound, named naturally after the place where I first got to know them. Each of my Tenants apartments have one or more of the following: 1. A shrub fence surrounding their private patio. 2. A trellis with vines doing the same. 3. An awning or trellis overhead of this patio for privacy and noise-control (I do allow a VERY little noise). The old style Quad had ONE patio area for everyone. I found my Star-Tenants didn't use this Public-Patio ... but they love my P.B. patios and are happy to pay more rent for them ... (and I never know my Tenants are on the Property).

Lastly on "privacy" ... I find the "candy store operators" deserve all the noise, commotion, and Property destruction that they get (through poor or no screening of Tenants ... and no strong heart-to-heart talk as to the rules of the Property (backed by the Tenants signed agreement together with two months rent as "security") ... forfeiture of this sizeable chunk of money if the Tenant "even looks cross-eyed" as to promises they have made and signed. I find that Star-Tenants enjoy my hard-line on the rules-of-living on my Property. I have even had a nice couple bring by a bottle of imported wine for the "tough Lease signing" ... as they said ... "other Property owners don't seem to care like you do Jim ... we want peace and quiet and a nice well run place to live which is as close to home living as possible. Jim Anderson ... you are a rarity and we want to live under your strict conditions, which will only benefit all four of us."

I also select my Tenants as to how often they are away on business. My old building where I live, and where I inherited a set of so-so Tenants ... now, by applying my 10 Chapters on fix-up ("show Biz decor"), I now have a fashion designer I hardly ever see, who travels to NYC and California monthly. She has a 2BR all to herself. She uses the second BR for her Artist studio. Similarly, another 2 BR is rented by a top commercial photographer. He uses the 2nd BR for a photo studio. The third apartment, I am the proudest of; this Publisher & Editor of Florida's top Designer/Architecture 4 color slick magazine uses my 1 BR only 3 days a week when they come to Miami from their mansion in Palm Beach to work on their regular magazine. These people have ultimate taste ... they could live in any stylish condo they choose ... they choose my Quadplex. GIANT OAKS GROW FROM ACORNS.

CHAPTER TWENTY ONE

HOW TO INCREASE RENTS:
"THE LEASE SECRET"

Some sort of written agreement is normally preferred. You could discover that all your tenants' good promises and intentions from your initial interview can be soon forgotten when Mr. Tenant takes possession of the apartment. And only count on what is put down on paper and signed by you both and a witness. This is the same advice as I gave to you when you made an offer to buy a building with the Contract For Sale form. Remember? Only count on what was put in writing and signed by both parties and a witness. This is good and proper advice for you to follow on any business dealings you enter. People are normally too casual and (not dumb for they really know better), its just laziness. And such laziness has no place if you intend to be in business for yourself.

I also know a lot of apartment owners who are against leases. Their main complaint is that they cannot kick out an unruly Tenant. I cover this very well in my "Lease Secret" below. Secondly, these owners say a lease does not give them the flexibility to increase rents. Well I would hate to be in such a "close" situation on Capital that I could not plan a year ahead on my finances which is the only term that I normally sign a lease for down here in Florida. I know that in New York City I used to want and ask for a three year lease with a renewal clause for the rent to increase "no more than X%". Then if business conditions deteriorated, potentially I could renew this lease at the current price or even lower. But down here I find it is a lot less sophisticated, and the one year lease just suits me fine and I have all the flexibility regarding rent increases.

One story which gives a good example "for leases" is the following. I was delighted with a new tenant I had just gotten when I was new in this business. She was an executive, recently transferred to Miami. She moved in a van of furniture and I felt that I had a solid long term tenant. But six months later her girl friend got divorced. These two decided to move in together, but they chose the other girl's apartment "because it was bigger." My tenant would have probably stayed with me . . . if she had a Lease. Maybe her girl friend would have moved in here if I had a lease.

You can secure a supply of Standard Lease Forms at most stationery stores for about 10 cents each. And I tell this fact to a tenant who feels a little uneasy about signing what may be his first Lease. When he realizes it costs 10 cents in a store, and it is not some sharp document prepared by some unprincipled lawyer, this seems to relax the tenant who is about to sign his first Lease.

Sometimes there are various Lease forms available with slightly varied wording and form. I would get the advice of a competent Realtor as to which form to use. In Miami my Broker friend pointed out that of the three Lease forms available . . . one of them contained the all important clause making the tenant responsible for stopped-up plumbing. This clause can save you a lot of money over the years in plumbing bills and your tenants will be more careful in not clogging up the plumbing. In fact I add an additional clause suggesting that the tenant do not put grease of food scraps down the drain . . . no hair in the "john", etc. Then I point out this plumbing clause in the Lease and have the tenant initial it, as clear legal proof that the tenant was so informed.

Also, one of these Lease Forms has an inventory check list on the back-side, which is helpful if you rent furnished apartments.

THE LEASE RIDER

This is my secret which I feel has contributed greatly toward me having mainly great tenants, which upgrade my property which continually allows me to increase rents.

I have put on a single sheet of paper various additional "rules of the property" which in today's more casual and lenient society has been very helpful to me in moulding my tenants into star-tenants. This sheet is also headed "Rider to Lease".

Such items that are listed may seem too basic, but remember . . . "if it is not in writing . . . don't count on it."

My rules of the property include "no loud radio, TV or noise ever, and especially after 10 PM" . . . "one off-street parking space". If you don't list this, tomorrow your new tenant may haul in his boat, or truck or motorcycle. In fact I add, "no boats, trucks or motorcycles." If you get a star tenant who later wishes to buy a motorcycle . . . then you are in the drivers seat and can allow him permission of a motor-cycle on your property "only as long as he is quiet with it, and the other tenants do not complain." So, Mr. Tenant is on the spot. He normally is not allowed a motorcycle, which is stated in the agreement and signed by him . . . however you will allow this motorcycle only if your rules above are follow-ed. Now Mr. Tenant will do your bidding. I give this example in detail, because it can be applied to any other special re-quest that later develops from Mr. Good Tenant.

More "rules of the property". "No papers or cigarettes or refuse can be thrown on the ground." (I don't want to be the janitor, and I state this to them, plus the fact that I only want neat tenants.)

"Security money is non-interest bearing." There is a possibility that you could be forced some day by some legal-beagle tenant to pay you Security Interest if you do not state this fact in the agreement. Most tenants will never bother you with this, but for that one out of a hundred who may . . . PUT IT IN WRITING.

Perhaps "no children or pets." Many of you probably have children, but as a new apartment building owner you must realize that often children can be destructive because of too-lenient parents. So, I stay flexible on this subject. Never be rigid. But I protect myself, IN WRITING, whenever the parent pleads to be allowed her child in the apartment, and you get all the grandiose statements about how well behaved the child is. I calmly say, "well I have a general rule against children, because normally the parents don't make them mind . . . but if you are willing to put it in writing (about the child's good manners), then I will allow the child. My special lease-clause goes like this... "Tenant is given special privilege for her 15 year old child to share this apartment which is normally for adults only, as long as parent's child is well behaved, well-mannered, and clean as guaranteed to landlord by the parent. This special permission will expire if my other tenants (your neighbors) complain about the poor conduct as stated above by your child. If child causes a nuisance, you and the child can be evicted on one week notice with loss of security money." Nice places are scarce to find where children are allowed, simply because most property owners have found that most of these children destroy the property, cause too much noise, and in general, degrade the property.

When you find a parent who will sign a tough statement, such as the one above... you know that you have found a good parent that has control over the child, and you have acquired another good tenant which will upgrade your property. I have found that about 25% of the parents will sign such a guarantee of their child's conduct. Only accept those parents that agree to this in writing, otherwise your property will depreciate with unruly and messy children, not controlled by thinking and orderly parents.

Similarly regarding pets, I tell the tenant-prospect that I will consider pets if we have a "good pet conduct guarantee" in the lease. My wording is such, and again tough, but if I give the favors I must get something in return. Here is my "pet clause." "Tenant is given permission to keep one small cat (be specific) in said apartment. Tenant says that the cat is quiet and will not cause wear and tear to the property. If cat damage does occur, tenant agrees to repair said damage immediately to the owners satisfaction. Furthermore, when the tenant vacates said apartment, tenant agrees to have rugs professionally cleaned to rid them of cat odor and hair, for the good pleasure of the next tenant. Obviously any rug discoloring caused by the tenants cat means that the rug must be replaced to the owners satisfaction. Tenant acknowledges that the rugs are in new (or good) condition. Further, tenant agrees not to let this cat roam the neighborhood alone...

only on a leash." When a tenant signs this, I am fairly well insured that I have a nice and happy tenant, because although I prefer singles, since it means less people on the property, I find that a single with a pet is a happier and a more solid and contented person. This is not to say that most people who live alone are not good prospects, but I am stating why I am not rigid to a tenant having a pet, wherein most apartment building owners simply have a flat rule . . . no kids . . . no pets. That is too rigid for me, and I will exert myself, to take the extra step with the protection this clause gives me against a lot of tenants who will casually promise anything, but will do little that is not agreed to in writing.

One of my "rider to lease" forms is included in the "exhibit section". I suggest that you tailor one to your own property needs. Good tenants do not mind such a strict lease . . . in fact they appreciate it because they know that all tenants are under the same conduct-code which they know will make for a pleasant surroundings and living environment.

Tenant reference information is covered in another Chapter, However I find it convenient and good for legal reasons to put down all tenant reference information right on the face of the lease instead of on a little scrap of paper. With my way, this information becomes a part of the lease agreement, and any misstatements by the tenant could jeopardize his lease. So type right on the lease "next of kin" and "work reference". . . . "drivers licence, State, and expiration date," and "Social Security number." Now heaven forbid that a year from now you will ever have to take this tenant to small claims court, but if you do, you have all the proper information for your court action. Also needed, "was tenant a veteran?"

SECURITY MONEY

Many apartment owners still use mistakingly the old phrase "first and last months rent required to move in." It should be written as "first month's rent and one month in Security money required to move in." This technicality is taught in real estate class because first and last does not properly protect your property the way it is stated. Further with "first and last," this infers that the tenant does not pay the last month rent because he has done so in the beginning. I want my tenants to pay the last month's rent . . . then as I clearly state in my rider-to-lease . . . that "if the apartment is returned to the owner in the same clean condition as it was turned over to the tenant, with nothing broken, discolored, etc. . . . then upon inspection of the apartment when tenant leaves and returns the keys to the owner . . . then the tenant security money is returned." "However, if work is required to return said apartment to the original good condition that the tenant acknowledged when he moved in . . . this repair and fix up and clean up will be paid for out of the Security money, with the remainder given to the tenant after all repairs to the apartment have been made."

Sometimes I will allow a new tenant to pay PART of the Security money over perhaps a three month period if otherwise the new tenant could not "swing" the deal. Example: on a $200 rent normally you would get $400 (first month plus one month Security). I don't like to accept a tenant that doesn't have $400 to his name, because he just is not truthful or does not really look out for his future. However, if you decide to compromise, and remember, there are a lot of apartments available without security money, or perhaps just a $50 payment . . . so in some cases I will allow a tenant to move in for perhaps $250, with the other $150 Security money to be paid to me, say, in $50 payments over the next three months. If you make a deal similar to this one, always talk it out clearly with the tenant, be certain that he can "swing the deal," AND PUT IT IN WRITING IN THE LEASE.

Further on "move in money" . . . some owners require three months rent to move in . . . first, last, and Security. I think this is a little steep. For when you figure that is $600 to move into a $200 a month apartment . . . I have seen condominiums that are advertised FOR SALE for just a little more than $600 (maybe $800 or $900). So, if you can get it, by all means do, because the more of your tenants money you have . . . the more control you have of the situation.

HOW TO INCREASE RENTS:
"THE LEASE SECRET"

However, don't sit with a bunch of vacancies because you are holding out for three months rent to move in.

If your tenant skips out owing you money from a bad check, or with damage to your apartment . . . don't just ignore it like many owners do. It is a very simple matter and just costs $10 (which the tenant will have to pay after you win your case in court). You go down to the Justice building where a polite Clerk will fill out all the forms for you. Don't be talked into "going home and filling them out yourself," because like all bureaucratic forms you will probably fill out something wrong, or make an omission and after several tries and a lot of lost patience and valuable time . . . you will give up. You have your dead-beat tenant's business place and address on your Lease, and you have the Court send his notice there. (Always keep your tenants job changes updated therefore.) This first embarassment at work will probably get your former tenant to settle out of Court. But promises are just promises. Get it in writing for possible future action (which now gives you more proof to the Judge that the tenant "acknowledges his guilt." And also if the former tenant has promised on a pay-schedule basis to repay you . . . get that in writing, with dates, signed by both with a witness . . . and (another secret) call the small Claims Court, tell the secretary that you "wish to extend and delay the date of the Court hearing since the defendent (former tenant) has promised to pay off." With this little call you save going down to fill out another claim form latter for an other suit, you save another $10 of your former tenants money . . . and you tell your ex tenant, that your will "delay the hearing" (you are not going to CANCEL the hearing). This puts Mr. dead-beat tenant's hands right on the stove, and he'll probably pay up on schedule.

Now, if the ex-tenant goes to Court remember that you must be calm and be well mannered, because Judges are very tough on ill mannered people in Court. State your case very clearly and truthfully (usually from notes or from a typed out statement of facts) and mention every time your case is proved by so and so "in writing" . . . "signed by Mr. ex-tenant."

Also do not hire a lawyer unless you feel you are totally inept at what I have described. The Judge will have less pity for your case if he sees you can hire a lawyer and the dead-beat cannot. That is why it is called Small Claims . . . ie, small suits usually practiced by the Plaintiff and Defendent themselves, with no lawyers present.

If you can provide a witness to back up your testimony, that is fine . . . but I have won all my cases by myself, even if the ex-tenant brings in some lying witness . . . since I always have my claim backed up in writing and signed by the ex-tenant. This is the primary legal point that the Judge will consider to decide.

Regarding damages, Small Claims will only judge in your favor to ACTUAL lost money by you. That is, apartment damage, loss of rent due to tenant leaving. I have tried to get Judges to rule in my favor for say the remaining three months on a lease, pleading that the tenant was irresponsible in signing a one year lease and did not fulfill his contractual obligation. However I have had no luck with position to date. My next attack will be to put a clause perhaps in my lease-rider, stating that the tenant "is responsible for the twelve months rent, regardless when he vacates" . . . to my feeling . . . this kind of committment from the tenant in writing would make the Judge rule in my favor for the entire amount of the remaining lease. My latest solution on this is to clause the lease thusly: "Tenant has right to choose between Winter rent Oct./Mar. of $300 Mo. and Summer rent Apr./Sept. of $100 Mo. . . . or at the average annual rental rate of $200. What this will do in Court is to get you a bigger settlement for the Winter months in lost rent.

And now the good news. You can find a good "back-alley-lawyer" that handles many small claims for small business if you attend one of the Small Claims Courts Pre-Trial Hearing. (Just call and get the next time and date.) In this pre-trial hearing you will note several lawyer types answering the call for many cases (not just one like you would have). Sidle over to this lawyer and ask his rates. I did this and now I don't bother. I pay about 30% of the settlement money I win, to the lawyer, and they charge about $50 for an eviction. Which is worth it, unless you enjoy paper work (and I do not). However, now that you know about what you should pay (from small claims type lawyers . . . not the fancy corporate types) . . . you can go to the telephone book to check prices. (But you'll miss the Court House adventure.)

Some thoughts and solutions about the few tenants who pay late.

Some unthinking tenants like to wait around until the tenth of the month to pay their rent. Psychologically, its really a case of rebellion. These tenants really don't want to pay rent and secretly wish they were the property owner . . . or at least that they had unlimited wealth with no worries about that monthly rent payment.

Many tenants also have visions that the landlord is filthy rich and really doesn't need his little rent money. (To these I answer . . . "take my building . . . take my mortgage.") Of course I like my situation, but to a tenant or a craftsman . . . this is a good answer about your "building wealth."

Incidentally (a little conscience-raising) I never refer to myself as "landlord," be it to a tenant, to the Government, or among friends. The word landlord has acquired a bad terminology of the "bad guys," who simply collects the rent . . . and continuously raises the rent, without ever improving the property or the apartments. The inference of "landlord" is . . . that if your air conditioner conks out just as Summer begins . . . you cannot count on its repair until Fall, at the earliest.

That description does not fit me, and I hope and trust it will not describe you. Don't be "penny wise and pound foolish" as they used to say. For that is the nearsighted approach not to continuously improve your property and its units. And why irritate a good tenant by delaying repair of the air conditioner (if it wasn't the tenant's fault) . . . you will have to do it sooner or later. This kind of delay and procrastination on your part is just harassment of the tenant. It's also stupid. If you are a procrastinator (and all of us suffer somewhat from this malady) as a new apartment building owner . . . as a new business man . . . decide to change those errant ways. The way I began was to keep a note pad by my favorite TV and reading chair. As I thought of the things I had to do I wrote them down. Then fresh in the AM (when I began to think, but forgot) what I had to do . . . I referred to this list . . . and whammo . . . I began to get things done. It works for me . . . try it yourself.

And so now, the word I use to describe myself to everyone is not "landlord" . . . but PROPERTY OWNER. It has a nice sounding ring to it, doesn't it? "Property Owner" gives you the distinction you deserve. Maybe one out of every ten thousand persons has been successful enough, enterprising enough, shrewd enough, saving enough, to be able to become an apartment building owner. So call yourself a "property owner." It will bring you dignity and the honor that you deserve. Also you will notice more respect from your tenants and all your business and government contacts.

RENT ON TIME

Rent on time is really very simple to overcome when you realize the problem's root and then consider solutions. Simply put in your lease, and get the new tenant to agree (before he moves in, when he is willing to agree to almost anything) . . . that there is a "ten dollar penalty for late payment of rent." Explain to the tenant that you must make your mortgage payment (and maintenance payments perhaps) on time or you have to pay a penalty. And if the tenants pay rent late, then you the property owner are sometimes forced into a "cash squeeze," and are forced to borrow short term money at a high interest rate.

When an explanation like this is carefully and slowly given to the new tenant, he will usually understand "the why" and promptly pay his rent on time. Too many property owners (as most business men) just spout-out "the rules" without giving "the why" (the explanation). This policy is good business practice in all respect of human contact person to person . . . give the reason-why . . . communicate . . . few people do.

Even with all this expertise (and you are becoming a lay-psychiatrist practicing on your tenants) you will still have an occasional tenant always late with rent (some people, poor souls, just can't get life together). If it is paid by the tenth of the month, I probably overlook it . . . if otherwise the tenant is a good tenant in other respects. Quiet enough. Neat enough. A no problem tenant.

But when the rent is not paid past the tenth of the month, you are flirting with the danger of a tenant skipping out (you still have the security) and in Florida we have a little "do it yourself legal paper" that usually does wonders in breaking loose that rent money from a holdout tenant; in fact it will probably "scare the Bejesus" out of your tenant to such an extent that you will never again be bothered with late rent from that errant tenant . . . and it will only cost you ten cents to apply this unusually strong pressure.

I feel that some tenants "test you" (more conscience raising) . . . they want to see "what you are made of." If you don't react firmly and do not act decisively, then the tenant becomes "in charge," and then look out, for you have lost command of your property.

Now this little ten cent legal paper, sold in your nearest stationery store is called NOTICE TO TENANT, so solemnly printed in Old English. (See copy in "exhibit section" of this book). This little Form looks very official, and it is. It demands the rent within three days (some. lawyers refer to this form as "the three day form"). There is a place for your name and your lawyers. I send out these notices myself and save the legal fee, but I always insert my long legal firms name (the longer . . . the more intimidating to the tenant). For sure TYPE up this form . . . hand written would not be impressive to a dead beat tenant. Nine out of ten tenants will cough up the late rent immediately . . . This three-day-notice works better than ex-lax. And since you have sent this notice about the 11th or 12th day late . . . with the rent due on about the 15th day late . . . the tenant has not delayed you long enough if he has decided "to skip" . . . so on the 15th he pays, because you have struck speedily . . . you have acted decisively and without procrastination. You have surprised your errant tenant, even maybe while he was planning to move, but on such short three day notice . . . he just gives up and pays the rent. If you procrastinate and wait till the 20th or 25th late rent day, the shady tenant will probably have already left his apartment.

Here is a little story as to why some "landlords" have gotten callous to all the tall-tales-tenants-tell. It was last year, my second year in this business, and I had just purchased my third apartment building in September, and now Christmas was approaching. One of my inherited tenants, that I didn't know too well, asked me if I would let him pay his December rent "after Christmas, so he could buy some gifts for his son who lived with his divorced wife." Pretty sorrowful tale wasn't it? I said, "of course," (wouldn't you?). . . not realizing that it was a tenant-con-job. Would you believe he skipped out the day after Christmas? I had his Security money of course . . . maybe he didn't trust me that I would return it to him, so he used up his Security money through a tall-tale, and then disappeared. What a waste of energy. You will find that tenants like to blame their problems on others . . . an ex-wife, a mother in law . . . usually a child works the best though. So after three years or more of hearing THE TALL TALES TENANTS TELL, I am now very objective. I give a little compassion, but now realizing that at least part of the tenant story is probably just that . . . "a story" . . . so I give a little, but past the 11th late rent day . . . and decisively on the 15th late rent day . . . I move quickly and decisively by sending out the "three day notice form" . . . this usually breaks the log-jam in 9 of 10 cases . . . otherwise after three days you can evict through your own action or through a fifty-dollar-special from a small claims lawyer.

Incidentally, save yourself a lot of wasted energy . . . go to post-office and purchase a supply of "Certified-Letter" supplies, ie, the Certified sticker with the certified number on it, the certified slip, etc. for you to leisurely fill out at home or office as the need occurs. Then take it by your PO next day for their stamp-proof . . . your certified letter is sent . . . and you have beaten old-man-procastination once more.

Certified letters I find good for notice to tenants of some rule that they continually disobey, however if they refuse to accept the letter, then simply hand the letter or notice to them personally. Incidentally, one other reference check I include for a need possibly later in case of a rare eviction is, "where you ever in the Service of your Country?" Your lawyer will need to know that if he evicts, and it is a lot easier to get that information from a new tenant than when you two have disagreed.

Incidentally, a certified letter works wonders if a tenant continually disobeys some previously agreed to rule of the house that offends you and your property. Simply tell him that "one more repeat of the offense and you will get a letter." This fore warning is just a fair practice which most tenants will appreciate; and they will usually stop whatever they are doing that annoys you. However, if they repeat again, after your verbal warning, send them a Certified letter (no receipt-requested needed)... in this letter state that "after five requests to stop such and such, he is hereby asked in writing to stop, because of disturbance to other tenants (which he agreed not to in his lease addendum), plus this disturbance is degrading your property which can become a much bigger claim against him." Further "if the tenant repeats same once more, he will be immediately sued for eviction by the Sheriff and liable for any rent loss, plus his security payment, plus damages. This will usually shake-their-timbers (for now the tenant has tested you and he knows you are not a push-over)... the insecure tenant probably won't even mention the letter, believe it or not, and will be as sweet-as-sin to you. He was just "testing." Kids are always testing their parents... tenants sometimes test their landlords. I am always reminded of the animal trainer in the cage at the circus with all those wild lions and tigers. The cats growl, scratch and make advances threatening the trainer. He looks them in the eye, cracks his whip, and voila... those huge ferocious lions and tigers meekly jump up on their pedestals, and even do all kinds of tricks, even where the trainer puts his head in one cat's mouth as the finale. I have often thought, if parents used his psychology (of an animal trainer) in training their children, then we would have better trained kids.

Apartment Lease

Note: A "Rider" is attached to this agreement.

THIS LEASE, made this .... day of .... A.D., 19....., by and between

JAMES W. ANDERSON ...., owner and

...., hereinafter called the Lessor, and

proprietor of the ...., or

his duly authorized agent, both of ....

of ....

hereinafter called the Lessee ....

WITNESSETH, That in consideration of the sum of .... * .... Dollars

paid by the Lessee ...., which said sum is hereby acknowledged to have been received as part payment of rents accruing

under this Lease, and in the further consideration of the covenants, agreements and conditions herein contained, on the part

of the Lessee .... to be kept, done and performed, the said Lessor does hereby lease to the Lessee .... Apartment No.

.... on the .... floor in the

The monthly rental is guaranteed for one year for rule-obeying Tenants

.........., situated ...., with the full under-

standing that .... family consists of .... adults and NO PETS/child One Auto and no more.

TO HAVE AND TO HOLD THE SAME for the full term of .... 30 day Lease .... from the

.... day of .... A.D., 19....., to the ——— day of ——— 19....., the said Lessee ....

yielding and paying to the Lessor therefor the total rent of .... Dollars.

And the said Lessee .... covenant .... with the Lessor to pay said rent in advance in .... payments,

the first payment of .... Dollars on the .... day of .... A.D., 19.....

which said sum has been paid and acknowledged herein, and the remaining payments as follows, namely:

* .... is for the first month's rent and two months security (interest bearing, provided tenant complys with this agreement fully) Sec-urity money is specifically NOT to be used for last months rent. Ten-ant is not liable for double rent for Winter months (Oct/Mar) should tenant have to leave during or after Winter months. Tenant

254

and the Lessor does hereby reserve the right to terminate this lease at any time this condition is permitted to exist; not to assign this lease nor sub-let any part of the premises here leased, except with the written consent of the owner and only at a price which shall be an amount not less than the proportional rate for the full term; not to use said premises for any other purpose than as a private dwelling for the members of ....family; and especially the cost of removing foreign substances from toilets and sinks.

................family; to pay the cost of repairing all damage to the apartment occasioned by the Lessee .... or any of ....

AND THE LESSEE................ hereby covenant ....and agree................that if default is made in the payment of rent as above set forth or any part thereof, or if said Lessee................or................family shall violate any of the covenants, agreements and conditions of this lease, then the Lessee................shall become a tenant at sufferance, hereby waiving all right of notice to vacate said premises, and the Lessor shall be entitled to re-enter and retake possession immediately of the demised premises, and the entire rent for the rental period next ensuing shall at once be due and payable and may forthwith be collected by distress or otherwise as provided by law; and will at the end of h................term without demand quietly and peaceably deliver up the possession of said premises in as good condition as they now are (ordinary wear and the decay and damage by fire or the elements only excepted).

SAID LESSEE................hereby acknowledges receipt of the articles enumerated on the reverse side of this lease and by agreement made a part hereof and further covenants and agrees to assume full responsibility for said articles and to make good any damage or deficiency therein at the expiration of this lease; to return all linens clean and pay for cleaning of same upon termination of lease.

One reserved parking place per parking memo. No overnight guest parking or they will be towed away at guest's cost. Further, no guest parking on neighbors lawns. Pets specifically not allowed. Also 2nd auto not allowed without an agreement in writing. Rent automatically goes up $100 per month for either pet or 2nd auto infraction. There is a $1 per day late-rent-penalty.

And the Lessor, upon performance of the said covenants, agreements and conditions by said Lessee ....hereby covenants that the said Lessee ....shall have the quiet and peaceable enjoyment of said premises, herein reserving the right to inspect said premises so often as shall be deemed necessary and to show the apartment at reasonable hours to prospective tenants during the thirty days next prior to the expiration of this lease.

Lessee agrees that if the Lessee is in default of any of the other terms, covenants or conditions of this lease, other than the default in payment of rent, and as a result thereof the Lessor reacquires possession of the demised premises, then all unearned rentals shall be retained by the Lessor as agreed upon and liquidated damages, the parties being unable to ascertain the exact amount of the damages that may be sustained by the Lessor as a result of breach of this lease by the Lessee. However, the Lessor agrees that in the event he can mitigate his damages by releasing of the demised premises, then and in that event, any monies that the Lessor may receive in mitigation of the damages shall be payable to the Lessee. In enforcing the terms, covenants and conditions of this lease, the Lessee shall be responsible for all court costs and attorney's fees incurred in connection therewith. All of the remedies under this lease and rider hereto shall be considered cumulative.

Witness our hands and seals this................day of................A. D., 19................

Signed and sealed in the presence of:

initial.

255

RIDER TO LEASE AGREEMENT

1. No children or not pets are allowed in apartment or on Property unless specified in a specified by a special set of written agreements between Owner and Tenant.

2. Utilities (Gas and Electric) are paid by Tenant. Water paid by Owner.

3. Tenant accepts this apartment in its "as is" condition. We agree to describe this apt. as
_____ condition. Further that this apt. is turned over to Tenant in a clean
and orderly condition and must be returned to Owner in same condition, or Owner will clean
apt. and deduct cleaning expense from Tenant Security Deposit. Cost to clean refrigerator is
$13, stove $17. Other cleaning costs will be billed to Tenant and deducted from Security.

4. Further in consideration of reduced rent, from a market value for this apt. of $_____
to your actual rent paid monthly of $_____, Tenant agrees to maintain his apt. by fixing
anything he or she breaks or destroys, such as broken windows, torn screens, marks or
holes on walls, floors or ceilings. Further, if you let the HUD Inspector inside your apt.
(you are not obliged to let him in unless you want to), and if the HUD Inspector reports any,
violations in apt., such as mentioned above, then it is your responsibility to repair them,
or Owner will be forced to repair violations, but will bill Tenant and deduct this amount
from Security. This again, in exchange for special reduced rental on this apt.

4. All your plumbing is in good and working condition, and as specified in your lease, you
the Tenant are responsible for any repair, immediately. If you don't throw hair down the
toilet, and grease and food down the sink, you won't have stopped pipes. If you don't let
drain-acids sit in the pipes, you won't have a leaking drain pipe. "P" drain pipes in this
apt. are noted as in _____ condition.

256

inal condition when vacating

6. Miami Sanitation Laws demand garbage be put in strong bags(plastic preferred), put in garbage cans provided, and the garbage can lid closed

7. Miami Peace Disturbance Laws and Owner Policy requires you not to disturb your Tenant neighbors with loud music, loud parties, loud arguments, loud TV, etc.

8. You must keep the front and rear outside entrances to your apt. neat, clean, uncluttered.

9. Light bulbs and fuses have been installed and paid for by Owner and must not be removed.

10. This APT.# _____ contains the following appliances/& condition described:

11. These appliances and fixtures must be left in the clean and operative condition described above, otherwise the cost to restore them will be charged to you.

12. For safety regulations and for the Owners necessity to maintain and improve his Property, Owner has access to your apt. This is also necessary for monthly inspection and occasional remodeling. No private locks can be allowed on your apt. for these reasons.

13. Since several Tenants moved out without returning the door keys, we must now charge a $5.00 key deposit, which will be returned when you return the keys, when you vacate the apt.

14. Your security deposit is xxxxx interest bearing, with full Lease compliance

15. Your rent is due on the first day of the month, promptly, so we can pay our Mortgage which is due the first of the month. There is a $1 per day penalty for late rent payment.

16. The Owner does not allow unauthorized persons to move in after you take possession. The Owner is concerned that too many people cause discomfort to all Tenants, and that his good tenants will leave, causing Owner financial loss. A guest, (no guest cars allowed) may reside in this apt. for two weeks, and Tenant must notify Owner when this occurs, and is not allowed more than twice per year.

17. General good conduct and good living habits are required of all Tenants, so all residents

257

will live in harmony, and in harmony with our neighboring Property Ownrs.

18. No signs of any kind are allowed outside apt., except for the name specified in this lease which will be put on your mailbox, in an orderly and uniform manner.

19. No public petting or drugs allowed on this Property.

20. No trucks, motorcycles, or noisy cars allowed on Property. No engines running on Property.

21. The Owner will have the right to make further regulations which in the Owners judgement are needed for the safety, care and cleanliness of the Property.

22. This lease is binding on Tenants, their friends and their visitors.

23. Any violations by parking a second, unauthorized auto overnight will require Owner to have this auto towed away at the expense of the violator. No tow-away signs are posted which Owner feels will degrade the esthetics of this Property.

24. Since this apt. is in the vacation land of the USA where Winter rentals are acknowledged to cost double the Summer rate; If you have a lease on a cheaper annual rate, and if you vacate before the cheaper Summer months rental basis, then you will be charged XXXXXXXX for your Winter months. Example; 4 Winter months on an annual rate of $300 per month, will cost you an extra $XXX XXXXXXXX, if you move out before your Summer lease months waived. Please initial it if you wish your

25. We post a note monthly giving notice of spraying for bugs. apt. sprayed. Some people don't because of allergys, etc.

26. The Owner intends to keep the rents low and reasonable to clean and responsible Tenants who do not violate these rules that we have reviewed in detail. If the Tenant breaks any of these rules and regulations, the Owner can evict Tenant, with loss of all Security and advance rents paid, and further, the Tenant will be liable for Legal costs incurred by Owner to enforce any Tenant violations of this lease. (Tenant)_____.(Owner)_____

258

(this form, properly filled out thusly, usually works "like Ex-Lax" to pry out rent from an errant Tenant)

_____, Fla., _____, 19___
   (City)   (Date)

TO ___ Tenant name on Lease, Apt.#, Apt.address,city,state,zip.
Your two month's Security will be used to evict you, per your
signed agreement. It is expensive to move; and certainly em-
barrassing to find your furniture on the street by the Sherrif.
Apartments are scarce too. Note:ONE NOTICE PER TENANT.NEXT TIME..."OUT"
You are hereby notified that you are in default in payment of rent in the sum of ___$300.00___

THREE HUNDRED _____ *Dollars, for the rent and use of the premises.*
If said rent is not paid in 3 days, we will immediately begin
Eviction proceedings.These Eviction proceedings cannot be stopped
once they begin; so if you present us the rent on the fourth day
we will not be able to accept it *County, State of Florida, now occupied by you, and*

that demand is hereby made for the payment of the said rent or the possession of said premises within three days

from the date of the service of this notice, pursuant to the Laws of the State of Florida.
If you follow the Golden**Rules that you signed at our Tenant
Interview all will be peaceful...it is up to you.

OWNER OR AUTHORIZED AGENT
JAMES W. ANDERSON. Proud Property Owner

RESERVED   PARKING ASSIGNMENTS,
(Actual form used...not made up just for this book)
Biscayne Bay Villas, ⬛ NE ⬛ St. Miami, Fl. 331⬛

"THE HOW TO LIVE RENT FREE BOOK" by J. ANDERSON

Please park in your assigned parking space ONLY.
If one person breaks the rule, then each other one must
also break the rules, and we have a "domino effect" of confusion.

There are other reasons for these assignments. The two
front lower apartments have the reserved parking space
right in front of their living room window so the car
lights of other autos will not disturb them.

Parking for guests and deliveries are provided in the
driveway which will hold about three autos, if the first
and second auto drives completely back to the garden-gate.
PLEASE TELL YOUR GUESTS THIS WAY FOR THEM TO PARK, BEFORE ▰▰
THEY EVEN ARRIVE.

I, the owner also use this driveway parking space, and
sometimes have heavy material to unload, so please take
this into consideration also.

If one of your neighbor tenants violate these assignments
⬛⬛ this sheet, if violations continue

260

Thank you for your cooperation for a better Biscayne Bay Villas.

Jim & Andree
Jim & Andree

FRONT BUILDING
(entrance)

| Parking Space #1
for Apt.#_____ |
| Parking Space #2
for Apt.#_____ |
| Parking Space #3
for Apt.#_____ |
| Parking Space #4
for Apt.#_____ |

DRIVEWAY

(Driveway also for Apt.#_____)
Driveway. For Owners & Guests
(tell guests to drive IN to
   allow another auto behind.)

Parking Space #5
for Apt.#_____
(Auto in this space must keep
   over to "left" so as not to
   block the driveway.)

(Parking assignments...
bottom half)

261

TO ALL TENANTS AT THE NEW YEAR, 1978; FROM, JIM ANDERSON; OWNER

At the beginning of this New Year, I wish you and yours a very
pleasant and successful New Year; and this important message to you.

Whether you live in an apartment, or your own Condo, your own home,
or even on your own ranch or estate; you will have neighbors to contend with. Neighbors, whose ideas are different from yours. Only
through adult consideration for others can there be harmony together.

Yesterday, I noticed the two extra lawn chairs I put in the garden
for your enjoyment, were missing. Unfortunately you are the losers
in this situation.

My message to you on this matter is that regardless of where you live
on this Planet you must get involved, and you must refuse to let
ill-mannered neighbors upset your serene lifestyle that we try very
hard to create for you. Last week, several of you complained of the
smelly cat litter on the ground by the garbage...when I told Bill
in #6 about it (and to clean it up,PRONTO)..his reply was:"nobody
complained to me"... and I told him: "Unfortunately they don't want
to get involved and prefer me, the owner to interceed. This, I am
happy to do whenever a problem is too difficult to solve between
yourselves for I own this Property and refuse to have it depreciate.

262

(Cont.)

I ask you all to be considerate of your neighbors, and when someone
is too loud, or violates your rights in some other way, your best solution is to quietly and with a smile talk it out BETWEEN YOU..., and
usually you will solve the problem much easier than you thought.

Recently at another Property that I own, I offered a good tenant a
larger vacant apartment. He quickly accepted and casually said that
he was considering moving, "because of his noisy neighbor-tenant."
When I asked him why he did not talk to his noisy neighbor, or to me
if that did not work...his answer, "I did not want to bother."...
Well, folks, we had better "bother", because if us good-guys don't
"bother"... "the bad guys" will run all over the "good guys." IF THEY
STEAL LAMP FURNITURE OUT OF YOUR GARDEN TODAY...SOULD THEY FOR STEAL
OUT OF YOUR APARTMENT TOMORROW ?

I continually urge tenants to be concerned with the Property where
they live...YOU DON'T JUST RENT HERE...YOU LIVE HERE...AND PER THE
LAW YOU ARE ENTITLED TO QUIET ENJOYMENT OF YOUR SURROUNDINGS. Example:
When you see a stranger on the Property (your home area);STOP THEM...
AND ASK FIRMLY AND DIRECTLY: "Can I help you?" or "whom did you want
to see?" I find that strangers get annoyed with these questions, but
so what...for that is better than you allowing a potential "set up
investigation" for a robbery of your precious keepsakes the next day.
Get involved. Protect your Property. You live here. You pay rent and
you are entitled by law to quiet enjoyment of your Property. All of
your neighbors have signed the same "rules & regulations".Let's comply.

FEDERAL CRIME INSURANCE PROGRAM

RESIDENTIAL CRIME INSURANCE POLICY

This Policy (of which this Application is a part) covers losses from burglary and larceny incident thereto, and robbery, including observed theft, subject to applicable limits and to a deductible, as stated below, and to Federal law and regulations.

FEDERAL INSURANCE ADMINISTRATION
(An Agency of the U.S. Government)
U.S. Department of Housing and Urban Development,
Washington, D.C. 20410

APPLICATION

(Type or print heavily in ball point pen)

Policy No.

(Insert Social Security Number and add suffix "O" for the first application. Add Suffix "A," "B," "C," etc., for each additional separate Application where multiple premises are involved.)

Insured's Name and Mailing Address, including County, Zip Code, Apartment No. and Telephone No. (If any):

Location of Premises, including County, Zip Code, and Apartment No. (if different from mailing address):

Effective Date:

(Not earlier than noon on day following date on which applicant signs Application.)

Expiration Date:

(One year from effective date)
Producer's Name, Address, and Telephone No.

Servicing Company's Name and Address (To be filled in by Agent or Broker):

1. If not a single-family residence, describe type of building (e.g., apartment house, rooming house):

2. Do three or more persons other than relatives of the named insured reside in premises? ☐ YES ☐ NO

3. Has applicant ever previously been insured under a Federal Crime Insurance Policy? ☐ YES ☐ NO

4. Amount of insurance applied for ($10,000 maximum): *(Check One)* ☐ $1,000 ☐ $3,000 ☐ $5,000 ☐ $7,000 ☐ $10,000

   NOTE: Coverage is subject to a deductible of $50 or 5% of the gross amount of any loss, whichever is greater.

PREMIUM COMPUTATION (To be filled in by Agent or Broker):

Territory: *(Check one)*   1 ☐   2 ☐   3 ☐   Amount of annual premium $ ☐   REMITTED HEREWITH $ ☐

264

PROGRAM UTILIZATION DATA:

(Check one)

1 ☐ WHITE
2 ☐ NEGRO/BLACK
3 ☐ AMERICAN INDIAN
4 ☐ ORIENTAL
5 ☐ SPANISH AMERICAN
6 ☐ OTHER MINORITY

(The information concerning Minority Group Categories is requested for statistical purposes so the Department may determine the degree to which its programs are utilized by Minority families, in accordance with 24 C.F.R. 60.2, 36 F.R. 10782, June 3, 1971.)

CERTIFICATION BY APPLICANT:

"I certify under penalty of Federal law for fraud or intentional misrepresentation as set forth in 18 U.S.C. 1001, (1) that the statements I have made in the Application, including the signature date set forth below, are true and correct to the best of my knowledge and belief, (2) that I have read the applicable eligibility requirements and the protective device requirements set forth in the Application, and (3) that to the best of my knowledge and belief the insured premises meet such requirements.

"I understand that if at the time of an inspection during adjustment of a loss the insured premises are found not to be protected in the manner required, this Policy will be considered void from its inception and only the portion of the premium not absorbed by administrative expenses in connection with the issuance of such policy and the inspection will be refunded." (GIVE THESE FORMS TO TENANTS, THEY LIKE) ⌐ able, is available in most cities & States for a very reasonable fee.

Leaders Note: This National Government Theft Insurance, Non-Cancell-
(when Uncle Sam does something right...he keeps it a secret)

_____
(Signature of Applicant)   (you should use it too)

_____
(Date)

STATEMENT BY AGENT OR BROKER:

"I certify under penalty of Federal law (1) that I am an agent or broker licensed in the State in which the premises are located, (2) that the date of the Application is correct, and (3) I have explained to the Applicant that compliance with protective device requirements is a prerequisite for coverage under this Policy. I also agree that in the event of cancellation of a Policy, I shall ratably refund to the Federal Insurance Administration commissions on the unearned portion of premiums at the same rate at which such commission was originally paid."

_____
(Signature of Agent or Broker)

_____
(Date)

HUD-1621 (3-74)

265

Notice to Quit

AND VACATE

(My theory on "forms" is that they are never filled out properly. When I buy another Quad the Lease agreements are really "candy store" variety. I want the Tenant to understand THE FULL CONSEQUENCES RIGHT AWAY. Herewith:

TO ___ Tenant name on Lease. Apt.#. Apt.Address, City, State, Zip.

Florida Statute Landlord-Tenant Law provides the Owner with the right to give a 15 day written notice to vacate (on your 30 day Lease)

You are hereby notified to **Quit and Vacate** *the premises described as follows:*

Within 15 days or no later than the end of the Month. The Landlord Tenant Law further provides the Owner an additional protection of DOUBLE RENT should you stay beyond this period. Remember: We hold two month's rent as secuiry for our protection in just such circumstances. Should you fail to vacate; your Security money will be used to Evict you by the Sheriff's office and the balance of your two month's rent will be applied to DOUBLE RENT for the extra days you stay beyond the vacate-date provided herein until the Sheriff's office physically removes your possessions from your apartment

on or before the _____ *day of* _____, 19 ___

This notice is given you under and by authority of Florida Laws, Chapter Eighty-three.

Dated _____, 19 ___

_____ Owner.

ANDERSON'S GOLDEN RULES OF LIVING

- I -

DO NOT DISTURB YOUR NEIGHBORS . . .
WHO ARE MY GOOD TENANTS

- II -

DO NOT DESTROY MY PROPERTY . . .
WHICH IS YOUR GOOD HOME.

- III -

PAY YOUR RENT ON TIME . . .
SO I CAN PAY THE MORTGAGE ON TIME

(To the reader: You will note the psychology in his bulletin, gives something to the tenant . . . and something to the property owner. It is suggested that you have this duplicated under your own name and posted in a few places on the property . . . and to also attach one to your lease-agreement . . . for you and tenant to sign.)

(whenever you get what will probably end up as one of those TALL TALES TENANTS TELL, like: "can I pay my rent after Christmas so I can buy my kid some presents"(only to have the tenant "skip" after Christmas.This happened to me. when I was innocent and impressionable)..."present" the tenant with this "form" to sign, confirming their agreement of fact.

RENTAL AGREEMENT

P.S. You will find that the "deadbeat" will refuse. The sincere Tenant who may have problems (as we all do from time to time) will gladly sign this to prove his honesty as to his problem—circumstances.

At this time I am renting _____
_____ . I realize that I am $ _____
(address)

from _____
(owner)

behind in my rent at this time. I promise that I will pay the above amount owed by the

day of _____, 19____.

In the event that I for any reason do not follow through with the above promise, I shall vacate my apartment immediately and no later than the above mentioned date. If I fail to do the above, I give my permission to said owner to change the locks on my door and allow the same to re-rent my apartment. If the apartment I am renting is unfurnished, I give said owner or agent my permission to remove the furniture from my apartment and set it out on the street. The owner will return all personal clothing and belongings to me. I realize it is my responsibility to pick up my personal belongings and articles no later than 48 hours after the locks on my apartment have been changed.

CHAPTER TWENTY TWO

SHOULD YOUR APARTMENTS BE
FURNISHED OR NOT FURNISHED?

Again, I am not rigid to either belief, because tenants like the general Public, are unpredictable. However, any smart apartment building owner would prefer unfurnished apartment tenants if and when they are plentiful because you are getting a more worthwhile committment from a tenant who moves in his own furniture. And secondly this tenant will be happier with his own possessions. And thirdly, this type tenant is more substantial when he owns his own belongings.

I don't like to lease one of my apartments to a tenant who more or less moves in with his toothbrush and suitcase. This type tenant is contributing little, while the apartment owner is giving everything.

The owner has spent advertising dollars. The owner has cleaned up the apartment and probably painted it or at least a touch up. Maybe even with a little remodeling or improvement to up the rent. This tenant with just the toothbrush comes along, you rent to him . . . you have taken this unit off the market . . . you have chosen this tenant over others who have applied. So, besides a lease and the Security money you have nothing else as a tenant committment. This situation works in a majority of cases however because that Security money does have some strength . . . however I am simply explaining the more desirability of a tenant who moves in a van-load of furniture and belongings. Obviously this is prefered.

Your tenant that moved in with a toothbrush could take off in the night and your only remuneration for all your work is perhaps the one month Security money. Additionally, in Florida, there are a lot of new people moving here (I understand that we will have an additional two million new residents from up North moving to Florida by 1980 . . . a lot

269

of this is a Sun-rush which will turn into a gold-rush for you as Northerners leave the Cold North with all its energy crisis worries). These transient tenants will ask for everything from sheets to kitchen equipment to a TV, etc., etc. As much as I like to help people ... my advice is not to give out all these additional items to a new tenant ... even if you have the items on hand. Formerly I did and I discovered that it is far better to get the new tenant hooked and committed and interested in his new apartment by letting him buy these items. I feel good when I see a furniture truck delivering a desk or a bookcase, etc. to one of my tenants apartments. I call it "nesting" ... that is, the new tenant is taking a real interest in his apartment ... this is the kind of tenant you want to work toward. If you provide everything "but the toothbrush" you have a less committed tenant.

There is another approach to the tenant who wants bedding, dishes and a TV however, and it can be doubly profitable to you. In Florida we call a "Seasonal Tenant" one who commits only for a four to six month period in the peak Winter Season sometime during the months of November through April. For this type of Seasonal Tenant you get approximately double the normal rent. This is traditional in Florida. And a "seasonal" at double the rent can perhaps pull you out of an upcoming budget problem, so again I repeat ... be flexible. Seasonals traditionally usually pay one half of the entire rental committment plus Security before moving in ... and the other half of the entire rental committment within the first month. Their Security money is returned to them in the normal fashion stated before.

Back to furnished or unfurnished ... I even go so far in flexibility to KEEP the furniture from an apartment or two stored nearby (try some inexpensive neighbor's garage) ... so I can go "either way" in looking for tenant WITH furniture, but agreeing to tenants that require furniture. You will find in Florida that you will have a lot of people relocating here who desire at least what I like to offer as "partly furnished." This means, and I explain it, as "the bare minimum, and that I want tenants who wish to own their own furnishings because they are better tenants and happier tenants". I also offer to give these type tenants tips where they can acquire their own furniture for "little or nothing" in money cost. Just a little interest and sweat to make their own little nest exactly to their liking and needs.

Also "partly furnished" means "as is," and again is stated in the lease-rider. And also that nothing more must be added by the owner to the apartment. Such as maybe the tenant later says he needs a desk . . . or a bookcase . . . or another lamp. "As is" means that . . . and I explain to them nicely that that is not our agreement to keep adding items to the apartment and then I tell them where to go to get the item they need at a bargain price. Lastly I tell them that doing it this way we are both happier since I think tenants are happier with mostly their own possessions around them . . . and "a happy tenant makes the owner happy too."

NOTES & QUESTIONS

HOW TO SAVE TIME AND MONEY. . . AND HOW TO GET THINGS DONE QUICKLY. . . ON YOUR SALARIED JOB. . . YOUR QUAD. . . AND IN YOUR PRIVATE LIFE

This chapter will be devoted to saving you time, since you now have two fields of endeavor. . . your salaried job. . . and your Quad (doesn't that sound like a nice and secure and orderly lifestyle?). Now you will want to get things done in a hurry, without the wasted time most people put up with throughout their lives. There are ways of getting things done in this day and age that I just know most people do not use. Besides saving your time. . . these secrets will save you money. . . because if you purchase an auto or a refrigerator. . . and it doesn't work properly. . . you will want to get it fixed fast, or get it replaced with a new one PRONTO. . . especially now that you have two endeavors. Althoug your Quad will not take that much of your time. . . these secrets are just important for all of us to know and use. . . especially for us DOERS. I am going to enjoy writing and telling this story also, because it will bring back some very fond memories of days gone by. . . when I was a part of the big business World.

One of the eight great men that I was fortunate to work for in New York City was the almost legenday character. . . J. Elroy McCaw. He was a Leader in the Radio and Television Industry and he made millions, much of which he invested in old mansions formerly owned by another legendary man, William Randolph Hearst.

When things got tough. . . or in a bad situation. . . "J. Elroy" would say to me. . . "Jim, YOU CAN MAKE THINGS HAPPEN". . . or. . . "JIM. . . YOU CAN GUIDE YOUR OWN DESTINY."

I worked for J. Elroy for a one year period as Vice President, General Manager of one of his Companies during a tough assignment to bring the company out of the "red," I broke my leg – three very bad spiral breaks... About three days after the accident I got a call from Elroy wondering when I was coming back to work? I was really feeling sorry for myself in this very uncomfortable and helpless situation... but old Elroy psyched me out of my gloom. He talked me into struggling into work the next day... and that afternoon, he invited me and several associates for cocktails. Elroy began to tell us one of his pitiful personal stories. Several years past, he had been in a bad auto accident... broken limbs... broken skull... the works. Doctors gave a gloomy prediction for his recovery in Seattle, when Elroy heard that his employees at his NYC Radio Station were going on strike, and further, were going to picket Yankee Stadium to prevent Elroy's Station from broadcasting their baseball games. (And in the 1950's, the Yankee Baseball on radio was very, very big money.) Upon hearing this in his hospital bed, old J. Elroy got out of bed... struggled to dress himself.... shocking the nurses as he telephoned and arranged for an ambulance to take him to the Airport. He flew on a stretcher to New York City and the high altitude caused him great pain and suffering because of his concussion. Nevertheless J. Elroy prevailed . . . . . he arrived in NYC... broke the strike at his radio station, which set future precedent for such matters in the industry. Was it all true? I think it was, but I never bothered to check it out... this story was good enough to psych me out of my self-pity "just over a broken leg." And I began to spend a very delightful and successful year... working ten hours a day in a leg cast up to my high-thigh.

Also at this little cocktail session, J. Elroy told some of his favorite stories about being drunk on his crutches. One night he said he overheard someone say... "What a pitiful sight to see a drunk on crutches." We all laughed heartily (especially me, drinking... and on crutches). Then he told his best story. One night, after a long session of business meetings, Elroy crutched out on Broadway... in was raining... and taxi cabs were scarce. Soon an empty taxi came zooming down the street. . . passed an old lady who was waving frantically. . . and pulled into the curb next to Elroy, looking pitiful on his crutches, in the rain. J. Elroy made it into the cab and announced. . . "the 21 Club please" (only the best restaurant in New York). . . to which the driver mumbled. . . "I don't feel sorry for you after all." I plan to write an entire book on that one year on crutches. . . but I just had to give you a little inspiration from a great man, who said to me, "Jim, you can make things happen". . . "Jim, you can guide your own destiny". . . and now I pass it on to you with the hope that old J. Elroy's inspiration (rest his soul) will help to make you a success in your endeavors. This entire Chapter deals with this very important subject. . . how to get things done. . . how to make things happen. . . and with a minimum of effort on your part, for you are too busy to waste time.

(*) Referring back to the Chapter where I said that later in the book, I would tell you how to "go high up to speak to executives important to you", I had given the example wherein I had to speak to the President of the Department Store to get my one year air conditioner guarantee extended for free service, because my good-tenant had not "bothered me" to tell me that this air conditioner had stopped working after several months. . . ("but we don't use air conditioning anyway, so we didn't bother you.") In this type instance, the air conditioning Manager can't help you, for he has his rules to follow, and rightly so. . . for as someone said in describing "the Army". . . "It was created by geniuses. . . to be run by idiots." Now don't get upset. . . this is not disrespectful. . . I didn't even think it up. . . but it is true. . . in the Army. . . or in business. . . if you just stop to think and analyze their problems. . . EVERYONE CAN'T CHANGE THE RULES. . . RULES MUST BE FOLLOWED OR WE WOULD HAVE COMPLETE CHAOS. . . (so if you know

JIM ANDERSON'S "HOW TO LIVE RENT FREE" BOOK

enough to analyze the problem... you can usually solve it)... in the case of the air conditioner... out of order; out of warranty, but hardly used... that kind of restitution decision must be made "by the top brass", who not only have the authority to change the rules... they also have the good old common horse sense (that scarce commodity these days)... to make a true, but out of the ordinary decision.

So I reached the President of this Department Store Chain (I'll tell you how to do that later in this Chapter, that is, how to get by "the Watchdogs"... "The Bodyguards"... commonly known as Executive Secretaries, but who have gone way beyond their intended bounds in "protecting" their boss from calls of customers or salespersons.) So now, I clearly explained my problem to the President... just as I stated above. Of course, I communicated quickly at the beginning of the conversation that "I was a good customer"... "the owner of apartments"... and then told him what this good-tenant unknowingly did to me. Would you believe that on-the-spot, this President said: "Well, Mr. Anderson, this is out of the ordinary, but I understand the situation, and I am going to extend your air conditioner warranty beyond the normal one year... and I will have our serviceman out there to repair it immediately."

Does this sound unbelievable or out of the ordinary to you? It doesn't to me because I do it all the time without having the least feeling of guilt. I feel I am justified... but I also know that not 5% of you would do such a thing or even have the vision that it could be possible... but I hope that I now conscious-raise you into doing it too . . . especially since it can save you money.

I even use this procedure on smaller things... because I have trained myself to "reach the top brass" easily. Recently, one of those heavy duty, outside door mats (made of heavy duty old tire strips) fell apart at our front door stoop after only about two years of wear. My wife wanted to throw it away (women are usually very poor managers with such problems, and must read this especially carefully and change their errant ways on such matters). I told the dear wife that I paid $7.50 for that mat. I bought it from Sears, who is known for backing up their merchandise. Further, that Sears would probably like to know of this faulty mat because they will then go to their mat manufacturer, and not only demand a new mat. . . but will also check the quality control of the mat manufacturer to see if their quality control is slipping. . . because if Sears sells too much shoddy merchandise. . . they know they will lose customers. . . and Sears is not our No. 1 merchandiser for nothing. So I called one of the top executives at Sears; they all know me from previous calls re-poor merchandise or poor or rude service from one of their employees. I explained to the executive exactly as I did for you. . . and added that "I don't know if there is such a thing as a one year guarantee on such a door mat. . . but at that price, I expected to get 5 to 10 years wear out of that mat. . . am I incorrect in my opinion?" And further that "the mat was at my particular doorstep, where I know it was properly cared for. . . and not at the doorstep of one of my tenants, where I could not have vouched for the proper care of the mat." I further did not even demand a new mat. . . "But wanted to advise Sears of possible poor workmanship in their $7.50 door mat." The store exec told me to "bring it in for a new mat at no cost." I graciously thanked him. Here again, the Manager of the Sears Mat-Dept. could not have made such a decision. . . (remember "the old Army Saying"). . . and in fact, when I returned this mat, the Mat-Manager was quite surprised until he called his boss "upstairs," to learn of the refund decision.

This little bit of conscious-raising can help you on all kinds of problems . . . big and small. . . throughout your life. Did you ever buy a new automobile which was a "lemon"? I did. . . and after giving the auto Agency several chances to fix the car (even the Agency President isn't high enough in this situation sometimes). . . I called the President of the auto company in Detroit. . . COLLECT. Of course I did not talk to the President (but sometimes I do), but in this case, one of his top Aides returned my call. . . and took care of my problems with my "lemon".

Want another? I had a faulty tire (a "bubble"), discovered by my trusty Gasoline Service Station. Right here, another important tip. . . I recommend that you set up a charge account at a nearby and trustworthy Station. . . use it as much as possible, so you are a customer in good-standing. . . just in case we have gasoline rationing again, as in World War II. . . people who remember back, can tell you of the extra "help" they got from their good friend at "their" gas station.

Back to the tire. . . so I called the local District Manager (I usually give a try to "one underling". . . hoping against hope that some Corporations extend a little latitude of common sense down-the-line). . . However, this Manager told me (almost reciting it out of the Corporate Manual like a robot) that "A refund would be given for the amount of rubber NOT used. . . plus a charge to mount the tire. . . and it would take a half a day.' I hung up in disgust and again (as with the Auto President in Detroit), I called the President of the Tire Company in Akron. . . COLLECT. Here again, the President did not answer my call. . . but one of his "top guns" did return my call. I got his name and Title, then recited the "recorded message" that I had received from his local District Manager. . . and added, that "I did not ask for or expect to receive a reject tire on my new $8,000 Station Wagon". . . further that "I had been risking my life by driving with such a faulty tire caused by your poor workmanship". . . and further, "that I was not about to pay for the mounting of the new tire, since it was the Corporation's responsibility to replace their reject tire on my car, not mine." Further, "I did not expect to purchase an $8,000 new car complete with your reject tire which now has about 25% wear and risked my life." And lastly, "I could, no way, waste a half a day waiting for the tire to be mounted, and that I demanded the tire to be changed at my convenience. . . and quickly."

I will say that these tire-people were the toughest I have encountered (you must stand firm to your guns if they don't agree). . . I guess that the tire people get many such complaints. Bottom line. . . I got my tire. . . . 100% free exchange and put on my auto. . . AT MY CONVENIENCE. I confess, I did reluctantly pay about $2.50 for the tire change. . . just figured I had won enough. . . for life is too short and beautiful to fight all the time for your rights.

I do find that "Service and Store People" will take advantage of you IF YOU LET THEM. Lets say you are getting the delivery of a new refrigerator (tip: get them at the "warehouse sales" of your biggest Department Store, and keep a back-up for emergencies). I buy mine for half price or less th , way . . . and I rarely spend much for repair later, this way. If I get 5 years use, and now the repair would cost $150 on a $500 frig that I had paid $250 for . . . I would call the Salvation Army to haul it away . . . then use my "reserve" frig while waiting for the next worthwhile "warehouse sale." Seriously, I save a lot of money this way on all major items. Now, back to the delivery of your sale-frig. It always seems to be the same . . . an unbelievably dumb person calls you to say, "hello, we are delivering your frig NEXT TUESDAY." I patiently say . . . "can you hit it a little closer than just Tuesday . . . about what time please?". . . Then the reply. . . (remember the "Old Army Game"), "Oh, we can't tell you that. Our delivery trucks are very busy, and we can't make appointments." (Sound familiar?) I reply with a few chosen remarks like, "I work too, and will have to take off work to wait for your delivery man (even if it isn't true, for you must fight fire with fire). . . "and further, if you can't make such a basic and common sense judgment to give me a definite time, I am sure your President will accomodate me, because he values my business if you don't." Would you believe that I don't wait a half a day or a full day for deliveries like the majority of people do. . . because I value my time enough, that I will solve such idiot problems caused by the Old Army Game. (And even if I just want to go fishing.)

Lastly, you will run into rude people all over. . . haven't you noticed? Don't you find rude waiters or poor waiter service in at least 50% of the cases? Well I have a policy on this situation that I have followed for about 20 years. . . I tip 15% for expected, good and friendly service. Do you know that tip, T.I.P. originally was the abbreviation for TO INSURE PROMPTNESS? Then, from a tops of 15% I grade downward and tip less for poor and unfriendly service. . . down to zero tip for lousy service. What I decry; is the majority of customers who tip 15% for lousy service. . . and go up from there, to 20% or 25% for normal (and expected) good service. An owner should fire a lousy waiter who is destroying the business that this owner worked such long hours; plus risking his life's savings to build this restaurant business. I can't understand owners who allow such. . . but they do. . . just like there are a majority of lousy Landlords also.

Further, I find that rude service people act "that way" just because they find that they can get away with it, because of "milk-toast" customers. My wife is a real milk-toast. . . nice. . . but a real milk-toast. . . In her French Homeland where she rarely speaks up for her rights with caustic service people. . . (But as DeGaulle said, "I love France. . . its the people I don't like.") . . . recently Andreé actually spoke up. . . and her reward was great. We were calling a Paris Hotel where friends were arriving from London. The Hotel switchboard operator was particularly rude and cold to my always-beaming and friendly, Andreé. Finally, for once (I hope not the last) Andreé spoke up and said, "You don't have to answer in such an angry fashion, do you?" Can you believe the reply from this obviously startled Hotel Operator who had probably spoken rudely to everyone for years? Her reply was. . . "That's my regular tone of speaking." Well at least she was honest, but she also had to be shocked BY JUST ONE PERSON SPEAKING UP. . . We had to call several more times to finally reach our arriving friends, and Andreé commented "how pleasant the Hotel Operator was, after that." The moral? If we would all do this more when we are treated rudely by "service people". . . and talk back. . . we would all find that the World around us would be a much more pleasant place to live.

And now, if you got this far. . . your reward is to learn my secrets on how to reach the "Boss". . . the "Brass". . . the President of the Corporation, who can help you and save you money. Salesmen will get a big bonus from this information.

First, you must understand the problem. . . then you can solve the problem. Top Executives are "protected" from you by "Watchdogs" or "Bodyguards" (this is what I have dubbed them). . . they are erroneously called "Executive Secretaries," however I see these watchdogs claiming far too much power and discretion as to controlling who speaks to her Boss. . . and I find her judgment full of errors (she is basically negative. . . her Boss is basically positive), as to who she admits through the hallowed-portholes and to the Boss's inner chambers. Quite often she admits only those who have "buttered her up." I chose cunning to get through to her Boss, in the form of a "game" that I have played, and refined, and then played over again for the past 20 years. I imagine, that in the past 20 years I have spoken to more Presidents of major Corporations (as a stranger) than anyone else in the World. In fact, during my television career days, it seemed that I was always the Manager of the low-rated station that nobody wanted to buy. . . remember the "Old Army Game," that is, my station couldn't be purchased for advertising by most Corporate Advertising Manager Types. . . for if he did the President would perhaps fire him "for making that lousy buy." . . . However, I found that if I communicated the complete story to the President or the Executive V.P., that I would come away with some very, verry big sales of Television Advertising. So, I spent about 20 years, outfoxing the "watchdog". . . or the "bodyguard", as I quickly dubbed the Executive Secretary. So then, here is some of my priceless knowledge and experience. . . once again, FROM THE FIRING LINE. . . AND NOT FROM THE IVORY TOWER (no "button pushing" here).

To find the Bosses names, first of all you make a preliminary call to get names of the President and Exec. V.P. by saying that you are with a research firm and are "updating your executive list." (Use the Co., "Standard Executive Directory, Chicago". . . if quizzed further.) Otherwise you can call the Library, and they will give you these names. The third Executive that usually is a "doer" and has power and common sense is the Marketing V.P. . . . however I have found most of the time, that Personnel and Public Affairs, and PR Executives are full of baloney. . . just a "whitewash" with no real power or understanding . . . just a waste of time. Then you call, speak clearly. . . ASSERT YOURSELF like you are in control of the situation . . . give your name if asked. . . sound completely legitimate. . . this will intimidate the "Army Private (the watchdog) on the other end of the line. . . and she will usually spout out information like hitting the jack pot in Las Vegas. Then I usually ask for No. 2, realizing that I can quickly ask to be switched to No. 1, the President. So if I get the rebuff from the watchdog. . . I quickly snap back. . . Mr. Big please (the Pres.) To my request, the watchdog usually stumbles and fumbles her defense and gives an alternate suggestion like "can I connect you with Mr. Nobody in Personnel". . . to which I reply. . . "no thanks, Mr. Big please." However, if she says to call back No. 2, because he is busy or out of the office, I will usually do this, if I have the time. Otherwise, I get switched to the President's office and say again, in a very own-the-place-type-voice. . . "IS HE IN?" This is a trick that I developed to get past the watchdog and it works quite well. If she (dares) asks, "who is calling?". . . I matter of factly say, "Jim Anderson." (Again, like I own the joint. . . or that I sound like an old friend of Mr. Boss.) If this doesn't work, and the watchdog suggests "an assistant". . . I will usually allow myself to be transferred ONE NOTCH DOWN. Assistants to the President usually have a lot of power. . . and especially with your complaint or needed adjustment. . . this person will work just fine. But caution. . . (the old Army Game again). . . don't allow this next person to then switch you to someone else. . . and even perhaps be switched downward once again. I also make certain that my problem is clearly stated . . . so that I get switched to the one proper person who can help.

To change the subject here for a moment while we are possibly waiting for the President to pick up his phone. . . I will pass along another "trick" I learned from a "very tricky person". . . his name is Bad-Billy. Once this person was looking for a very high-up and specialized job. He would send his resume to the Presidents of many Companies where he would like to work. . . (with a scribbled, hand written note at the top to the President. . . "Harry, thought this guy may interest you. T.S." Who is T.S.? . . . Bad-Billy didn't know a T.S. either. . . but it stopped a lot of Presidents' to take a minute to look over his resume. . . Bad-Billy got past a lot of watchdogs this way, because they couldn't judge either who an

obvious friend of the Boss was; this "T.S.". . . so the watchdog, in her command position shot through the resume to her
Boss. . . and would you believe that one of those Presidents
hired "Bad-Billy". . . for most important people even like and
enjoy "the chase" by clever and creative people.

I will tell you one of my best personal stories about how
this technique worked for me and for the benefit of Frank
Sinatra. I was a "young turk" selling Network Programs and
advertising for ABC, N.Y. City. For back in 1960, ABC was
a very poor No. 3 among the 3 Television Networks. We had
"Wyatt Earp" and that was about it. During this 3 year
period I really refined my technique to get past the watchdogs . . . and to the Boss; because we were dealing with a $3
million to $5 million decision on every presentation. . . and I
guarantee you that neither the Advertising Agency or the
Corporation Advertising Manager could or would make such
a decision in favor of the lowly ABC.

ABC had committed and purchased five Frank Sinatra one
hour "Specials". . . but of course, in 1961 (as Sinatra con-
firmed on a Barbara Walters interview recently. . . "this was
one of the lowest points in his career."). Leonard Goldensen,
ABC's Chairman of the Board (a wonderful person) was
calling his good friends like Charles Revson the President of
Revlon, to attempt to "unload Sinatra" and to prevent
another money loss to ABC if Sinatra was not sold. However,
no one was about to risk a $3 million investment (would be
$10 million today) on Sinatra, a singer who had just bombed-
out in his 13 week series for "Chesterfield" on the NBC
Television Network.

So here was where my ability to get past the "watchdogs"
paid off in the highest way. I had the Timex account, but
they had never bought ABC. . . always bought their Specials
on NBC and CBS. Obviously their Ad Agency (remember the
Old Army Saying) would not risk making a $3 million deci-
sion to buy a questionable singer on an iffy Network. I felt
that Sinatra would not flop a second time . . . that he was too
much a pro to let that happen. Being a "fan" besides, I
decided to get my Sinatra pitch to the Timex Brass. I started
with the Executive V.P., Mr. Bob Mohr (how can I forget

him). I called him several times, but his watchdog was un-
flinching in her determination not to let me pass. However, at
this high level contact, I found that I could get a lot of
helpful information about Mr. Big that could help me reach
him. Always on a very important mission such as this... I
would always ask the watchdog "what are the business hours
of Mr. Big and his private telephone number"... and they
usually always tell me not realizing that these are "keys" to
get past her. In this case, she said, "Oh, Mr. Mohr gets in the
office very early... at about 8:15 A.M." This is really early
for New York City, where they told me on my first job there
(with MetroMedia) "not to come to work before 9:30 AM, or
you will spoil it for all of us." I had been used to arriving at
work at 8:15 AM in St. Louis... so now I had the key to
reach Mr. Mohr... the next morning, I call him at 8:15
AM... he picked up his own phone since the watchdog had
not arrived yet... and would you believe (as I usually found)
that Mr. Mohr was a very pleasant person. I stated my case
quickly and precisely. I wanted to see him about "an unusual
advertising opportunity that would sell a lot of Timex
watches." He very matter of factly scheduled me in for an
appointment at 8:15 AM the next morning... and at 8:15
AM at Timex, in the beautiful black steel Seagram's Building,
in one of the Penthouse Offices high above Park Avenue... I
sold the five Sinatra Specials to Bob Mohr of Timex. These
Sinatra Specials were very successful... helped to build
ABC... and they did sell "a lot of Timex watches", although
as it developed only three of the five Specials could be
scheduled. Incidentally, another little part of the "game"
with the watchdog, is to get Mr. Mohr's DIRECT number, I
would not have gotten through at 8:15 AM, because the
Timex switchboard was not open yet.

So this is a message to any watchdog out there... and to
their fine Boss... to say that much commerce is lost and
foiled because a watchdog guarded the gates to the Boss...
the decision maker... to the detriment of the Corporation... and I further suggest that you Bosses have a "discussion" with your watchdog to CLARIFY HER ROLE. You
may even have a friend call you (on a game plan) to see if

your watchdog lets your "unknown friend" through.

Now let me take this important subject more down to earth. I discovered that my first Quad was the boyhood home of a famous local Judge of today. I wanted to invite this Judge by for a visit since I was certain that he would like to see his beautiful old homestead restored probably back to more beauty than even the Judge remembered. Also I figured that the Judge probably never even drove by; not wanting to be disappointed by the "ruins" of a possible beautiful childhood dream. So I called the Judge. . . and told his watchdog "that I had a very personal and private invitation for the Judge and could I please speak with him?" In the Judge's watchdog's opinion (very dangerous and overused) my request was not good enough. . . or maybe I did not give enough information in her opinion. However, I felt I said enough. For I did not want to expose the Judge's personal childhood (even to his watchdog). Well. . . the watchdog never gave my message to the Judge. . . and since it was not that important. . . (actually it was just a thoughtful remembrance). . . I forgot about reaching the Judge.

It is now one year later, and I was near the Chambers of this Judge. . . and when I saw this elegant Judge stroll by. . . I walked up to him. . . introduced myself, and explained (with his watchdog at his side) that I had left several private and personal messages for him last year but never heard from him. . . and that I wanted to invite him to visit his boyhood home which I had magnificently restored. I showed him the photo of this building which is in the front of this book, which I carry in my wallet. The Judge was delighted. . . and accepted my invitation, while his watchdog was sputtering excuses like "it was all a mistake" and "I never saw this man", to which I replied, "of course you never SAW me. . . we only spoke on the telephone." Thirty minutes later, without the Judge present, the watchdog searched me out, and almost accosted me. . . again claiming no knowledge of my calls to the Judge. I merely brushed her off with the comment that she "was just another overprotective and inefficient watchdog, that made too many erring judgments for her boss." As she growled back at me, she even threatened to hit me with anything handy. (What decorum for a Judge's watchdog?) I hope that these examples point up the problem of the watchdog. . . and how to pass her by.

OTHER WATCHDOG PLOYS . . . AND THE "007" SOLUTION

"I'm sorry, but he's on the phone". . . my quick and firm reply. . . "I'll wait." (At least she has admitted that Mr. Big IS IN the office). . . however, the very cunning watchdog will have more excuses to counter with. . . like, "sorry, he just had to rush into a meeting". . . or, "sorry, he had to take an emergency long distance call". . . to which I reply (firmly). . . "I'll wait."

Another watchdog ploy: "I'm sorry, but he's away from his desk." (Usually for No. 2 or less, because THEY COME to No. 1). I firmly reply to this unbelievable statement, "will you please look for him and I will wait?" I find that many of these executive watchdogs are a little lazy, and they prefer not to get off their derriere, whenever they can possibly avoid it. Would you believe, that 8 out of 10 will get up and look for their Boss, WHEN ASKED THIS WAY. . . and most will return to the phone with their "found" boss. This is how silly this game can get.

Oh also, when they say he's on the phone, I matter of factly say. . . "will you let him know I'm holding; and see if he wants me to wait?" Those words are golden. . . chosen and developed after many misfires at the beginning days of this cat and mouse game. That statement is saying. . . "get off your assumptions. . . walk into his office. . . put a note under the Boss's nose, saying, "Jim Anderson is on the other line, do you want him to hold?" Would you believe that in the majority of cases, the Boss hangs up almost immediately and takes my call? This possibly shows that a lot of unimportant monkey-business phone calls go on in the heirarchy. This technique can help you on the telephone in your personal life too. . . as a good friend challenged me several years ago. . . "don't make 'nothing' phone calls". . . in other words, when you take the time to make a call. . . GET SOMETHING ACCOMPLISHED.

"HOW TO SAVE TIME AND MONEY . . .
AND HOW TO GET THINGS DONE QUICKLY."

Another watchdog-standard; "I'm sorry, but Mr. Big is out of town." To which I shoot back a quick and firm reply: "When will he return?" and secondly. . . quickly, firmly and slowly. . . "Who is in command when Mr. Big is not in town?" Would you believe that many salesmen spend 50% of their time, talking to persons who can't even say "yes" to their deal. . . because he did not ask at the beginning point blank: "Can you make this decision?" Why guess as to who to talk to next when the Boss is out of town. . . maybe there is someone "hidden in the woodwork"; for I have found some of the best executives keep a very low profile and you hardly know they exist. . . you could call these types the "no frills doers". . . and so when Mr. Big is out of town. . . this gives you the perfect opportunity to get this new informa- tion. Also you want the correct spelling of his name (ask until you get it right). . . and his complete Title. As most people. . . executives are irked about having their names or Title spelled incorrectly. Also don't forget, you already have the names of the published No. 2 and No. 3. . . but when you can get more information to use against the "enemy". . . the watchdog. . . by all means use it. . . just like 007 James Bond would do.

I have another high-echelon policy I use with great success in getting an important decision. I will only be stepped-down ONE notch in my quest for a qualified decision. . . and it works like a charm. Let us say you reach and talk to No. 1 or No. 2. . . you quickly tell him your story. . . and your prob- lem. . . now sometimes it is quite necessary that he transfer you to his "lieutenant" in charge of the proper Department. (Its just like the Army, only more efficient.). . . For Mr. Big wants his proper lieutenant to handle the matter. Mr. Big will normally refer you to the proper person. . . don't argue with Mr. Big at this moment. . . but listen carefully, for he will probably make some powerful statement that many people normally would not even listen for. . . he will say something like: "I'm sure that Mr. No. 3 can make you satisfied." Then, do not hesitate to repeat Mr. Big's comment to No. 3. . . CORRECTLY AND EXACTLY. I even write down his exact words and repeat them to No. 3, for when you talk to the top brass you will find that they are very honorable (unlike in the movies). . . and they are much more flexible and cooperative than most flea-bag bureaucrats that I just cannot get a decision from. . . and my only solution to that problem is. . . VOTE THEM OUT.

Business is run quite differently from government. Business must survive on its own gift of wisdom. . . the bureaucracy survives in spite of its dumbness . . . they just tax more. . . and print more money, which creates more inflation. You will find great satisfaction in dealing with big business. . . I am sorry I have not found a key to satisfactory dealings with Government Officials. . . that is why I say. . . VOTE THEM OUT.

Here is another little "funny" about most watchdogs who really don't consider themselves as secretaries. . . but rather, "the second in command." If and when Mr. Big is out legitimately, and I choose to leave a message, I always say to the watchdog. . . "I will leave a message. . . do you have a pencil?" I do this, because after a vast number of actual experiences, the watchdog will say. . . "wait a minute". . . in other words. . . this executive secretary is not very executive-like because she isn't even ready to take down a message. I discovered this only because at the beginning, when I would leave a message (I always wanted to insure its correctness) when I asked the watchdog to repeat my message. . . it was always incorrect (making me look like an idiot to Mr. Big). . . or the watchdog just did not care about taking down my very important message, and just wrote and repeated, "Jim Anderson called." Then they would confess that they did not have a pencil and just "winged it." (And maybe would even forget to tell the Boss I called.) So, my experience in 20 years of asking secretaries to get a pencil. . . most of them say. . . "wait a minute". . . try it. . . you will be amazed at the inefficiencies you must overcome.

Here is a humorous way to reach Mr. Big when he is difficult to get to. Most of them work late. Get his direct telephone number which you probably have anyway. Call him in the evening about 7 PM or so. . . you will normally get such relaxed and attentive response to your call. . . for he is lone-

some on the job. . . for all his young-turks have left the
ship. . . the Captain is alone and lonely at the helm. I have
reached many No. 1's this way, and get big success and
response from such talks with No. 1. A tip: At this relaxing
and quiet evening hour, I try to keep the conversation light
and humorous. . . no panics. . . no ultimatums. . . the light
mood seems productive in the evening.

Here is another example in solving a problem with a Corporation which can be used often in your every-day-life. A
dear friend was flying into Miami from New York City, but
when I called the airline to confirm arrival time. . . they
could not tell me anything for they said the airport was
"closed because of bad weather". I replied: "My friend may
be crashed on your runway, and yet you won't help me find
my friends' alternate plane route". . . and so I snapped back
at the ticket Agent. . . please transfer me to Frank Borman
(the former Astronaut and now the very successful "people
oriented" President of Eastern Airlines). . . the Agent
sputtered something about: "Can I transfer you to our Head
Ticket Agent?". . . to which I gave my standard reply in such
situations. . . "Miss Blue. . . I only waste my time with one
worker. . . and then I go to the top. . . for I am busy, and
cannot waste my entire day on this matter." . . . The end of
the story? . . . I didn't talk to Frank Borman. . . but I talked
to one of his assistants (which is all I really needed in this
case). . . I told him my need and the poor service from Miss
Blue. . . the assistant said: "I'll call you back in 5 minutes."
He did so, I got the information on my friend. . . did my days
work. . . still met my friend on time at the Rescheduled
Flight. . . I got it all worked out, because I now know how to
"make things happen". . . as J. Elroy McCaw used to say.

MORE ABOUT GETTING THE NAMES OF
THE PERSON YOU SPEAK TO ON THE PHONE

Have you ever noticed that sharp corporations . . . intent on
giving real service. . . answer the phones like. . . "good morning, this is Eastern Airlines, Miss Jones speaking. . . can I help

you?" Unfortunately, most callers (maybe you) just ignore the fact that this person gave you her name. I repeat it to her several times during our conversation, just to let her know that I consider it important to know to whom I am speaking. . . in fact. . . I MAKE IT A FIRM POLICY, NEVER. . . NEVER. . . TO SPEAK TO ANYONE ON THE PHONE WHO WILL NOT GIVE ME THEIR NAME. (What are they hiding?) There will be a few who will refuse. . . mumbling something like they are not required to. . . or its not necessary, etc., etc. With these dolts I simply ask to be transferred to the President. Usually here we get "disconnected" or they use some other delay-ploy. . . but don't give in. . . you are a "doer". . . call back. . . get the President's name. . . talk to his office, report the happening to a responsible person. . . believe me, the front office does not want to allow such employee conduct, and they will act on your complaint. . . unlike the "dreamer" who is convinced that "one person can't change things". . . to this I say baloney. . . I change things all the time. . . just me, myself and I. . . and you can too! Do you think all of this conscious-raising is silly? Think about it. Lets say that you are requiring some important information. . . you talk to "this person" (no-name that I call, "the irresponsible mystery voice on the other end of the line"). . . Let's say this "mystery voice" gives you some important information. . . Like an Airline schedule and a ticket sale. . . then when you are in one city, doing business or visiting, and you then return to the airport for your next connected flight on your ticketed reservation. . . you find that the airplane is not scheduled, and your day and your next appointment are ruined (by that "mystery voice"). So it isn't to silly, huh? This exact situation happened to me in Columbus, Ohio. I had stopped there to visit some friends. . . then was taken to the airport to catch a plane to visit my mother in St. Louis. I was met at the airline ticket counter in Columbus by confusion and a warm of 50 other people, just like me, who had also been ticketed on this nonexistent flight to St. Louis. Obviously, one agent. . . or a group of poorly managed agents had not kept up with their changing flight schedules, and had sold 50 people a flight that was not scheduled. I talked to the airline exec who was at the counter trying to help. . . appease customers, etc. . . I told him that I had the name of the ticket agent who sold and scheduled me on this nonexistent flight. The airline exec almost kissed my feet in gratitude. As he scribbled down her name, he mumbled. . . "wait till I get a hold of that agent." It was "funny" wasn't it. . . that of all these 50 people standing around the airline counter. . . terribly inconvenienced. . . that I was the only one who had the name of the ticket agent. Does this sound like a lot of work for usually nothing? I don't think so. . . it actually saves me a lot of time, aggravation. . . and money, by usually getting more reliable and correct information in this "age of mediocrity." Also, I get every name, unconsciously. . . through habit. . . and I write it down on my secretarial notebook that I keep by the phone as my daily diary. (No bits of scrap paper lying around my telephone). I know that I get a lot better and more accurate service. . . everywhere. . . BECAUSE I ALWAYS KNOW WITH WHOM I AM SPEAKING. . . else I don't talk, and I transfer my call to the President's office.

Ten years ago, in NYC, I wrote the President of the telephone company suggesting that they should answer their operator assistance calls this same way that the airlines do. . . if they really want to be service-oriented as their ads portray. . . I got no response from the telephone company. Now, recently, in St. Louis, while calling "information", I was greeted by this operator who said, "this is information. . . Miss Green speaking." I was shocked, because I have found that one of the most immovable objects in this world is the telephone company. I asked her in a startled wave, "why she had volunteereded her name to me. . . for that, to me, was new." Her reply, "well we just started this policy, and we were given our choice of using a name or a number. . . and I chose to use a name, because a number sounds foolish." Bravo, Ms. Green . . . you are correct . . . and when will the rest learn this. Corporations take note: with this policy, your profits will increase through a more efficient operation.

All of these ideas, tips, and examples will help you, dear reader, in more efficiently running your life, your salaried job. . . and your Quad. I especially suggest that young people and women-alone read this over again. Tip: I always get acquainted with several executives at the Power Co. and the Telephone Co. very quickly because I want to help serve my tenants when they have an aggravating problem that I can help them solve fast. Remember, you don't have to do it. . . but I like to help, when I can. . . and I figure that I will have tenants who don't have my experience, so why not help when I can. Say your new tenant wants his Utilities turned on "yesterday" (everybody is the same on this). . . A call to your friend-utility-exec will get your good tenant much faster service. . . again. . . only if you want to, and if you have the time. But there is an old and true saying: "Give another job to a busy person, if you want to get it done." . . . Very, very true. Another tip: most people don't know that Utilities have an evening hook up service for working people who can't stay home and wait for them during the day. The Utilities don't advertise this because it means more expensive worker over-time pay. . . but it is normally available. . . and when I am too busy, I advise my new good-tenant of this night-service. Also when I need anything from a Utility, they are about the worst in playing "the old Army Game" by saying. . . "We will be out to see you on Tuesday". . . with these disinterested "Army types" I have found great help and courtesy from my Utility-exec-friends. . . who in general, really want to be of service. . . its just the underlings who aren't interested in doing their job. . . and that's just human nature . . . "for after we understand the problem. . . usually we can solve it." I apologize for adding this long section to my book. I hope it

wasn't too long and drawn out. But by giving actual exam-ples, I am using the proven way taught in the great Dale Carnegie executive course. . . that "if you want to gain more attention and impact from your listeners. . . GIVE AN EXAMPLE. . . and don't pontificate by just giving rules and regulations. . . this is a "turn off." And it takes time to explain, because it took me years to successfully develop these techniques. . . and I do believe that these "secrets" will save you time and money.

"HOW TO SAVE TIME AND MONEY . . .
AND HOW TO GET THINGS DONE QUICKLY."

If this subject interests you more. . . consider buying Dr. Wayne Dyer's book "Pulling Your Own Strings." I have not read the book, but I heard Dyer discuss the subject matter on a TV talk-show, and I was surprised to see similarities in what I have just written. I put some of this conscious -raising in this book, instead of writing another book on this subject. . . Now with Wayne Dyer's book, I believe, on the same subject matter.

HERE IS ANOTHER RECENT NEWSPAPER STORY ON THIS BOOK

The Secret To Rent-Free Living?

Author: Anyone Can Live Rent-Free

'JUST STICK OUT YOUR HAND, PALM UP'
. . . to collect rent checks, Anderson says

He has been selling the idea of economic freedom and his book for the past six months to radio and newspaper audiences around the country.

An Associated Press article on the Miami author has appeared in over 400 newspapers, Anderson boasts.

The headlines: *Florida Man Beats His Rent by Collecting It From Others*; *Ex-New Yorker Finds Key To Living Rent-Free*; *Landlord Says Owning 4-plex Makes His Job as Easy as Accepting Checks.*

SALES OF the 320-page paperback (distributed nationally by Ingram/Nashville, Dimondstein/New York and Southern/Miami) have been encouraging

Anderson makes no pretense about his audience — he's not writing the book for the armchair businessman with expensive bookstore tastes.

"I call my book the McDonald's approach to commercial real estate," Anderson says, the mass-merchandise approach aimed at "the working guy."

The one-time marketing man and television executive says "only 5 per cent of the people in the country have tax shelters. If "doctors and lawyers can have them, why not the working stiff?"

ANDERSON, WHO spent much of his television career renting an expensive apartment in New York, calls the American dream of owning a single-family home an economic disaster.

"I finally realized that my home was a real luxury for which I paid the taxes, the upkeep, the insurance and everything else," he writes, "just for me and my wife to live there and to try to keep up with the mortgage payments."

He calls that single-family home a "millstone" that drags down the average working guy.

Instead of spending $80,000 or $100,000 to own a fancy home in the suburbs, Anderson preaches the doctrine of apartment investment.

"If you can afford a home, you can afford to own your own apartment building," he says, "and live there rent free.

"I was amazed three years ago when I decided to release myself from that big old millstone around my neck (my home) by buying an apartment building, that I could afford the apartment building for actually less money than the equity I had from the sale of my house."

ANDERSON'S APARTMENTS mostly rent in the $180 to $255 a month range. He says the highest mortgage payment he has is around $380 a month.

In a typical four-unit apartment building, called a quad or a fourplex, Anderson says rent from two of the units pays the mortgage, interest and taxes.

Rent from the third apartment covers maintenance and the rest is profit.

And he never buys an apartment property with financing from a bank — he always has the owner take back a second mortgage.

"Plus, there's the tax shelter advantages," he says. (Interest paid on the mortgage is tax deductible, and so is depreciation on the investment plus some maintenance expenses.)

Anderson, who got his Florida brokers license last year after three years as a salesman, doesn't have much use for "so-called real estate experts."

ONE OF his favorite targets is the broker who advises others on property management but owns nothing himself. He quotes his version of the 1930s Packard automobile jingle: "Buying income property? Ask the man who owns one."

He's started offering his services as a consultant to others looking to buy rental property and offers a 90-day satisfaction guarantee on his book, dispensing replies to inquiries about his advice.

Anderson debunks a lot of the "old wives tales in this business," including the one about all the headaches of being a property owner/landlord.

"Brokers tell me as reasons why they don't own ... 'I don't want to clean the johns, and I don't want those Saturday night calls.' To this I reply, as I laugh myself all the way to the bank on a leisurely Monday morning, 'I don't clean the johns, and I don't get those Saturday night calls.'"

IN ANOTHER interview, Anderson emphasized "I'm not a *landlord*. I'm a property owner. I do nice things for my tenants, and I expect them to do nice things for me ...."

"I don't allow tenants to run my buildings," he says matter-of-factly.

HIS NO-NOSENSE approach to landlord-tenant relations includes the dictum about security deposits — 'an absolute must.' He gets three months rent in advance just to keep his people honest and never rents furnished apartments.

"Why put in furniture to promote gypsies," he says.

ANDERSON CONCEDES that much of his advice is not new. Others have become rental property owners and have been far more successful than Anderson. But few have had his gift for promoting the idea of living rent free.

The biggest hurdle for most people is not finding a place to buy or finding a way to finance it, he says. The biggest problem is overcoming inertia.

"The guy paying up to $1,000 a month for a mortgage on that millstone (home) is thinking about his job, his family and his golf game. He looks straight ahead, not looking one degree either way to see how he can survive financially any other way," the Miami landlord says.

"I'm not preaching a get rich quick scheme. Just something so you can keep working if you want, have a roof over your head and live rent free the rest of your life."

CHAPTER TWENTY-FOUR

CONCLUSION

May I say in conclusion that of all the interesting jobs I have had in my lifetime so far . . . that I think that apartment building ownership and management has made me happier and more secure than I have ever felt before. The independent feeling you get from the knowledge that you own BUILDINGS is truly uplifting.

Then the satisfaction of putting more value into your building than the past owner has thought of is very rewarding.

Then when you see a better class of tenants applying because they like your improvements inside and out, that is a nice reward.

When an architect or a decorator or a writer rents from you, you feel that creative people like that like what I am doing . . . "so I must be on the right track."

And now my newest reward will be to help you to get into this most satisfying of all businesses without the big risk that can be involved when you go it on your own.

And remember "caveat emptor" (buyer-beware). That real estate Agent is representing the Seller and not you the buyer. This is too large a step for you not to have someone on your side. Don't go it alone, just because you have purchased "a few houses" or had "some other business."

I recently spoke to one of the top lawyers in town about this new service of mine, wherein I represent the Buyer on a fiduciary relationship basis and at no cost since I as a Broker qualify to share in part of the Listing Broker's Commission . . . this lawyer said . . . that he had "often wondered when someone would offer this Service to the Buyer . . . because we all know that the real estate Agent really represents the Seller, not the Buyer, and the Agent is bound in a fiduciary relationship with the Seller . . . not the Buyer. And

Who should, and who should not begin on this project? I would really not want to discourage anyone... even the procrastinator ... for they could change their wasteful ways, as others have done, to be completely rewarded and fulfilled by this new lifestyle.

However, on the plus side, I think It would be a marvelous new lifestyle for the hundreds of thousands of salesmen. Your income can vary with your sales; and this QUAD-cushion could be just the remedy for 30 years of peace and tranquility.

Women alone? Of course. Conscious-raise a minute; There are probably more women involved in the sale of real estate than men... they love the home, and are identified with it more than a man. And they can certainly communicate with people (as well as tenants). As a matter of fact, I ask my wife to handle many tenant matters since I may be too brusque. However, an introverted woman must learn to speak up, and not allow tenant-intimidation. As far as investment money? ... statistics used to show that women own 80% of the Nation's wealth (it could be 90% today), so the women can buy a lot more Quads than we men. As far as repairs and maintenance... how many times have you heard a wife say of her husband: "Harry doesn't know one end of a screw driver from the other"? (Actually Harry is just being smart in his lazy way... he doesn't want to work around the house)... so the little woman does all the little house-repairs. Secondly, what the woman alone can't fix herself... she gets her low cost maintenance cráftsman to fix for her (as she "bats her eyelashes, in helpless abandon").

"The Middle-Class Poor" are good candidates for this project. Graduating students are some of the first to adopt this new lifestyle; since being young, they are not "old and set in their ways"... and they have been terribly worried about how they were "going to make it in the cruel, cruel World."

More "types" who should consider this life-style are SELF EMPLOYED PROFESSIONALS, such as Craftsmen, Artists, Musicians, accountants, bureaucrats (who will have their own energy and Union wage increase inflationary pressures), and

Union workers who will have the energy and bureaucratic waste inflationary pressures. Any self employed person who has a fluctuating income will find this project a wonderful solution. A QUAD or a Duplex will give financial security to these people whose incomes fluctuate.

Self employed shop-keepers are some of the first to buy a QUAD. For they are already "doers", for they are already in business and they can easily handle a QUAD, on the side. The "Own Your Own Business" Expo regularly hires me to speak at these Expos, where people pay admission to visit the various franchise-booths where they can learn how to get into their own business. The Expo Management sees me NOT AS A COMPETITOR. . . BUT AS A PERFECT COMPLEMENT TO OWNING YOUR OWN BUSINESS. So, purchase the franchise, or the distributorship. . . but also own and live in your own QUAD (instead of your millstone) and you will really have the World on a string. Your business will always be a gamble, however. . . YOUR QUAD WILL NOT BE A GAMBLE. . . so at the least, you are hedging your investment.

PROCASTINATION . . .
THE PUBLIC'S No. 1 ENEMY

Whenever a person or a couple come over to visit me and to look over my properties (and I welcome this) . . . the first thing I tell them when we sit down for a chat, is to tell them that . . . "only one out of 5 who comes here, and sits there, will ever do anything about buying an apartment building . . . and it won't be because of lack of cash . . . it will be procrastination."

Most of you who are reading this book do have the $15,000 required to buy building No. 1 . . . but it will be your procrastination that will stop you from becoming financially independent and to live rent free.

Sometimes my visitor (all enthused) will begin to project toward building No. 2 (he hasn't even bought No. 1 yet) . . . I try to keep his mind on the "game plan" just like a football coach who must channel his players minds on next weeks game, and not the big game two weeks off. That is why that next game (against an inferior opponent) was lost. It was thinking about the game TWO weeks off. So often you see a pass-receiver let a beautiful pass just slip through his hands, and it would have been open field for a touchdown. Why? Because the receiver was not concentrating on CATCHING THE BALL . . . he was, too soon, concentrating on running over the goal for a touchdown . . . so, concentrate on the "next game" . . . in your case . . . it is building No. 1, and nothing else.

We need a lot of Indians and few Chiefs. We need only a few Shepherds to control hundreds of sheep. In the same way we have 99 salaried workers for every person who goes out for himself and does something on his own.

Luckily we need the "sheep" . . . for they are the workers . . . they will be your tenants if you break out of the procrastination rut.

I do many things every day with "relish" . . . for I love my work and I am not any longer a procrastinator . . . I kicked the habit. (Incidentally I also kicked the smoking habit three years ago, never to take another puff. I was a heavy smoker, and I blamed procrastination for not quiting sooner. Have not you put off quitting many, many times?)

My tenants are procrastinators and I just grin to myself as I take that next rent check. They get impetuous if there is a delay in repairing something (it usually is beyond my control) . . . then perhaps we make a deal for them to repaint their apartment and I am to furnish the paint. I have seen the paint just sit in the corner of their apartment for six months. Their excuse? "I have been too busy." Baloney, they are lazy procrastinators.

I have talked to many New Yorkers who dream of coming to Florida and living in a condominium, so they "don't have to mow the lawn, etc." To those people especially I say stay out of my business for you will be a failure.

THE BRIGHT SIDE . . .

On the other side of the coin there are people among you who are salaried and have been working for someone else too long but have hesitated in a major move because of the risk to your life's savings. You people are the one's I have written this book for (so procrastinators give this book to someone you know that fits the above description and maybe when your "doer" friend buys a building . . . there will always be a unit at a discount price for his procrastinator friend who gave him this book).

There are clever people out there (usually about 5 out of every 100) who are just wasting their time working for someone else . . . but just needs the right vehicle to get started on their own. I understand that problem very well. For I went through this agonization too. Have you seen that "tire com-

PROCASTINATION . . .
THE PUBLIC'S No. 1 ENEMY

mercial" where the dummy and his wife were in the big car, driven by a clever chauffeur. After one more dumb remark from the "master" . . . the wife said to the chauffeur "Stanley . . . have you ever wondered why YOU are up there (driving) and HE is back here?" That's the kind of person I would like to help . . . the clever person who just hasn't found the right thing in which to channel his resources and some of his time.

At a lecture Seminar recently where I was on the program with a Professor who instructs adult evening classes on owning your own business, I asked this Professor, "what percent of your hundreds of adult students that take your course on owning their own business ever actually DO own their own business. His answer . . . "about 10%," Imagine, adults even take their valuable relaxing time in the evenings after work to go to adult class to learn about owning their own business; only 1 out of 10 ever does anything about it. What a waste of time, energy, etc. Procrastination is the main reason.

About one month after a radio interview on a talk program wherein I was interviewed about this book and the concept of living rent-free . . . I got a letter from a listener (one month later) excitedly ordering my book with the big long story that she had mislaid my address and could not find me listed in the phone book (I have an unlisted telephone number) . . . that she had called the radio station one month after the interview to no avail . . . and that she poured out all the junk from her drawer (probably her procrastination drawer) and still could not find the note with my name and address on it. Finally when all was lost, she found the paper wedged inside the chest of drawers. What a waste of energy. Enclosed with the book I addressed her as "Dear Procrastinator" AND challenged her to "kick the habit." In her case she blames her husband (like all good "alkys" do). I would not work with her on buying a building. It would be all frustration.

300

... And now the rest is up to you. This project is possible by the 120,000,000 workers (and graduating students, soon to be working) in the U.S.A. However, separating the "doers" from the 90% "dreamers" ... that leaves about 12,000,000 workers in the USA that can and should purchase a Quadplex or a Duplex. About 60,000,000 of the 120,000,000 workers either own a "millstone" or have the $15,000 equity necessary to purchase a Quad. The remaining 60,000,000 will have to take the first step I recently developed for one of my tenants who said to me: "Jim, how can I live rent free?" ... So included herein is that solution: HOW TO OWN YOUR OWN DUPLEX... EVEN IF YOU DON'T HAVE THE DOWN PAYMENT... AND SOON LIVE THERE RENT FREE... WHILE YOU PAY LESS INCOME TAX ON YOUR SALARY... ALL APPROVED BY UNCLE SAM.

Considering all of these "box car" numbers thrown out above... you may say... WOW... that's a lot of people buying Quad's and Duplexes... however, as a student of human nature and an observer of procrastination... even though this overlooked solution has the strongest and the most basic appeal to the 120,000,000 workers in the USA, ie, LIVING RENT FREE... PAYING LITTLE OR NO INCOME TAX... 30 YEARS OF HAPPINESS... INDEPENDENCE... SECURITY... STATURE AND PRESTIGE IN THE COMMUNITY... FINANCIAL SALVATION AS WE GO INTO THE INFLATIONARY SPIRAL OF THE 1980's... AND A SIMPLE AND JUST OVERLOOKED SOLUTION TO ALL OF THIS ABOVE... WITH NO TRICKS... NO MAGIC... NO MIRRORS... NO GET RICH QUICK SCHEME... JUST GOOD OLD MIDWESTERN COMMON SENSE FROM A PERSON JUST LIKE YOU, WHO DID THIS OVERLOOKED PROJECT, THREE TIMES IN THREE SUCCESSIVE YEARS, WITHOUT ANY PREVIOUS EXPERIENCE, AND THEN PUTTING DOWN IN DETAIL IN THIS 100,000 WORD REFERENCE BOOK, STEP BY STEP, AS TO HOW YOU CAN DO IT TOO...

with all of this primary appeal to the 120,000,000 work-
ers . . . I feel that about 1% or 1,200,000 workers will get
into this project within the next year . . . they will have
2,000,000 to 3,000,000 tenants (some of the "dreamers" do
make nice tenants) . . . AND THIS "HOW TO LIVE RENT
FREE" PROJECT WILL CHANGE THE LIVING HABITS
OF AMERICA WITHIN THE NEXT FIVE YEARS . . .
THEN ABOUT 1,000,000,000 (1 Billion) OF THE WORK-
ERS OF THE WORLD CAN DO THIS . . . 10,000,000 WILL
POSSIBLY DO IT.

AT SCHOOL LECTURES, STUDENTS TELL THIS AUTHOR... "WE ARE INTO THE ERA OF QUAD-SOUND... AND UNLIKE OUR PARENTS, WE ARE GOING INTO QUAD-LIVING FOR OUR OWN FINANCIAL SALVATION IN OUR ERA... THE INFLATIONARY SPIRAL OF THE 1980'S, AND STOP WORKING FOR UNCLE SAM FROM JAN. 1 'TILL MAY 11th OF EVERY YEAR WHICH IS WHAT THE AVERAGE TAX PAYER DOES."

Anderson's book conscious-raises the old impractical goals after graduation "of living in the boondocks (suburbs), in one of those little-boxes (overpriced luxury homes). This "unproductive millstone" (home) will become your financial tombstone in the inflationary spiral of the 1980's... you ain't seen nothin' yet (inflation)."

THE ALTERNATIVE... purchase a QUAD (4 unit) apartment building (for about the same cost as the millstone, beleive it or not)... live in one unit, rent free... and rent out the other 3. (See Chapters on "Getting Star Tenants" and "The Lease Secret")... also see Chapter on "No-Frills Financing". Your tenants rent pays all your expenses.

If the student does not have the $10,000 down payment normally required to purchase the QUAD... the Author has a conservative and simple solution, entitled: HOW TO OWN YOUR OWN DUPLEX EVEN IF YOU DON'T HAVE THE DOWN PAYMENT; AND SOON LIVE THERE RENT FREE."

Additionally, two "singles" living together develops another financial problem of higher income taxes from two-working-single-adults. But your QUAD or Duplex ALLOWS YOU "LEGAL TAX DODGES" (shelters) provided by Uncle Sam in his great wisdom to encourage Property Ownership which is the backbone of this Country, and what made it strong and great. In this purchase you can easily create your own "divided ownership."

Within a few short years, and by following the Author's sound and simple problem solving advice on SUCCESSFUL APARTMENT BUILDING MANAGEMENT... these rather recent working adults will have a much happier, secure and independent life than their Parents had (or have), living in their unproductive-millstone as we approach the inflationary spiral of the 1980's. Your job security will not be the only answer to your personal financial salvation . . . more vacations and more pleasures of life . . . versus the past generations that were trained that the goal in life was that millstone in the boondocks, is no longer true. You may even like this sideline . . . .save up more money from your salaries . . . purchase several more buildings . . . and quit your job altogether . . . and manage your Property, like I do.

This reference book also simply solves all the old wivestales about apartment buildings, and why perhaps your parents never bought one . . . "problem tenants" . . . "maintenance" . . . "vacancies" . . . "location" . . . "5 point inspection" . . . "How To Increase Rents", many, many more.

Students always ask the same question after the lecture . . . "Your plan sounds so good that everyone will buy QUAD'S and Duplexes, and there will be no tenants." Anderson replies, "There are 90% "Dreamers" and 10% "Doers" (that's just human nature) . . . the doers will own the QUAD'S and Duplexes . . . and the dreamers will be the renters."

To readers of the new book: HOW TO LIVE RENT FREE, by J. Anderson

If you fill this out and mail it to me, I will put you on my NEWSLETTER MAILING LIST ... FREE ... to receive occasional newsletters on apartment building ownership ... such as: trends, financing, maintenance, managing, etc.

1. I □ did; □ did not know that I could purchase a 4 unit apartment building for the equity in my home or: for about $15,000 cash

2. I □ did; □ did not know that I, as an apartment purchaser could obtain the no-cost professional services of an advisor-Broker to help.

3. I □ did; □ did not know that this Advisor-Broker would also assist me in the building inspection; the negotiation; the Contract-For-Sale; the Closing; plus initial advice on the professional management of my new apartment building after the sale; also at no cost to me.

4. I □ did; □ did not know that this same no-cost Advisor-Broker would confidentially give me his list of dependable low cost Craftsmen for maintenance work.

5. After reading the book, I need more information on the following subjects. (Check all subjects that interest you)

   □ Living on the premises.

   □ How to find the right apartment for me.

   □ How to know what is a fair price.

   □ Proper Building Inspection.

   □ Location advice.

   □ How to negotiate down, the price.

306

- ☐ What are my tax advantages?
- ☐ Other topics of interest to you.
- ☐ What is the best way to finance.
- ☐ Contract-For-Sale help.
- ☐ "Closing" help.
- ☐ Management advice.
- ☐ Management service.
- ☐ How to increase rents.
- ☐ Other_____
- ☐ Other_____

6. I ☐ would; ☐ would not be interested in information on your "NO-FRILLS SEMINAR" through a Broker in my area.

Fill out questionaire above, and send with coupon to: BRUN PRESS, BOX 370034, Miami, Fl. 33137.

NAME_____

ADDRESS _____

CITY_____ STATE_____ ZIP_____

FURTHER COMMENTS: _____

_____

_____

MONTHLY NEWSLETTER ON RENT FREE MOVEMENT

$50 PER YEAR

QUAD-PLEX OWNERS of AMERICA

DEDICATED TO ASSIST AND ADVISE FUTURE, NEW OR CURRENT QUAD-PLEX OWNERS
IN THE MANAGEMENT OF THEIR RENTAL PROPERTY.

701 N.E. 67 STREET
MIAMI, FLORIDA 33138

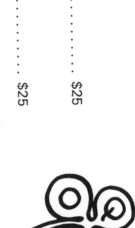

TELEPHONE
305 - 756 - 6249

Membership &
initiation fee $25

$5 annual dues
for five years $25

Total $50

YOU GET:

1. ANNUAL REPORT ON THE GROWING QUAD-PLEX BUSINESS.
2. INTRODUCTIONS TO OTHER QPOA MEMBERS IN YOUR AREA.
3. LOCAL HELP FOR LOCAL PROBLEMS.
4. PERSONAL CONSULTATIONS, AT COST.

FOUNDER: **JAMES W. ANDERSON**

AUTHOR OF "JIM ANDERSON'S HOW TO LIVE RENT FREE BOOK"
MAJOR NEW MASS REFERENCE BOOK ON "INFLATION-SURVIVAL"
Library of Congress Catalogue Card No. 78-113752

NAME _____

ADDRESS _____

CITY/STATE/TEL. _____

308

ORGANIZED PROUD PROPERTY OWNERS OF AMERICA.

OPPO Contributors will receive an annual report as to OPPO Progress.

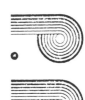
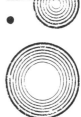

PLATFORM

1. Put the bureaucrats in jail for stealing taxpayers money; as our government now puts the tax-evaders in jail. O.P.P.O. will sponsor this bill.

2. Stop and reduce government growth and bigness through new amendments sponsored by O.P.P.O.'s members. Simple bills such as limiting government employees to 1% of the population. Currently it is nearing 2% in some areas; and overstaffed everywhere.

3. O.P.P.O. will sponsor legislation for more punishment for the criminal and fines for most offenses which will eliminate judicial corruption and lawyer shistering. O.P.P.O. will sponsor legislation to remove, fine and jail corrupt judges.

4. O.P.P.O. will support a new breed of government executive. Men and women who will lead the USA up to becoming a No. 1 Nation again. Limit. One term in office.

Please Xerox this sheet 100 times and send it to your friends/employees. A Property Owner Revolution begins and grows just from small seeds of discontent, fostered by organizations like OPPO into A STRONG NATIONAL ORGANIZATION AMONG THE 47,000,000 PROPERTY OWNERS . . . & VOTERS . . . TO MAKE THE U.S.A. No. 1 AGAIN.

NAME _____

ADDRESS _____

CITY/STATE/ZIP _____ ($5 enclosed)

309

THIS 1000 WORD FEATURE STORY APPEARED IN 400 NEWS-
PAPERS COAST TO COAST, AFTER A REPORTER FROM THE
WORLD'S LARGEST NEWS GATHERING ORGANIZATION SPENT
THREE HOURS WITH JIM ANDERSON, INVESTIGATING, INTER-
VIEWING, AND THEN WRITING THIS STORY.

He's Telling His Secret of Leisurely, Rent-Free Living

Practically everyone has at one time or another dreamed of living free and easy. Maybe it's in a place by the sea or high in the mountains. James Anderson's idea of the good life is Miami where he lives - free. While most Americans are putting in a hard day's work, Anderson turns his palm upward, collects the money and enjoys the good life.

MIAMI—While most Americans are putting in a hard day's work just to keep a roof over their heads, James Anderson is off to Europe for a month or at home sipping a cocktail, gardening and enjoying the beaches.

Anderson is no millionaire. He lives rent free in a luxurious Spanish villa "just two doors from the Biscayne Bay" on Miami's northeast side. He affectionately calls the apartment his "gushing oil well."

He insists that anyone can enjoy such a lifestyle—with a little planning and work.

"I live better today than I ever have before," Anderson says, showing off his home's wooden floors, arched entryways, overhead wooden fans, 40 louvered doors and butcher-block counter.

On a typical morning, the 52-year-old former New Yorker and author of "Jim Anderson's How to Live Rent Free Book," enjoys the morning newspaper over coffee, makes a leisurely trip to the bank and gets a few chores out of the way.

Then he spends the afternoon deep-sea fishing, answering his mail or working on a pet project. He's often in demand for talk shows.

Anderson says the secret is to sell that single-family home he calls a "millstone around your neck" and put the money into a four-unit apartment building called a quad-plex.

"Owning your own home has been profitable in the past, but the 1970s inflationary spiral is making the No. 1 concern of most Americans just making ends meet," he says.

310

"I'm telling you to get out of your millstone and buy a quad-plex. You'll live rent-free and your financial problems will be solved."

Rent from the first two units pays off the mortgage, interest and taxes, he says. And the third apartment takes care of maintenance. The rest is free and clear. Depreciation and inflation make it a tax shelter, too, Anderson adds.

Families, he notes, can find quadplexes in which one unit has three or four bedrooms or live in two units. Of course, then they have to pay themselves "rent."

Improvements just make it easier to raise the rent and increase the profits, he says. Anderson bought his first quad about four years ago and now owns three such buildings. He says he has more than doubled the rent through improvements.

He readily admits that one of his secrets is to keep his quads so nice looking that he never lacks for tenants and sometimes even has people waiting for spots.

His personal favorite is to cover the grounds with trees and other tropical plants, which he calls "turning greenery into greenbacks."

Friends scoff at the prospect of dealing with tenants, cleaning bathrooms and taking Saturday night calls when the plumbing goes out of whack, he says.

That, he says, happens only in operations that are "run like a candy store." He points out that preventive maintenance takes care of most such problems, and emergency calls just haven't been a problem.

And the rent from the third apartment is used to hire what Anderson calls "craftsmen" who take care of roofing, plumbing, carpentering and other needs so he doesn't have to do it himself.

"I don't clean the johns or take Saturday night calls," he says. "I'm not a landlord. I'm a property owner. I do nice things for my tenants, and I expect them to do nice things for me . . . . Some of my best friends are tenants."

Best friends and relatives, to be exact. His 80-year-old French mother-in-law lives above the one-bedroom apartment he, his concert-pianist wife, Andree, and their Russian wolfhound, Natasha, occupy.

The mother-in-law calls it her "tropical paradise" and couldn't wait to get back during a recent trip to her homeland, Anderson says. A decorator friend liked the place so much he tried to get Anderson to evict her.

Anderson says the hard work comes at the beginning, but it gets so easy he estimates that the management of his three buildings takes up about 20 percent of his time now.

He says he quit his job with a Miami advertising agency when he got into the quad-plex business. Before that, he spent 20 years in the television business. He worked for the ABC TV network and stations in New York, Washington, Minneapolis, Philadelphia, San Antonio, Panama and the Phillippines.

Anderson says he had only a small savings account to help him get started. Persons who want to get into the business, he advises, need about a 10 percent down payment—once you get started, the rent from the first two units should take care of the rest.

He collects the rent checks and handles other details for his tenants, but says it's not like work because he's careful who rents his property and he likes all the tenants.

"Stick out your hand, palm up," he orders. "That's how easy it is. It shows you can pick up rent checks."

If it's such a lucrative business, why does he want to share his secret?

"I don't care if they buy my book. I just want them to get the idea that a millstone is not the answer. They can have four homes for the price of one."

CBS
NEWS

CBS TV News sent their film crew and investigative reporter to Jim Anderson's "gushing oil well" (quad plex) to see, if indeed, he does "live like a millionaire, in luxury, but rent free." (As reported by 400 newspapers).

The CBS film was very generous and expansive in showing throughout most of this feature report, Jim Anderson's "millionaire lifestyle, rent free living". . . "the arched entryways". . . "the wooden floors". . . "the 40 louvered doors". . . "the butcher block counters". . . "in his elegant Spanish Villa along beautiful Tropical Biscayne Bay.

Anderson says, "CBS TV News filmed everywhere but inside my closets. It was a very thorough TV News Report."

CBS TV NEWS AUDIO SCRIPT

(Anchorman introduction). . . "THE AUTHOR OF A BOOK ON "HOW TO LIVE RENT FREE" GETS DOUBLE ROYALTIES. . . ONE FROM THE BOOK. . . AND THE OTHER FROM NOT HAVING TO PAY RENT. . ."

(Reporter). . . "IT'S A LUXURIOUS SPANISH VILLA TUCKED AWAY IN MIAMI'S NORTHEAST SECTION. . . CERTAINLY IT MUST COST A LOT TO LIVE IN. . . NOT TRUE. . . IT COSTS THE OWNER NOTHING. . . ACTUALLY THIS IS NOT A HOUSE AT ALL. . . IT'S A "GUSHING OIL WELL", OR AT LEAST THAT'S WHAT ITS OWNER CALLS IT. THIS IS PART OF A FOUR UNIT COMPLEX CALLED A "QUAD-PLEX". THE MAN WHO OWNS IT, 52 YEAR OLD JIM ANDERSON IS A FORMER NEW YORK CITY TV NETWORK EXECUTIVE. HE SAYS IT HAS PROVIDED HIM RENT-FREE LIVING. . . AND IT HAS GOTTEN RID OF A MILL—STONE AROUND HIS NECK, THE SINGLE FAMILY HOME, WHICH IS NONPRODUCTIVE AND IS BEING PRICED OUT OF THE RANGE OF MANY AMERICAN FAMILIES."

CBS

(Author Anderson speaks on CBS TV News)... "WE ALL AGREE THAT "THE MILLSTONE" HAS BEEN OUR BEST INVESTMENT... NOW I SIMPLY SAY... DO IT AGAIN... BUT "TIMES FOUR"... BUY A "QUAD" AND YOU'LL REALLY HAVE FINANCIAL SALVATION IN THE INFLATIONARY SPIRAL OF THE 1980'S WHICH ALL RECENT MAJOR SURVEYS REPORT IS AMERICA'S No. 1 CONCERN. WITH YOUR "QUAD"... YOU LIVE IN ONE SPECIAL UNIT... FREE... THE RENT FROM TWO UNITS PAYS YOUR MORTGAGE, TAXES AND INSURANCE... YOUR THIRD UNITS' RENT WILL PAY YOUR MAINTENANCE AND IMPROVE-MENT COSTS... YOU CONTINUE ON YOUR JOB, SINCE YOUR QUAD WILL ONLY TAKE SEVERAL HOURS OF SUPERVISION WEEKLY... AND NOW YOU HAVE A TAX SHELTER LIKE YOUR RICH DOCTOR. ONLY 5 PERCENT OF THE PEOPLE IN THIS COUNTRY HAVE A TAX SHELTER FOR THEY ARE FRIGHTENED TO DEATH OF LOSING THEIR INVESTED PRINCIPAL."

(Reporter)... "ANDERSON SAYS, "QUAD-PLEXES" ARE UNDER-PRICED PLENTIFUL, AND USUALLY MORE CONVENIENT, AND CAN BE FOUND ALL OVER THE COUNTRY. THEY ARE TEN TO TWENTY YEARS OLD, BUT WITH NEW DEMAND, BUILDERS ARE COMING UP WITH ELEGANT NEW QUAD DESIGNS. ANDERSON PUT DOWN JUST $10,000 FOR HIS FIRST "QUAD"... AND NOW, 3 YEARS LATER HE OWNS 3 QUADS, WHICH HAS ALLOWED HIM TO QUIT WORKING ALL TOGETHER. HE SAYS HE SPENDS LITTLE TIME SUPERVISING HIS "QUADS" AND CRAFTSMEN DO ALL THE MAINTENANCE WORK FOR HIM... AND HE CHOOSES WHO WILL LIVE IN HIS UNITS SINCE "QUADS" ARE NOT SUB-JECTED TO FEDERAL-TENANT GUIDELINES... HIS BOOK, "JIM ANDERSON'S HOW TO LIVE RENT FREE BOOK" IS NOW IN ITS THIRD PRINTING... C B S NEWS... MIAMI."

HOUSING TRENDS IN THE 1980's

The current imbalance of home owners will gradually reduce as the 47,000,000 home owners of the 75,000,000 total households in the USA will see a better lifestyle in Quadplex and Duplex living.

Creative builders will capitalize on this phenomena and build speculative Quad's in just about every environment conceivable. We will have Quad's by the parks; Quad's by the water; Quad's by the Golf Courses; Quad's by the seaside; Quad's by the rivers and lakes, Quad's in or near the Central City for busy people bored with long commutes and cannot afford $2 per gallon gasoline. Quad's Midtown . . . the only place I do not see Quad's . . . is in the boondocks, which will turn into the blue-collar slums of tomorrow, as is currently happening in the major Cities of Europe (see Europe report in Chapter on "Location").

The Creative/Speculative builders will also conceive beautiful designs for these new Quad's and Duplexes . . . they will look more like mansions than apartment buildings . . . and not with two or four visible front doors . . . but the 2 or 4 entrances, creatively placed on 3 or 4 sides of the building and looking more like a Villa, than the current "motel look" of many today. I live in a beautiful Villa-Quad.

Downtown, and near the Central Cities, redevelopment will accelerate at a much more rapid pace than in these late 1970's. As is currently a big thing in Europe, the middle class will purchase these older but better built structures, and convert them into Quad's as has been going on in New York City for almost 50 years, where the 4 story "Brownstone" home at the turn of the Century is now 4 or more apartment units, and the lucky owner spends most of his time on the Riviera.

In my lectures at Universities I talk to a lot of students who say "we are into Quad sound, and we are going into Quad-living, so we can work less, and enjoy living more." . . . I don't see anything wrong with that thinking from our future generation.

Families that desire more room for themselves will own two duplexes on the same lot . . . Retired people will own a Quad or a Duplex to finally solve the problem of their fixed income, because their tenants increased rents as the economy increases takes care of these Senior Citizens.

I see local Governments "relaxing current zoning" on their big, oversized single family homes in very nice areas, where the owner, possibly a Senior Citizen, wants to keep the beautiful and nice old structure, but can't use all the space. So, forward thinking City Governments will allow these types of large old homes to be converted into Duplexes with a set of very strict zoning stipulations to not only keep the area exclusive, but through more income for the owner, actually see these areas rejuvenating. I have talked to creative City Managers, and they see nothing wrong with this idea with the proper set of tight rules (in writing, remember?), such as; a minimum square footage per living unit. (Perhaps 1200 square feet, or whatever is agreed upon.) Also a limit on people living in a building . . . perhaps three per unit and a total of no more than six persons per old building. No more than 2 or 3 cars should be allowed, and strict rules on noise and living standards should prevail. If City Fathers do this, they will patriotically be saving resources of this Country by not tearing down these perfectly good, but too big single family homes . . . and the City Fathers' coffers will increase also, because now they collect taxes on a duplex, instead of that old rose covered millstone.

The housing I do not see continuing to flourish is large apartment complexes and large condominium complexes . . . They remind me of an "Alcatraz" type prison . . . and if these residents would only conscious-raise some night (perhaps when coming home from a party) . . . let them fantasize that there are guards marching along the roof of their chic? large apartment or large condominium . . . armed with tommy-guns, as they do at Alcatraz. This, anyway, is the vision that I see whenever I drive up to one of these monstrosities. I also call them a three-ring-circus, with all their noise, car pollution, etc. that you cannot avoid when you have maybe 20 or 50 apartment units on a very small piece of ground.

Some people call this type apartment . . . luxury living . . . I call them jungles. Also they are built poorly, with paper thin walls where you can even hear a burp from your neighbor. Low ceilings; no better charm than any motel I have stayed in . . . and many people call this . . . luxury living? I call it a Micky Mouse investment . . . and a Micky Mouse Lifestyle. For many of you apartment-freaks . . . stop paying rent . . . and start collecting rent . . . and let your tenants send you to Europe, or wherever you choose, every year. Yes, there is a better way of life, that has been completely ignored by the Mass population . . . for if you like the apartment life-style . . . don't live it in a 3 ring circus atmosphere . . . own your own Quad Plex . . . and you will own 4 of your condominium type apartments, for about the price of just one of your little jail-cell style apartments that some of you call luxury apartments (we have been making rich builders and developers for too long). It will happen, and give a beautiful new lifestyle to those who can see beyond the mass rush to condominium or large apartment type living of today . . . Your Quad will be your charming home.

The unproductive millstone? (your home if you ar just book browsing) . . . well I think if we read any newspaper with any intellectual observation over the past few years . . . we can see it on the endangered list as our American Bald Eagle. But unlike the Eagle . . . the millstone will not be revered nor missed.

In the 1950's, 7 out of 10 families could own their own nonproductive millstone . . . today in the 1980's; less than 2 out of 10 families can own their own nonproductive millstone. Doesn't that tell us all something? It tells me that we had better devise a better way of living . . . a way of living that will even surpass what we all thought we had with our nonproductive millstones over the past few generations. If two out of three households live in their own millstones to-day . . . I predict that it will reverse in the next 20 years when 2 out of every three households will live or rent their Quad Plex or Duplex in a very agreeable atmosphere, even surpassing the millstone, which really had not too much more going for it than log cabin living in pioneer days. For you log cabin freaks then, the future lifestyle is not for you . . . however, there will be a lot of "log cabins from the pioneer days" (nonproductive millstones) selling at bargain prices out in the boondocks . . . and you can pick one up real cheap.

I see the necessity for Quads on farms. Either new Quads to be built or Quads converted from the current old-and-good, but oversized "main house." While driving through the USA recently on a personal appearance tour for this book; I noticed all kinds of make-shift housing, near or next to the old main-house on the farms. I saw house-trailers; campers; rec-vans; motor homes; . . . even tents . . . I saw everything but the overlooked and obvious solution. . . A QUADPLEX, OR TWO ON THE FARM. There certainly is no land scarcity there. . . and if the zoning laws must be changed. . . get your local bureaucrats to change the laws to help you. . . the tax-payer. Then besides the shelter-need for two or three family units that usually run today's farms. . . there is need on these farms for low cost and convenient shelter for the hired farm hands. . . and better help will be attracted to our farms, if good and reasonable shelter is available there. I also see some retired people just relishing the opportunity to move into a quad out on a farm. Back to peace, tranquility, relative safety from big City crime and muggings. . . and back to real nice living. . . Country Style.

Owners of two Quads will be the ultimate. . . one in the City and one week end type Quad near or on the grounds of your favorite recreation. . . golf, tennis, water, etc. With some of your City-tenants also renting their week end Quad from the same owner.

If the 10,000,000 "doers" of the 120,000,000 U.S. workers buy their own Quad-Plex or DuPlex . . . then we will already have achieved a better balance in living . . . and this will be our long term "shelter" solution over the next 20 years; even over the next 50 years and longer, because this lifestyle is for today's people who want to work less and enjoy life more . . . and we won't have as many long term widows around, because the "old man" in his new and more relaxed lifestyle, without all the pressures of keeping up his nonproductive millstone . . . he will live as long as his wife . . . and in a better and happier lifestyle too. Isn't that really what life is all about? Here's to your next 30 years of happiness.

Now here is an example of a big builder jumping on the bandwagon to satisfy the new "quad" demand created by this book. Remember, I state that I strongly urge you to buy an existing quad for your first venture. It is easier to plan your income and expense... and you will not go broke with unexpected overruns which happen to the majority of first time builders. Plus expensive delays due to construction deadlines missed.

But I also stated that "Developers and builders border on genius and they will react to this new demand for quads." So after my book hit 400 newspapers Coast to Coast, and then followed by 250 CBS TV News Station telecasts... I immediately got many calls from Builders and Developers... their conversation-line was all practically the same... i.e., "people aren't buying (or can't afford) our $60,000 boxes in the boondocks (I call 'em Millstones)... and coincidentally we saw your 'live rent free' story in newspapers (or TV)... and we want to begin building quad-plexes... can you give us some advice?" So, I can say that Builders are reacting Nationally to this new demand for Quads.

This Builder I mention here, happens to be a "Quad-Plex-Factory" and I was sent this information just the other day and am happy to slip it in this 4th Printing. This factory, per the Photo, is as big as an auto assembly Plant, and I guess they can ship you a Quad... anywhere. Oh, some misinformed people have already mumbled... "Oh, it's a pre-fab?" Well, pre-fabs are big business in homes these days... and to my mind, in reading over their literature... they take away all the problems of building... even the price, which comes in at 8 times annual rental... wherein I say in the book... "if you must build, you must look at 10 times annual rental... and just hold your breath for two years for current high building costs to catch up with inflation and higher rentals." However, these Quads come in at 8 times annual rental, and the other problems they say they solve are: all materials are designated; no hidden or surprise costs; plans are stamped by a licensed registered engineer; quicker and dependable construction time with no costly delays; facilities and product inspected by responsible third party Agencies; this Builder arranges financing up to 90% or 95% (100% for veterans). I called this Quad-Factory and got the following information... a Quad with lot costs as low as $95,000. The four, 2 bedroom apartments will rent for $235 to $275 each monthly, depending on the rental demand in your area. So at a $250 average rental base... that delivers you $12,000 annually. At an 8 times rental, that's $96,000... and is right on target... and this factory just took away all my normal reservations about building your first Quad if all is true. Caution: don't put up too much money in front, and have your lawyer look over the entire agreement so you are totally protected, if you go into a deal such as this. (Note: We are not endorsing this Quad-Factory... we don't even mention his name/location. There are/or will be many.)

Fourplex

Note the attractive exterior-look that Anderson encouraged Builders to adopt (in his book). This Quad looks like a "Villa," and not a "Motel."

America's first "QUAD-PLEX-FACTORY."

Pache-

 ABOUT THE AUTHOR

This 1963 photo of author, James W. Anderson was taken in the Republic of Panama with his 15 foot pet boa constrictor, "Jimboa." Your author was sent there by Worldvision Inc., a Division of the American Broadcasting Co. in New York, to stabilize and manage their new Panama television station.

Anderson in 1977 is a Registered Real Estate Broker in Miami, but not an ordinary Broker ... he represents the Buyer (not the Seller) ... and only works on apartment building purchases for his clients, which he knows professionally as the owner and operator of his own three apartment buildings.

Your author's business slogan is taken from Packard auto in the 30's ... he says, "Buying income property? ... Ask the man who owns one."

320

Author, James W. Anderson gives you simple humorous and easy to understand solutions to the "old wives tale" problems you may have heard about owning apartment buildings. He observes . . . "ever notice that most real estate Brokers don't own their own apartment buildings? . . . And conversely, "most apartment building owners aren't Brokers." Anderson has ideally put the two talents together to knowledgeably represent the Buyer, in this most important personal decision (as you consult your lawyer).

Your Author was educated and spent his early business years in St. Louis, and has kept those solid middle-America ideals through his adult life. He has proven himself to be a professional problem solver in business ever since graduating from St. Louis University. After sales and marketing stints with Philip Morris Co. And Westinghouse Appliance Co. Anderson entered the then-new television industry. His 15 year television career was brilliant and he became known as an industry leader, an innovator and a problem solver. He was the No. 1 executive responsible in turning seven television stations from losing money (even bankrupt ones) . . . all into moneymaking situations . . . each in six months or less. These TV Stations were in such major and competitive markets as: WNTA TV New York City; WTTG TV Wash. D.C.; WPHL TV Phil.; KMSP TV Minneapolis; KWEX TV San Antonio; Panama, "Tevedos"; and DZBB TV Manila. Anderson was also a TV Network executive for ABC in New York City, and Metro-Media in N.Y.C. and Wash., D.C.

Through all of these very competitive situations Anderson was known as "the problem-solver . . . the innovator." Anderson has now concentrated his problem solving expertise into the apartment building ownership and management field. He is now pleased to share his experiences and successes with you, with his invitation: "buying income property . . . ask the man who owns one."

This is no get rich quick scheme . . . just a very basic but overlooked solution to our financial survival problems. Anderson says, "I did it 3 times in the past 3 years without any previous experience . . . and you can too. I am going to make 1,000,000 winners this next year . . . and I hope you will be among them."

PAPER BACK $15.00   **HARD COVER $25.00**

"IF YOU CAN STICK OUT YOUR HAND
TO PICK UP THE RENT CHECKS . . .
THIS BOOK WILL DO THE REST."

(Continued on next page)

The next question usually is, "what if you don't have the down payment?" Here are the three answers Anderson gives for the three major groups of workers.

"First. Those 47 million home owners (2 of 3 families) have made $10,000 to $50,000 profit on their home in just the past few years. If this large segment of the USA does not want to give up their suburban-box-in-the-boondocks, they can refinance their home and with just a part of this windfall profit ($10,000 to $20,000), put a down payment on a quadplex. People don't know that their current low F.H.A. loan on their home can be refinanced to get them cash."

Second. For people who don't have money for a down payment, Anderson suggest a method outlined in his book (published by Brun Press, New York.) See Chapter 1.

Third. "Do you know that there are 20 million veterans who have never used their no-money-down G.I. Bill privilege? They can buy up to a $100,000 quadplex with no money down. (G.I. Bill Law says up to 4 units is O.K.) Over the years those real estate brokers always discouraged us from using the G.I. Bill . . . right? Now I know why . . . too much paper work for then, plus the bureaucracy delayed their commission checks. Maybe those Brokers did us a favor though, for now is the time these 20 million veterans can use this no money down bonanza to invest in real estate."

Additionally, Anderson reveals for the first time, there are another 10 million veterans who have bought one home, using their no-money-down G.I. Bill loan; but now are entitled to buy another with no money down . . . and they don't even know it." Anderson expands this: "Think of all the youngsters with no big promise of a glowing future. Heck, I tell them to 'join up' for two years and learn a profitable trade. Then upon discharge, they've got a good paying job, plus they can use their G.I. Bill privilege to buy a quadplex, with no money down, and they have made a very smart three year plan for a lifetime of peace and prosperity."

"THINK-4"

323

ANDERSON'S RENT-FREE-MOVEMENT IN A NUT-SHELL

MIAMI, Dec. 17 — Jim Anderson, a real estate investor and author of the book "How To Live Rent Free", predicts his ideas "will change America's lifestyle in the next decade as people begin to realize that neither the single family home nor the large apartment house is the answer to ideal living conditions."

"After being asked the question 'How do you live rent free' hundreds of times in the past year," says Anderson, "I can now pretty well condense my book into a few simple steps."

First, he says, you buy a suitable four-unit apartment building (quad-plex) and live in one unit rent-free. "And dont think I've downgraded my standard of living," he says. "One news story about me said 'Anderson lives like a millionaire rent-free along scenic Biscayne Bay in his Spanish Villa type quadplex.'"

"Second. Very quickly the rent from two units will pay your mortgage, taxes and insurance. The rent from the third unit will pay for upkeep and improvement costs, so you can legitimately raise the rents. Also inflation is now your partner instead of your enemy, because inflation also raises your rents, even if you are the lousiest business person. Meanwhile your mortgage is going down (due to the inflation) until your tenants have paid it off completely. Then it's off to the Riviera.

"Third. You continue on your job (for a few years) and now you have a tax-shelter like your millionaire Senator. Only five percent have a tax shelter since they worry about losing their investment in some get rich scheme. Now instead of working six months a year for Uncle Sam, your new tax-shelter quad cuts your taxes in half, or more, and that money saved goes to you instead of our giant-government-waste machine.

"Fourth, you continue working because your quadplex takes only about two hours of supervision weekly. If your roof gets a leak . . . you just call the roofer; because your tenants' rent pays for that. However, if you live in a non-productive home, you will probably have to climb up there yourself to repair the leak.

"Incidentally, homes are overpriced, due to the mad and misguided rush to buy them. However, quadplexes are under-priced because they have not been discovered yet. A nice quadplex, believe it or not, costs little more than a single family home," Anderson says. (Continued on next page)